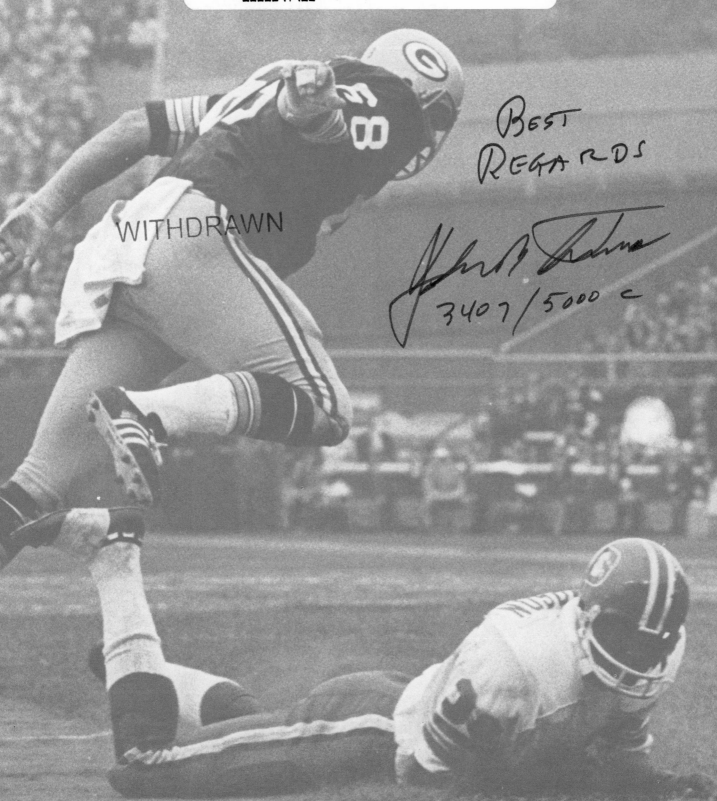

Best
Regards

John B. Torinus
3407/5000 c

THE PACKER LEGEND:

AN INSIDE LOOK

An Account
of the
Green Bay Packers

by

John B. Torinus

LARANMARK PRESS
1982

A Division of Laranmark, Inc.

Neshkoro, Wisconsin

LARANMARK PRESS

A division of
Laranmark, Inc.
Box 253
Neshkoro, Wisconsin 54960

First Printing July 1982.

Printed in U. S. A.

In memory of
George Whitney Calhoun
my mentor, my friend

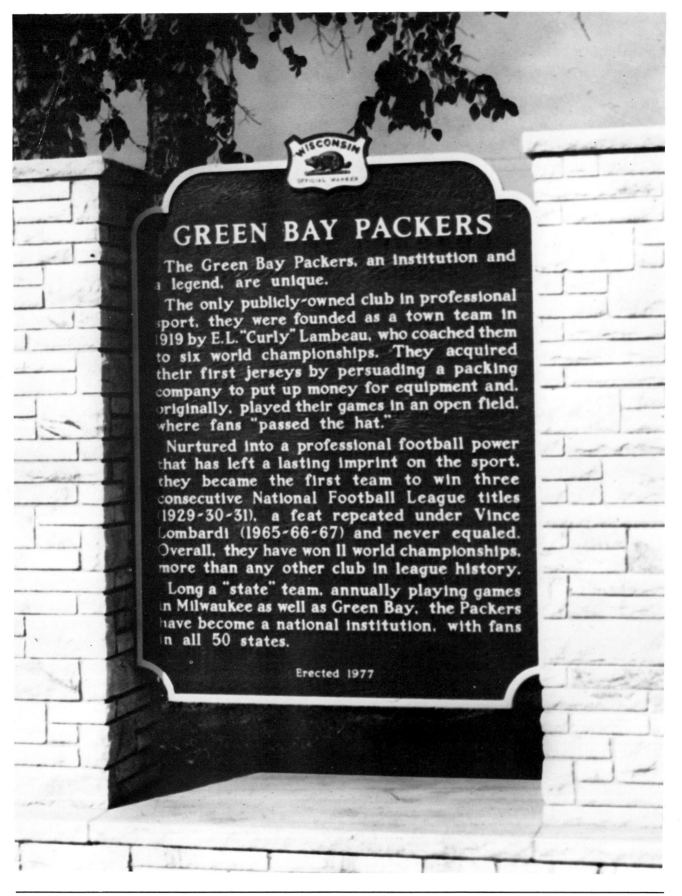

GREEN BAY PACKERS

The Green Bay Packers, an institution and a legend, are unique.

The only publicly-owned club in professional sport, they were founded as a town team in 1919 by E.L. "Curly" Lambeau, who coached them to six world championships. They acquired their first jerseys by persuading a packing company to put up money for equipment and, originally, played their games in an open field, where fans "passed the hat."

Nurtured into a professional football power that has left a lasting imprint on the sport, they became the first team to win three consecutive National Football League titles (1929-30-31), a feat repeated under Vince Lombardi (1965-66-67) and never equaled. Overall, they have won 11 world championships, more than any other club in league history.

Long a "state" team, annually playing games in Milwaukee as well as Green Bay, the Packers have become a national institution, with fans in all 50 states.

Erected 1977

Acknowledgements

I received a great deal of help assembling this material and the accompanying pictures from several people: Former and present newspaper associates and Packer employees; photographers Hank Lefebvre, Vern Biever, and Emery Kroening; Art Daley and Lee Remmel, former associates at the Green Bay *Press-Gazette*; Mike Michalske, the former All-Pro; Bart Starr, Tom Miller, Bob Harlan, and Dick Blasczyk of the Packers; friend Robert Flatley who inspired me to write the book in the first place, and John Hammer who encouraged me to finish it; my editor and publisher Larry Names; my agent Peggy Eagan; and finally the person who took all my tapes and rough notes and put them together, over and over again, Patti Trinkner.

To all of them, my thanks.

George Whitney Calhoun

INTRODUCTION

This is more a collection of recollections than a history of the Green Bay Packers. Rather than citing dates and places and games and scores, I have attempted in this book to give you some of the flavor, the drama, yes, the poignancy of this story of the most unique professional sports organization in the world.

This is the book which my great and good friend, George Whitney Calhoun, should have written and almost did. In his retirement years after leaving full-time employment at the Green Bay *Press-Gazette*, he often told me that he was at work on such a book. But after his death, his attorney and close friends and I searched in vain through his papers for the proof sheets which he told me he was reviewing. This book then was written before in Cal's imagination, and I shall try to do him justice by putting into type many of the stories which he related to me when I was his young assistant in the "Black Hole" at the *Press-Gazette*.

My close connections with the Packer organization began when I worked summers for Cal while I was still going to school, and one of my earliest and fondest memories is spending the Thanksgiving recess traveling with the Packers when they made their annual trip to New York and Philadelphia. Cal gave me board and room in exchange for helping him with his duties as chief publicist and traveling secretary of the Packers.

I continued to help Cal in those responsibilities when I began my full-time work at the *Press-Gazette* in 1934. In 1949, Andy Turnbull, the general manager of the *Press-Gazette*, asked me to take his place on the Packer Board of Directors and Executive Committee, since he was retiring and was going to live in California. That was Curly Lambeau's last year as coach and general manager of the Packers, so that in my span of time on the Executive Committee I have seen the full gamut of Packer Coaches come and go.

I was elected Secretary of the Corporation in 1954. In 1962, I left my position as Executive Editor of the *Press-Gazette* and became Editor of the *Post-Crescent* in nearby Appleton, but I have continued my close relationship with the Packers as Secretary and a member of the Board and Executive Committee.

I write this book because I am one of the few persons left who is intimately familiar with the Packer organization from its earlier days to the present time. And I hope this volume will prove of interest to the many Packer fans not only in Wisconsin but all over the country. I know Cal would have liked it.

SPORTS

J. Dempsey's mother says he's no hobo and never was. He didn't act much like a bum that afternoon in Toledo.

while Fahlier and Glick will be the battery for the Northwest tribe.

The Boilers and the Barkers will clash on Oneida field. The former team is promising to shake off the hoodoo which has prevented it from winning a game so far, while their opponents are eager to grab off a win in order to catch up to the Northwest leaders. The batteries will be: Peters and Stack for the Boilers and W. Kraft and E. Kraft for the Barkers.

The Delce Calks and Toilers will fight it out at the league park. Lancelle and Marks will be the battery for the Calks and Janssen and Decker will work for the Toilers.

At the De Pere Driving Park, the Oneidas and Whales will battle. Batteries: Gervais and McKenna for the Whales; Brenner and Gavin for Oneida.

FLEMING BACK AFTER LONG NAVAL SERVICE

Edward Fleming, who has been in the navy two years and four months, arrived in the city yesterday. He is a son of Mr. and Mrs. Lawrence Fleming. His father is a member of the city fire department. The young man was stationed for considerable time during the war at the submarine base at New London, Conn., as a first class electrician. He attended an electrical school in Minneapolis after being at Great Lakes Naval Training station, and afterwards was in the Brooklyn Navy yard.

Racing.

Summer meeting of Saratoga Racing Association, at Saratoga, N. Y.

Trotting.

Grand circuit meeting at Philadelphia. Great Western Circuit meeting at Sedalia, Mo.

BASE BALL

THURSDAY'S RESULTS.

American Association.
Louisville 7, Milwaukee 4.
Kansas City 1, Toledo 0.
St. Paul 5, Indianapolis 3.
Minneapolis 5-5, Columbus 4-1.

American League.
Boston 15, Chicago 6.
St. Louis 6, Philadelphia 1.
Cleveland 4, Washington 3.
New York 5, Detroit 4, (15 innings).

National League.
New York 2-5, Cincinnati 1-3; first game 14 innings.
Chicago 2-0, Brooklyn 0-1.
St. Louis 4-6, Philadelphia 2-3.
Pittsburg at Boston, no game, rain.

TODAY'S GAMES.

American Association.
Louisville at Milwaukee.
Indianapolis at St. Paul.
Toledo at Kansas City.
Columbus at Minneapolis.

American League.
Boston at Chicago.
New York at Detroit.
Washington at Cleveland.
Philadelphia at St. Louis.

National League.
Cincinnati at New York, two games.
Pittsburg at Boston, two games.
St. Louis at Philadelphia.
Chicago at Brooklyn.

TEAM STANDINGS.

American Association.

	W.	L.	Pct.
Indianapolis	63	41	.606
St. Paul	63	41	.606
Louisville	59	46	.564
Kansas City	56	49	.533
Minneapolis	50	56	.472
Columbus	52	64	.448
Milwaukee	38	65	.364
Toledo	38	67	.362

American League.

	W.	L.	Pct.
Chicago	62	39	.614
Detroit	57	42	.570
Cleveland	57	43	.570
New York	54	44	.551
St. Louis	52	45	.541
Boston	45	52	.469
Washington	40	61	.396
Philadelphia	27	70	.278

National League.

	W.	L.	Pct.
Cincinnati	68	33	.673
New York	61	35	.635
Chicago	54	44	.551
Pittsburg	47	50	.485
Brooklyn	48	51	.485
Boston	37	55	.402
Philadelphia	35	57	.380
St. Louis	35	59	.372

Boxing.

Pete Herman vs. Jack Sharkey, 10 rounds at Milwaukee.

Harry Greb vs. Larry Williams, 12 rounds at Boston.

Benny Leonard vs. Jimmy Duffy, 10 rounds at Buffalo.

CURLY LAMBEAU CHOSEN CAPTAIN OF FOOTBALLERS

Indian Packing Corporation Squad Meets; First Game on Sunday, Sept. 14.

"Curly" Lambeau, former East High and Notre Dame football star, was elected captain of the Indian Packing Corporation's team at the meeting last night of the city footballers in The Press-Gazette. G. W. Calhoun will again manage the eleven this season.

Close to 25 pigskin chasers attended the conference last evening and there was a good deal of enthusiasm displayed among the candidates. It was the unanimous opinion that, if Green Bay doesn't get away with state honors this year she never will.

Practice will start September 3, the Wednesday following Labor day, and from then on it will be held three times weekly, Mondays, Wednesdays and Fridays.

Providing a suitable opponent can be secured, the Packers will open the season on Sunday, Sept. 14, at Hagemeister park. Up to date the only game closed on the schedule is with Marinette here on Oct. 26. Many other arguments are now pending and it is expected that at least three more arguments will be booked during the coming week.

Shooting.

Close of Grand American handicap tournament at Chicago.

Tennis.

National doubles championship tournament at Boston.

Brother Moose.

Howdy-Pap! Don't miss the big meeting, Friday night. Class initiation followed by corn roast and smoker. Officers and members should attend. Chas. J. Williams, Sec'y.

Girl for house work, 709 School Place.

Not ffer from Catarrh

drive the catarrhal poisons out of your blood, purifying and strengthening it, so it will carry vigor and health to the mucous membranes on its journeys through your body and nature will soon restore you to health. You will be relieved of the droppings of mucous in your throat, sores in nostrils, bad breath, hawing and spitting.

All reputable druggists carry S. S. S. in stock and we recommend you give it a trial at once.

The chief medical adviser of the Company will cheerfully answer all letters on the subject. There is no charge for the medical advice. Address Swift Specific Company, 251 Swift Laboratory, Atlanta, Ga. Adv.

PROGRAM

The Packer Legend

PART I

THE

LAMBEAU

ERA

1919 - 1949

Earl L. (Curly) Lambeau

Lambeau started the Green Bay Packers with the help of George Whitney Calhoun, the sports editor of the Green Bay *Press-Gazette*. He was a player from 1919 until he finally hung up his cleats after the 1930 season. As head coach from 1919 through 1949, he compiled an amazing record, one that has yet to be matched. His Packer teams won six National Football League titles, three in a row from 1929 through 1931, then again in 1936, 1939, and 1944. He compiled a 31-year record of 248-108-23 for a fantastic winning percentage of .685. As a player, he was a devastating running back, and as a coach, he was an innovator of the passing game. He was inducted into the NFL Hall of Fame in 1963, its first year in existence, then was inducted into the Packer Hall of Fame when it was founded in 1970. He is also in the Wisconsin Hall of Fame. The contributions he made to the game of football, the NFL, the city of Green Bay, and the state of Wisconsin go without saying. He was simply a man among men.

Lefebvre-Stiller photo.

Chapter One

THE

BIRTH

OF THE

LEGEND

A severe case of tonsillitis...

A chance conversation over a glass of beer...

A heavy rainfall that was one one-hundredth of an inch too little...

All these incidents had a bearing on the founding of the Green Bay Packers, the most unique professional sports organization in the country.

The badly infected tonsils belonged to a young Green Bay athlete by the name of Earl L. (Curly) Lambeau. The Lambeau family had come to Green Bay from Belgium in the 1870s and settled on the northeast side of the city which was almost a solid Belgian community. As such, Curly attended Green Bay East High School and in his four years there became the school's athletic hero.

Lambeau lettered all four years in football and was captain of the team in his senior year, 1917. He was also the team's unofficial coach. The previous coach did not return to East that year and the teacher assigned to the job had no football experience. He told Lambeau to take charge of the team "while I go out and find a book I can read on football."

Lambeau was a triple-threat back. He ran and passed from the tailback position in the single wing and employed the now long-forgotten art of drop-kicking for field goals and extra points. Testimony to his athletic ability was the fact that he won the shotput, discus, and hammer throw in the conference track meet his senior year.

In the climax game that senior year, Lambeau's team beat arch-rival Green Bay West, 7-6, with Lambeau making two-thirds of

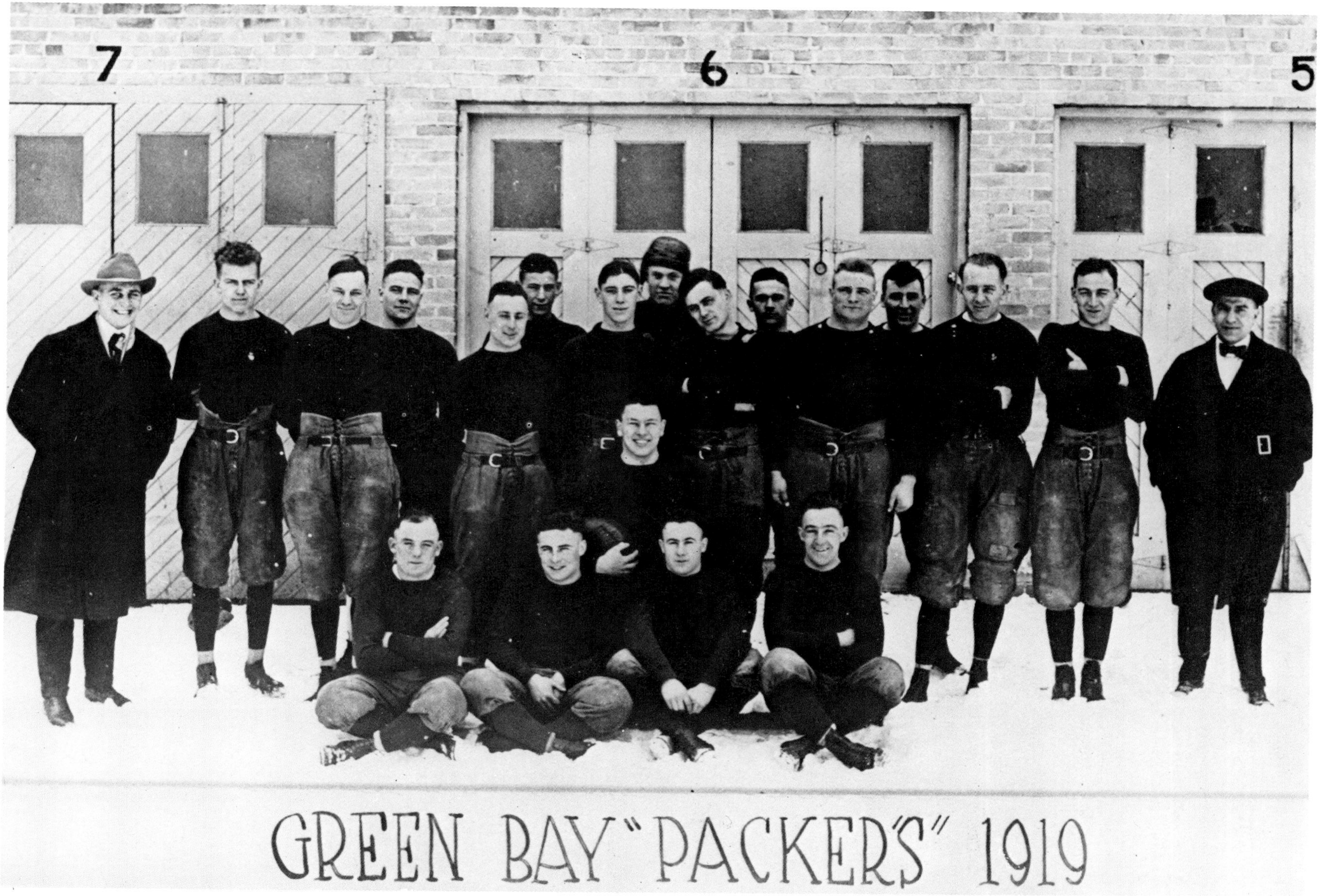

GREEN BAY "PACKERS" 1919

The First Packer Team, 1919. Packers 565, Opponents 12, 10-1. Left to right, front row: Martin Zoll, Wes Leaper, Carl Zoll, Herman Martell, Tudy McLean, Nate Abrams, Jed Medley. Middle row: J.H. Tebo, Al Petchka, Fritz Gavin, Cowboy Wheeler, Curly Lambeau, Wally Ladrow, Buff Wagner, Jack Dalton, George Calhoun. Back row: Joe Deloye, Sam Powers, Rig Dwyer, Herb Nichols, Gus Rosenow, Milton Wilson, Charley Sauber, Neal Murphy.

Lefebvre-Stiller photo.

The Packer Legend

the gains, scoring the touchdown, and kicking the extra point.

Lambeau enrolled at Notre Dame in the fall of 1918, and as a freshman he made the varsity team at fullback under Coach Knute Rockne. After the Christmas holidays, he came down with an acute case of tonsillitis and came home for treatment. The physician told him his tonsils had to come out but that he couldn't operate until the infection subsided. By the time Curly recovered it was too late to go back to college that semester.

Curly took a job with the Indian Packing Company, a war-time industry in Green Bay. He was paid the momentous sum of $250 a month and said afterward he thought at the time that that was all the money any person would need to live on. College became further and further from his mind, but he had a lingering ache to play football again as the summer of 1919 began to fade into fall.

The chance conversation over a glass of beer took place with George W. Calhoun, sports editor of the Green Bay *Press-Gazette*. Cal knew Curly well from his playing days at East High, and as a frustrated athlete himself due to a severe case of juvenile arthritis, Cal could sympathize with Lambeau when he told Cal about missing playing football. "Why not get up a team in Green Bay?" Cal asked. And he added, "I'll help you put one together, and I'll give you all the publicity you need."

The deal was made on the spot and sealed with another beer.

Cal was as good as his word. He ran stories for several weeks, inviting football players to an organizational meeting. He even ran a list of names of players he hoped would show up. From the tone of the articles, Cal more or less demanded their presence and insinuated that if they failed to show they would be unwise to meet him on the street. Cal knew the power of the press.

The meeting was held in the news room of the *Press-Gazette* building on Cherry Street on August 14, 1919. Some 25 players attended. Lambeau was elected captain, and Calhoun agreed to serve as manager.

Cal wrote in the next day's *Press-Gazette*: "Close to 25 pigskin chasers attended the conference last evening and there was a great deal of enthusiasm displayed among the candidates." The first practice was set for September 3, and they agreed to practice three

Early Year Action. The Packers played in an open field next to the Hagemeister Brewery those first few years, but there were a few bleachers and a scoreboard. *Lefebvre-Stiller photo.*

The Packer Legend

First NFL Team. The Packers entered the National Football League in 1921 and finished with a record of 7-2-2. Left to right: Herman Martell, no college; Rummy Lambeau, Curly's brother; Jim Cook, Wisconsin; Nate Abrams, no college; Bill Dumoe, Beloit; Cowboy Wheeler, Ripon; Buff Wagner, Northern Michigan; Frank Coughlin, Notre Dame; Norman Barry, Notre Dame; Joe Carey, no college; Dick Murray, Marquette; Curly Lambeau, Notre Dame; Dave Hays, Notre Dame; Cub Buck, Wisconsin; Art Schmaehl, no college; Milt Wilson, Wisconsin Teachers; Wally Ladrow, no college; Lynn Howard, Indiana; Fee Klaus, no college; Sam Powers, Northern Michigan; J.E. Clair, President, Acme Packing Company.

Lefebure-Stiller photo.

The Packer Legend

nights a week.

Then Cal added: "Indications point to the 'Indians' having the greatest team in the history of football in Green Bay and there is no doubt but that gridiron fans will see a great exhibition of football chasing at Hagemeister Park this fall."

How's that for a send-off? Cal was anything but modest. But the words he wrote that day turned out to be prophetic.

The name Indians didn't stick. Curly talked his boss, Frank Peck, at the Indian Packing Company into providing jerseys for the team, and the company also gave them the use of a next-door field for practice. The Indian Packing Company is long gone, but the Packers live on after more than 60 years of professional football competition.

That first season the team won 10 straight games, piling up a total of 565 points to their opponents' six. They played teams from nearby cities New London, Oshkosh, and Sheboygan; plus Racine and the Milwaukee Athletic Club in Wisconsin; and Menominee, Ishpeming, and Stambaugh in Michigan's Upper Peninsula. The closest score was against Stambaugh, 17-0. But that was before the final game of the season against a team from Beloit with the improbable name of The Fairies, who won, 6-0. Cal raved and ranted in the *Press-Gazette* the next day because the Packers had crossed the Beloit goalline three times, and each time the hometown official called a penalty and revoked the score. On the first two touchdowns, the ref said the Packers were offside. So the next time the team was on the Beloit five yardline, Curly told everyone to stand absolutely still. He took the ball and crossed the goalline standing up. The same referee said the Packer backfield was in motion.

The record in 1920 was almost as good; the Packers going 9-1-1, and this time around they beat Beloit the first game in Green Bay, 7-0, but lost the home-and-home encounter in Beloit, 14-3.

Curly continued to coach at East High from 1919 to 1921, while coaching the Packers. At East, he inherited a halfback named Jimmy Crowley, who went on to become one of the famous "Four Horsemen of Notre Dame" and returned home to play with the Packers for one season in 1925 before going into coaching.

Lambeau was a pioneer in developing the passing game in football. He came to believe it was the easiest way to gain yardage. After that East-West game, West fans complained: "Run

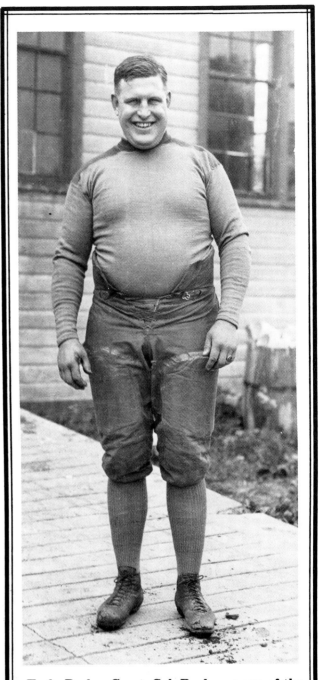

Early Packer Great. Cub Buck was one of the first big-time college players recruited by Lambeau. He was a huge man and graduated from the University of Wisconsin. From 1921 through 1925, he anchored the Packer line, first as the center. Curly Lambeau moved him to the tackle spot when Jug Earp joined the Packers in 1922. Off the field, he was a jovial giant, but on the gridiron, few opposing linemen could handle him, whether he was on offense or defense. *Lefebvre-Stiller photo.*

The Packer Legend

the ball, that's not football."

Lambeau would pass on first down or from behind his own goalline. He passed 75 percent of the time. He recalled one game at Stambaugh when he ran three running plays in a row and a different player suffered a fracture on each play. "I never called another running play," he said, "but after every pass I had to run for my life. Those miners were tough."

By then, Curly had heard about the organization of the American Professional Football Association, formed September 17, 1920, in Canton, Ohio, with the famous Jim Thorpe as president. After the 1920 season, Curly talked his boss into applying for a franchise, and it was granted to J. E. Clair of the Acme Packing Company on August 27, 1921.

In their first year in the National League, the Packers compiled a record of 7-2-2, playing against such teams as the Chicago Boosters, Rockford, Rock Island, Minneapolis, Evansville, Hammond, the Chicago Cardinals, the Decatur Staleys, and Racine. But the team was not nearly as successful financially as it was on the gridiron, and by the end of that season, Clair forfeited the franchise.

Actually, it was the league that forfeited the franchise. By then it had been renamed the National Football League at the instigation of George Halas, who had moved the Decatur Staleys to Chicago and renamed them the Bears. Halas was leading the movement to adopt some rules of conduct regarding such matters as the clubs' rights to players and limits on the number of players per team. But the most difficult problem was the use by professional teams of players still in college. Halas wrote in his autobiography: "From the very first the League had declared its opposition to using collegians, but we did not enforce the rule."

The league made an example of the Packers, who were accused of using two collegians in a game. "We revoked the Green Bay franchise and demanded an apology from Curly," Halas wrote. "Fortunately, Curly found another sponsor and with cash raised by a friend who sold his car applied for a new franchise. We supplied it."

Lambeau went to the league meeting in 1922, apology in hand. He drove to Canton with a close friend, Don Murphy, whose brother Brick was an investor in the Acme Packing Company. The league accepted Curly's apology, but there was another hitch in renewing the franchise. Curly didn't have the $250 a franchise cost in those

days. Murphy told him he would sell his car, a Marmon, and loan Curly the money on one condition, and that was that he could play in the opening game of the season that year. Don sold his car, raised the cash to pay the league and to buy train fare home. The franchise remained in Green Bay. It was the personal property of Lambeau, however, until the corporation was organized and took over in 1923.

Lambeau kept his part of the bargain with Murphy. He was in the lineup when the Packers kicked off to the Duluth Eskimos that fall. Don ran down the field, then veered off and headed for the bench. That ended his brief professional football career.

With the recruiting of college players, Lambeau made the town team into a truly professional outfit. In that first year, 1919, the players split the profits for the season, and each one came away with $16. But joining the pro league suddenly changed the whole picture, and Curly had to start guaranteeing players a season salary.

In 1922, he signed quarterback Charley Mathys of Indiana, a former Green Bay West great, plus center Jug Earp from Monmouth, and guard Whitey Woodin of Marquette. The year before his first major import was tackle Cub Buck from Wisconsin. The first real superstar hired by the Packers was Verne Lewellen of Nebraska, a big-back halfback and super punter, who came in 1924.

The Packers were the first team to institute daily practice, which they did in 1922. Mathys said that when he played with Hammond, they would only practice on Saturdays or on Sunday mornings before the game.

The rainstorm which was one one-hundredth of an inch too light came in the middle of the 1922 season when one of the Packer home games was rained out and the insurance company would not pay off because the official amount of moisture was one one-hundredth of an inch short of that required in the policy.

Later in the season, however, another heavy rainstorm proved a blessing in disguise. The Packers were scheduled to play the Duluth Eskimos in Green Bay. It had rained all Saturday afternoon and night and was still at it Sunday morning. Lambeau and Calhoun met in the *Press-Gazette* office to try to figure out what to do. If they played the game, they would have to pay the Eskimos their guarantee, and with the prospects of almost no gate at all, they didn't have the money.

At that point, Andrew B. Turnbull, the business manager of the *Press-Gazette*, came into the office. He listened to their troubles and told them that if they ever hoped to put professional football on a permanent basis, they would have to play the game. He also told them that he would advance them enough money to pay the guarantee and that before the next season he would attempt to rally support from the businessmen of Green Bay to help solve their financial problems.

Turnbull was as good as word. By the next summer, he had enlisted the financial support of several Green Bay businessmen who subscribed to stock in a corporation to be formed to back the Packer football team, but the formation of that organization is a remarkable story in itself.

Curly Lambeau, the Player. Lambeau was coach, quarterback, and drop kicker. He was a muscular 175-pounder and a fine all-around athlete. He made the Notre Dame first team under Knute Rockne in his freshman year of 1918, then dropped out of college. In 1919, he organized the first Packer team. *Lefebvre-Stiller photo.*

The Packer Legend

The Most Unique Organization

How can a small city the size of Green Bay support a team in the National Football League?

That question has been asked countless times. The answer lies in the extraordinary structure of the Packer football corporation.

The original *Articles of Incorporation for the Green Bay Football Corporation*, were filed with the Secretary of the State of Wisconsin on August 18, 1923. Business manager Andy Turnbull had corralled several of his cronies to meet at the *Press-Gazette* office several weeks before that to organize a corporation to give financial support to Curly Lambeau's young Packer football team. The group became known as the "Hungry Five" since they were always out begging for the Packers.

The articles provided that stock would be sold for $5.00 a share but would be non-profit, that is, pay no dividends and that all profits would go to the American Legion. Stockholders elected 15 directors who elected the officers and an executive committee of five.

At a meeting of stockholders in the assembly room of city hall, September 17, the directors chose Andrew B. Turnbull, president; John Kittell, vice-president; and Lee Joannes, secretary and treasurer. Dr. W. W. Kelly and George DeLair were added to the executive committee, and George W. Calhoun was named team secretary.

The original corporation went into receivership during the Great Depression, and a new corporation, *Green Bay Packers, Inc.*, was formed in January of 1935. The original articles were restated in an expanded version, but the concept that it would be strictly non-profit was retained and outlined in the following articles:

Article I:

The undersigned have associated and do hereby associate themselves together for the purpose of forming a corporation under Chapter 180 of the Wisconsin Statutes, and that this association shall be a community project intended to promote community welfare, and that its purposes shall be exclusively charitable, and that incidental to its purposes, it shall have the right to conduct athletic contests, operate a football team, or such other similar projects for the purpose of carrying out its charitable purposes.

This is the remarkable feature of the structure of the corporation. The original purpose in forming the corporation under the laws of Wisconsin applying to charitable corporations was to insure that the corporation would be exempt from payment of various taxes, but the long term effect of this unusual purpose has been much more significant.

Article VI:

The corporation shall be nonprofit sharing and its purpose shall be exclusively for charitable purposes. No stockholder shall receive any dividend, pecuniary profit or emolument by virtue of his being a stockholder.

Should there be a dissolution of the Green Bay Packers, Inc., the undivided profits and assets of the Green Bay Packers, Inc., shall go to the Sullivan-Wallen Post of the American Legion for the purpose of erecting a proper soldier's memorial, either by building, clubhouse, hospital or other charitable or educational program, the choice of which the directors of this corporation shall have advisory control.

Article VII:

The Board of Directors shall have the right to create a capital reserve to provide for the acquisition and maintenance of its plant, equipment and players and said funds shall be preserved and no distribution made to any donee under the charitable clause of the Articles of Incorporation, except when in the judgment of the Board of Directors it shall be deemed advisable.

It is these *Articles of Incorporation* which answer the question posed above.

The only way Green Bay could have lost the Packer franchise in the National Football League would have been through bankruptcy. National Football League franchises are granted irrevocably. As long as the Packers were solvent, they would remain forever in Green Bay.

Wisconsin statutes provide that a corporation cannot sell or dispose of its major assests without the approval of the stockholders. Can you conceive of the stockholders of the Green Bay Packers, most of whom live in the Green Bay area, approving a sale or transfer of the franchise when they would not only receive no profit from such a sale but would not even recoup their original investment?

The stock certificates of the Green Bay Packers, Inc., state on their face that no dividend will ever be paid on these shares and that in the event of dissolution of the corporation all remaining assets shall go to the American Legion as the *Articles of Incorporation* provide.

So if Packer stockholders had ever voted to sell or transfer the franchise, they would not even have gotten their bait back.

This non-profit provision was challenged on at least one occasion, and it led to the final break between Curly Lambeau and the Packers.

The important fact is that the fans in the Green Bay area were so proud of their team that they would never yield to insolvency. They proved that on a number of occasions when they bought stock in a corporation upon which they would never recover a return.

Packers Are Incorporated. This is a stock certificate from the original corporation formed in 1923, the Green Bay Football Corporation. Stock sold for $5 a share, but a purchaser also had to buy at least six season tickets. A. B. Turnbull signed as president; L. H. Joannes as secretary. *Lefebvre-Stiller photo.*

The Packer Legend

Co-Founder, Character Extraordinaire. George Whitney Calhoun presides in the "Black Hole", the wire desk at the Green Bay *Press-Gazette*. **On the side, he was traveling secretary and chief publicist for the Packers. He was the man who encouraged Curly Lambeau to form the Packers in 1919, then gave Lambeau every assistance he could to make the Packers a success. Here he visits with Packer assistant coaches Lou Rymkus (left) and Ray (Scooter) McLean.** *Green Bay Press-Gazette photo.*

Chapter Two

THE
WRITER
OF
LEGENDS

Curly Lambeau was not the sole founder of the Green Bay Packers. He was a co-founder. The other man who played an equally vital role in the birth and early promotion of the Packers was George Whitney Calhoun, a remarkable character in his own right.

As already written, it was a conversation over a beer between Lambeau and Calhoun which bred the idea of starting a professional football team in Green Bay. Maybe the word *professional* is stretching it a bit, for in those early years the players split whatever was left in the pot at the end of the season, which usually wasn't much.

Cal, as he was known, was sports editor of the Green Bay *Press-Gazette*. As is so often the case with sportswriters, he was also a frustrated ex-athlete. Cal was afflicted with a severe case of rheumatoid arthritis when he was still in college.

He had been a fine athlete and was on the varsity hockey team at Buffalo University. The attack of juvenile arthritis left him badly crippled in his hands, arms, and legs. It also affected his personality.

Calhoun's gruff exterior was an attempt on his part to keep people from feeling sorry for him. He adopted an outer crust of terrible temper to protect what on the inside was a very warm and emotional person. He spoke in streams of profanity, chewed and ate cigars instead of smoking them, and spit the juice into a brass spittoon always handy to his desk.

The *Press-Gazette* erected a partition to separate Calhoun's working space from the rest of the news room, although the women who were employed on the newspaper at that time really did not need much protection. Cal's office was

Railbirds. Enclosed stadiums were still dreams when the Packers were formed in 1919. Most of the fans stood along the fence, which was nothing more than a rope sometimes, in those early years, and Calhoun would go around passing the hat to finance the team. Then as now the ladies really outdid themselves with their fall football finery.   *Lefebvre-Stiller photo.*

dubbed the "Black Hole". I was assigned to the "Black Hole" when I started working summers at the newspaper while going to college, and naturally that became my assignment when I graduated and began my journalistic career there in 1934.

I well-remember my first morning on the job when I stood at attention before Cal's desk, and with the ever-present cigar butt in his mouth, he looked up at me and said, "Sit down, Dartmouth, and I will see if I can teach you how to write a seven head."

A seven head in the type style of the *Press-Gazette* at that time was two lines of 14-point type, the smallest headline in the newspaper's format. It was Cal's way of dressing down a brand new graduate of an Ivy League college, and in later years, I came to thank him for the post-graduate education in journalism I received sitting across the wire desk from him.

Cal taught me a couple of other things which have stayed with me the rest of my life.

Cal never went out for lunch at the office; it was too difficult for him to get around. So he sent

out to a nearby tavern generally for sandwiches, pickles, and so forth. One of his favorite sandwiches was a very thick slice of Limburger cheese contained between two slices of rye bread. Those were the Depression days and I didn't always have enough money to go out for lunch, so on lots of occasions I would work right through the lunch hour along with Cal.

I remember him looking over at me one day and saying, "Dartmouth, I can't stand to see you sitting there and starving." With that, he took the Limburger sandwich in his gnarled hands and tore it into two pieces, throwing half across the desk to me. "Eat that," he snarled, "and I won't feel so damn sorry for you."

Not only was it very old and stinky Limburger cheese, but in the process of tearing the sandwich apart, Cal had kneaded it with his hands until the cheese was squashed into the bread.

To this day, I like not only Limburger but old brick and some of the other famous Wisconsin cheeses.

The other cultural trait I learned from Calhoun was how to drink beer. He was the all-time champion, in my opinion, and he taught me early on how to drink a bottle of beer without swallowing. You merely tip your head back and open your throat and let the beer guzzle down.

Cal's wife had divorced him not long after he came down with that terrible case of arthritis, and he was very cynical about women from that time forward. He lived primarily a life among men, although he did have several loyal girlfriends who used to do errands and favors for him.

Several taverns in the Green Bay area were nightly haunts. One was presided over by a character named Shamus O'Brien, a real son of Erin whose place was out on Main Street. A gang of us from the *Press-Gazette* met there every Wednesday night for our weekly game of hearts. There was always a lot of good-natured kidding between Cal and Shamus; both men took it as

well as dished it out and all in fun.

Later on, Cal transferred his thirsty affections to an establishment just across the Walnut Street bridge on the near west side owned by Harold Brehme. Cal's relationship with him was the same as with O'Brien. Brehme stuttered, but that never hindered him from laying it on Cal real good. They were quite a pair; Cal with his crippled limbs and Brehme with his speech impediment.

Cal wasn't the only notable person to grace Brehme's tavern. Every year when the Chicago Bears were in Green Bay, Papa George Halas always visited Cal there sometime the evening before the game. It was a long-time tradition that was only broken when Calhoun passed away.

Despite his severe physical handicap, Cal was fiercely independent. He got himself around in his own car and up and down stairs at the

Calhoun At Work. Cal was always the first staffer in the news room to check his day's paper. The vest is not exactly natural, but the John Ruskin cigar is. *Green Bay Press-Gazette photo.*

The Packer Legend

GREEN BAY PRESS-GAZETTE, MONDAY

GREEN BAY PACKERS LOSE INITIAL GAME OF SEASON AT BELOIT; SCORE IS 6-0

Champions Are Robbed of Victory by Referee Zabel in Rough Battle; Three Touchdowns Taken Away.

CROWD ALL OVER PLAYING FIELD

Capt. Lambeau Crosses Goal Line Twice, Gallagher Once, But Scores Are Not Allowed by Official.

"Nothing short of highway robbery," said G. A. De Lair.

"I wish to go on record as saying that it was the most deliberate steal I have ever seen," said C. N. Murphy, Green Bay official. "Green Bay had the ball over the goal line for clear little touchdowns on three different occasions, and each time home officials ruled off side. It was a cut and dried deal to give Green Bay the worst of it, and they succeeded one hundred per cent."

"I talked to a business man from Janesville," said W. J. Ryan, the Packers' coach. "He said: 'I was over to the robbery this afternoon.' This expresses the sentiment of everyone from Green Bay that saw the game, as well as a number of people from Janesville who were neutral. The boys displayed wonderful fighting ability, but it was simply a case of too much Zabel. One of the players put it well when he said: 'Beloit had the game won before the teams stepped upon the gridiron.'"

(By Staff Correspondent.)

BELOIT, Wis., Nov. 24.—The Green Bay Packers met defeat at the hands of the Beloit Professionals at Morse park here on Sunday by a score of 6 to 0 before a good sized crowd of spectators.

Capt. Lambeau's team was robbed of victory by Referee Zabel of Beloit. This official penalized Green Bay three times after touchdowns, refusing to allow the scores. The Packers were twice on the verge of leaving the field but decided to play it out. Every time the Packers had the ball, the crowd would sweep out on the playing field, leaving practically no room for a forward pass offensive and of course, in this way, putting a big check on the Packers ground gaining machine. Just before the close of the game, McLean got away for a long run, headed goalward, close to the sidelines, when a Beloit spectator gave him a foot and the Packer quarterback fell to the ground. This was just one of the many obstacles that Green Bay had to combat with during their stay in Beloit.

The team were evenly matched in weight and both squads were exceptionally fast. The Packers made good on a number of forfard passes while Beloit's gains were made mostly on smashing line plunges. Scheibel, fullback, was a corking good plunger.

Packers Win Toss.

Capt. Lambeau won the toss and chose to kick to Beloit. The Packers cut short Beloit's offensive and he punted on the fourth down to McLean in midfield. The Packers got going

five yard line. Capt. Lambeau bucked tackle for as clean a touchdown as has ever been made on a gridiron. After the whistle blew, Referee Zabel took the ball and set it back 5 yards claiming the forward motion of the ball had stopped before Green Bay's captain went over the line. It was here that the riot started. For a time, it looked as if there would be a great little free-for-all. After a lengthy dispute, the teams went at it once more. Capt. Lambeau warned every man on the Packers to keep his hands to home and guard against off side. On this play, the Green Bay leader shot across the goal line with three yards to spare. As he did, Zabel once more blew his whistle, called an off side on Green Bay, penalized the Packers 5 yards and gave the ball to Beloit.

Decide to Play Out Game.

This was the straw that broke the camel's back. The Packers came within an inch of leaving the field, but at the last moment, decided to fight it out at all costs.

After the rumpus, Beloit kicked out of danger and the Packers, fighting like demons, once more started to waltz down the field. Twice in last ten minutes of play, the crowd blocked touchdowns for the Packers. Gallagher made a pretty catch of a forward pass and was headed for the goal when crowd bunched out in front of him and halted his progress. McLean got away again in the closing minutes of play but as related above a Beloit spectator spilled him while he was en route for a score. Final time was called with the ball in Beloit's possession in mid field.

Negotiations for another game on Dec. 6 were started in Beloit on Sunday night by the Packers' management. Green Bay is willing to play Beloit winner take all and a $2,000 side bet on any neutral field in the state with neutral officials.

Lineup of Teams.

The teams faced each other as follows:

Green Bay	Beloit
Dwyers-Abrams, l. e.	l. e. Van Kuren
Leaper, l. t.	l. t. Stubengen
Wilson, l. g.	l. g. Van Geldeer
Gavin, c.	c. Walsh
M. Zoll, r. g.	r. g. Yohrs
Powers, r. t.	R. T. Zeibell
Nichols, r. e.	r. e. Demoroski
	Sparks
McLean, q. b.	q. b. Witte (Cap.)
Gallagher, l. h. b.	l. h. b. Phillips
Lambeau, r. h. b.	r. h. b. Everson
Ladrow, f. b.	f. b. Scheibel
Rosenow	

Summary—Referee, Zabell, Beloit. Umpire, Gharrity, Beloit. Head linesman, Murphy, Green Bay. Linesmen, R. Lambeau and Jackson. Timekeepers, Wheeler and McCarthy. Touchdowns, Witte, Beloit. Time of periods, 15 minutes, each.

CITY IN BRIEF

Visiting in City—Mr. and Mrs. M. P. Jacobsen of Oak Park, Ill., have arrived in the city for a week's visit with relatives. Mr. Jacobsen left Sunday evening for Ironwood, Mich., to inspect a new warehouse being constructed in the northern city. He will return to this city Wednesday and spend the remainder of the week here.

Case Is Dismissed—The case against John Miller, accused of threatening bodily injury to John Pakanich, was dismissed by Judge Monahan on Saturday when it developed that the threat was not made in earnest.

Parents of Daughter—Mr. and Mrs. Arthur Harris announce the birth of a daughter, Genevieve Clara, on Nov. 16.

Cal called it robbery when the 1919 team lost its last game to the Beloit Fairies, 6-0. Cal wrote that the Packers crossed the goal three times, but each time were called back by a local official.   *Press-Gazette photo.*

Journalistic Magic

Here's a sample of Cal's weekly press releases:

The Green Bay Packers have strutted their stuff for Lambeau and company in a shroud of secrecy all week as they girded their loins for a 'battle royal' against their arch enemies, the big bad Chicago Bears, at City Stadium in Packertown next Sunday, at 2 p.m.

All Packertown was agog over preparations for the classic fray, but Boss Lambeau said 'nothing doing' to excited fans who begged and pleaded for a chance to watch the beefy bruisers go through their paces. The masterminder even warned his hirelings to 'take it easy' and not 'spill' any dope that might be welcomed with open arms in the 'Windy City.'

Plenty of fans will be on hand to give the two 'play-for-pay' teams the once-over at 2 o'clock next Sunday. They have been beating a path to the ticket office windows, literally bowling themselves over, in the rush to get ducats. However, there are still tickets available and reports about a sell-out are unfounded, according to Packer management.

The victors will have the 'inside' track to the Western division bunting in the National loop, and boosters here think conditions are 'ripe' for the Lambeaus to take the starch out of the Windy City Bruins. Nearly everybody believes that this will be a banner year for the Green Bay 'spoke' in the post-graduate organization.

Players and coaches have toiled long hours on the practice field turf in the shadow of the stadium, and Curly Lambeau was sure that his gridders would reel off their plays like clockwork by the time Sunday afternoon rolls around.

Lambeau and his assistants burned an ocean of midnight oil going over plays and strategy. They left no stones unturned as they went over a mountain-high pile of data and statistics, and everything points to a bumper crop of aches and pains for the invaders.

newspaper office without ever asking for help. I remember one night when we were sitting at a bar drinking beer and he had to go to the men's room. He started to get down from the bar stool, and a fellow next to him took his arm and tried to assist him. Cal swung around with his elbow, checking the fellow right in the jaw, and he hollered, "Get your damn hands off me!"

Cal did not drive at night, however. During the summer season, he was also the secretary and publicity man for the Green Bay Green Sox, an amateur baseball team which played in the Wisconsin State League. I used to drive him to some of the out of town games, particularly to the ones in nearby Kaukauna because we always wound up after the game at a tavern across the street run by John Coppes. He had a burlap bag full of peanuts in the corner of his bar which in those days were free to any customer and the bar room was constantly littered with peanut shells.

If you were a friend of Cal's, you also had to be a friend of his Boston terrier, Patsy, because Patsy went everywhere Cal went outside of working hours. She would sit by the hour on a bar stool alongside Cal, obviously as entertained by the conversation as everyone else in the bar was.

One night at Coppes' tavern when Cal went to the men's room, an old pal of his, C. O. Bates, who was president of the Wisconsin State League, took Patsy and hung her on a coat hook on the wall. When Cal came back, he went into a furor because he thought someone had taken his dog or that she had wandered off. Everyone but Cal had a good laugh when he found her hanging by her harness.

It was Cal's philosphy as sports editor of the *Press-Gazette* that he should become personally involved in any of the sporting efforts in the city, and besides the baseball team, he was also secretary to the Green Bay team in an amateur hockey league which played other cities in the area in the winter. In addition to publicizing Packer games in the newspaper, Cal became the traveling secretary and publicist for the team, and in the early years he passed the hat among the crowds who stood along the sidelines at the old Hagemeister Park where the Packers played their home games.

When I first became connected with the Packers through Cal, the total staff of the organization consisted of Lambeau, who had a full-time insurance business in Green Bay; his secretary; and Calhoun. The American Legion supplied the team with volunteers who did all the other chores in return for free admittance to the park. That is how the idea of making the American Legion post beneficiary in the event of dissolution of the corporation occurred to Andy Turnbull and attorney Jerry Clifford when they wrote the original *Articles of Incorporation*.

In the mid-1920s some frills were added. Curly's father, Marcel Lambeau, was a contractor, and with the help of Legion volunteers he erected some wooden stands on one side of the field at Hagemeister Park. The Packers opened a ticket office in the Legion building which was just one block down the street from the *Press-Gazette*, and a Legionnaire by the name of Spike Spachman became their ticket director. Jack Neville, another Legionnaire employed at the Kellogg-Citizens Bank, talked some of his fellow tellers into manning the ticket booths at the games on Sunday.

Calhoun originated the idea of writing a weekly newsletter about the Packers and mailing it out to daily and weekly newspapers throughout the area. It was printed for free by another Legionnaire at the Landsmann Printing Company, Fred Gronnert.

Calhoun used a number of the other employees at the newspaper as runners or go-fors. I was one of them. When I would carry his copy for the weekly newsletter over to the print shop, the next day he would send one of the other runners to make sure it had arrived all right.

One of these go-fors was a line-o-type operator by the name of Clem Collard, who was quite an athlete in his own right, particularly in amateur baseball circles. In the early days out at the stadium on the east side, Collard began helping Calhoun with the so-called press box, although in those days there probably were not more than three or four writers who covered the games and many of them were stringers for as many as three or four newspapers at the same time. Clem began bringing a few sandwiches and some hot coffee from home to serve to the reporters between halves. This custom grew year by year as the press corps expanded, so much so that Clem's wife was making several hundred sandwiches for the games every Sunday. In 1981, Clem observed his 60th year in the Packer press box.

Calhoun's florid style of writing would put modern-day sportswriters to shame. He tagged the Packers the "Big Bay Blues" (their colors were blue and gold back then), and the Bears

SPORTS

The baseball war is mighty costly. The press agents fighting the battles have worn out a dozen type mills already.

HAMMOND BATTLES THORPE'S ELEVEN TO TIE YESTERDA

CHICAGO FOOTBALL ELEVEN BEATEN BY PACKERS, 46 TO 0

Windy City Pigskin Chasers Unable to Check Green Bay's Offensive.

HARD FOUGHT GAME; INJURIES NUMEROUS

Invaders Fought For Every Inch; Fair Sized Crowd Witnesses Argument.

"GETTING AN EYEFUL"

Among the spectators at yesterday's game were nine members of the Stambaugh football team, who came here to get a line on the Packers. They had a chance to "look 'em over" all right, but they are apt to see a whole lot more next Sunday when Green Bay faces 'em on their home gridiron.

It's getting to be a regular weekend habit for the Packers to win a football game and running true to form. Capt. Lambeau's team walloped the Chicago A. C. eleven of Chicago by a score of 46 to 0 yesterday afternoon at Hagemeister park. This makes nine straight wins for Green Bay.

The visitors were, by far, the best team that has played here this season but they were unable to check Capt. Lambeau's squad. Chicago fought for every inch of ground and, at times, it seemed as if they were going to break away for a score. Both aggregations played straight football. The soggy condition of the playing field prevented open play. Forward passes and trick plays were thrown into the discard and it was an old fashioned line smashing gridiron argument.

Bays Get Quick Start.

Chicago won the toss and received at the west end. The Bays were off to a quick start and Capt. Lambeau's outfit put across the first marker in five minutes of play. The second score came quicker. A forward pass to Dwyer, aided materially in this count.

The visitors braced after the two first scores and the ball see-sawed up and down the field. Green Bay's line played their best game of the season and the Chicago backfielders were generally smothered before they got a chance to get started. Green Bay scored one more touchdown before half time and the goal was kicked.

Smashing Offensive.

The Packers opened up a smashing offensive in the last half and the vis-

tors were soon beating a hasty retreat. Coach Ryan made a number of changes in the lineup during the final quarters and the fresh men, "just rarin' to go" made it rather uncomfortable for the Windy City footballers. Towards the close of the battle, the play roughened up a bit and injuries were numerous, a couple of visitors getting badly banged up.

Lineup of Teams.

The teams lined up as follows:

Green Bay (46)	Chicago (0)
Dwyer, l. e.	l. e. Wright
Leaper, Martell	
Wilson, l. t.	l. t. R. Loss, Posey
C. Zoll, Des Jardien, l. g.	l. g. Carlson
Gavin, Leaper, c.	c. Hussers
M. Zoll, Sauber, r. g.	r. g. Jorgenson
Powers, r. t.	r. t. Murphy, Jones
Nichols, Abrams, r. e.	r. e. Loss
McLean, q. b.	q. b. Berg
Coffeen	McKenna
Rosenow, l h. b.	l. h. b. Fetz
Martin, Gallagher.	
Lambeau, r. h. b.	r. h. b. Mundson
Ladrow, Bero, f. b.	f. b. Logan

Referee, Murphy. Umpire, Stewart. Head linesman, Lande. Linesman, Dorschell and Jacobs. Timers, Abrams and Collette. Time of periods, 15 minutes. Score end of first half, Green Bay, 19, Chicago, 0. Touchdowns, Rosenow, 2, Lambeau, 2, McLean, 1, Ladrow, 1, Bero 1. Goals from touchdowns Lambeau 3, Gavin, 1.

TAG DAY AT COLLEGE NETS SUM OF $200

(By Associated Press.)

APPLETON, Wis., Nov. 10.—Tag day at Lawrence college netted $200 for expenses of the Lawrence homecoming, Nov. 15, when Ripon and the blue and white meet for a gridiron tussle on Lawrence field. Chester Hartlett, Wausau, is in charge of the entertainment.

Sport Calendar

Racing.

Continuation of fall meeting of Maryland Jockey club, at Pimlico.

Fox Hunt.

Annual meet of New England Fox Hunters' club opens at Belchertown, Mass.

Boxing.

Benny Leonard vs. Soldier Bartfield, 8 rounds, at Jersey City.

Johnny Dundee vs. Mel Coogan, 8 rounds, at Jersey City.

Al Roberts vs. Dan O'Dowd, 8 rounds, at Jersey City.

Battling Levinsky vs. Johnny Howard, 10 rounds, at Montreal.

Pal Moore vs. Mike Ertle, 10 rounds, at St. Paul.

Jack Britton vs. George Doig, 10 rounds, at La Salle, Ill.

Jeff Smith vs. Jack McCarron, 10 rounds, at Toledo.

Mike O'Dowd vs. Butch O'Hagen, 10 rounds, at Detroit.

Joe Benjamin vs. Johnny Drummie, 6 rounds, at Philadelphia.

MARQUETTE PREPS ARE HELD TO TIE BY WEST SIDERS

Purple Battles Famed Milwaukee Academy Eleven to 7-7 Score Saturday.

RYAN'S PUPILS START STRONG BUT WEAKEN

Cream City School Team Stages Stiff Comeback in Second Half.

In one of the most fiercely contested games, ever staged on a local griddle, the Marquette Academy eleven, and the West High scholers battled to a 7-7 tie at Hagemeister park Saturday afternoon, before a crowd of 500 brave football fans. Both teams were evenly matched in weight and speed and gave the small crowd some excitement at times.

The game was begun by Coleman, Marquette's husky fullback, who kicked off to L. Klauss. The Purple evidently got the jump on their opponents and immediately started to march down towards their goal posts. The backs alternated carrying the ball and this mixed with some perfect forward passes, brought the pigskin to the line. Shaughnessy scored a few seconds afterwards on a line buck. McGinn kicked an easy goal. Score West, 7; Marquette, 0.

Allaire booted to the Preps, but they were held for downs and the Westerners received the oval. Marquette in turn did the trick and it was returned to them, in the center of the field. Marquette fumbled the ball and Rocheleau recovered. Sustman brought the oval to the ten yard line, just as the quarter ended.

Second Quarter.

Again Marquette braced up and their forward wall held like concrete. Coleman punted from behind the uprights, to Shaughnessy, who was downed in his tracks. The West Siders began another march down the field, but in a critical moment, Klauss fumbled the oval and lost it. Marquette recovering. Coleman punted a few minutes afterward Quinn let the pill slide through his fingers, Fisher falling on it. Here the Preps fumbled and Patenaude recovered. The first half ended just as Marquette was trying forward passes. Score, West, 7; Marquette, 0.

Third Quarter.

The Marquette Preps bolstered up by a spirited talk from Coach Connie Hanley came back in the second half, determined to win. They started off in a rush and soon worked the oval goalwards. A long forward pass advanced the pigskin to the line and Markwiese carried it over on another pass. Coleman kicked the goal, tying the score.

The third quarter ended just as Coleman punted to M'Ginn. Shaughnessy muffed the pigskin and a Marquette gridder fell on the ball. The rest of the game was a series of fumbling and exchange of punts.

Marquette came near clinching the victory in the last few minutes of play on an on-side kick, which brought the ball to the five yard whitewash. The Westerners line held firm and Marquette lost the ball on downs. The time was called as McGinn threw a forward pass to Sustman. Score, West High, 7; Marquette Academy, 7.

The lineups:

West (7)	Marquette
Sustman, l. e.	l. e. Markwie
Allaire, l. t.	l. t. Lu
Platten, l. g.	l. g. Gramli
	Sea
F. Klauss, c.	c. Morris
R. Welsh, r. g.	r. g. Kritt
Clark, r. t.	r. t. Krie
Patenaude, r. e.	r. e. Da
McGinn, q. b.	q. b. Dur
Shaughnessy, l. h. b.	l. h. b. Fisch
Rocheleau, r h. b.	r. h. b. Benne
Quinn	
L. Klauss, f. b.	f. b. Colema

Summary—Officials, Referee, Rosenow, Green Bay Umpire, Lr. Garnow, Marquette University. Head linesman, Fitzgerald, Marquette. Linesmen, Lande, Green Bay and Mehigan, Marquette. Timekeepers, Coffeen, Green Bay and Crowley, Marquette. Touchdowns, Shaughnessy, 1, West High Markwiese, 1, Marquette. Goals kicked McGinn, 1; Coleman, 1. Time of quarters, twelve minutes. Substitutions, Marquette, Sears for Gramling; West, Quinn for Rocheleau. Score at end

HAMMOND BATTLES THORPE'S ELEVEN TO TIE YESTERDA

Stars of National Fame Play to 3-3 Standstill Before 10,000 Fans.

CHICAGO, Ill., Nov. 10.—In a terrific struggle featured by the hardest kind of tackling and blocking the Hammond All-Stars, captained by Shorty Des Jardien, and Jim Thorpe's Canton Bulldogs battled to a 3 to 3 tie yesterday at Cub park.

It was by far the greatest exhibition of professional football ever seen in Chicago. The game was witnessed by 10,000.

"Wyman to Baston."

Hammond was the first to score. After Captain Thorpe had won the toss and received the kickoff an exchange of punts left the ball in midfield. Hammond, strengthened by Baston and Wyman, the great Minnesota players, called the combination into commission almost immediately. Wyman hurled a beautiful forward pass over Thorpe's head to Baston who was stopped on the Canton twenty yard line.

Barrett and Wyman then were sent against the Canton line, but the position yielded only four yards in three attempts. Quarterback Ghee and Barrett then dropped back to the Canton twenty-six yard line and Barrett drove the ball between the posts for the first score.

The third quarter ended just as Coleman punted to M'Ginn. Shaughnessy muffed the pigskin and a Marquette gridder fell on the ball. The rest of the game was a series of fumbling and exchange of punts.

First Victory Over Chicago. Cal waxed boastful over this 46-0 victory over the Chicago Athletic Club eleven in 1919. This win and the 53-0 shellacking the Packers gave a team from Milwaukee a week earlier helped to create that enigmatic, measureless commodity called "Packer Pride." Beating the brains out of such small town teams as Sheboygan, 87-0, and Oshkosh, 85-0, meant nothing compared to beating the big city brawlers from Chicago and Milwaukee.

Green Bay Press-Gazette photo.

were the "Big Bad Bears" or better yet, the "Monsters of the Midway." He wrote that the Packers one season were going to "lock horns with every spoke in Bert Bell's wheel." He described one lineman as "a huge fellow who stood firmly with both feet on the ground and never rocked the boat," and he told of a defensive back who "moved in for the tackle and collared him around the knees." When Lambeau won a championship, he said to him, "I'll bet you wouldn't even change places with Jesus Christ on the cross." And when Lambeau was having a losing season, he described him as "always walking around like a chicken laying an egg."

Calhoun really came into his own when the Packers hit the big time and started traveling to major cities in the country like Chicago, New York, and Philadelphia. Cal could talk newspapermen's language, and in those days when professional football attracted little attention in prestigious papers like the New York *Times* or *Herald-Tribune*, Cal got more ink for the Packers than any other team in the league could muster.

I was fortunate in that the Packers at that time made an annual swing through the East at Thanksgiving time, playing the New York Giants the Sunday before Thanksgiving, the Philadelphia Yellow Jackets on Thanksgiving Day, and the Staten Island Stapletons the next Sunday. Cal would give me my board and room if I would help him with his publicity duties.

When Cal would arrive in New York City, he would order up cases of beer and a block of ice and fill up his bathtub with ice water and beer. He always brought along a daisy of Wisconsin cheddar cheese. Then he would get on the telephone to Art Daley and John Kieran of the New York *Times* and Red Smith at the New York *Herald-Tribune* and announce that the Packers were in town, the beer was in the tub, the cheese was on the dresser, so come on over.

Cal had one thing going for him in New York. Red Smith was a native of Green Bay and a built-in cheerleader for the Packers in the "Big Apple." But over the years Cal built a relationship with the sportswriters in league cities that almost guaranteed sell-out crowds wherever the Packers played.

Cal could also teach the big city sportswriters something about the art of drinking beer. He was a champion among champions in his native Green Bay and the state of Wisconsin. Cal perfected the technique used by top-notch beer drinkers of being able to open his throat and pour down a whole bottle of beer without swallowing.

One evening after the Packers had lost a very tough game to the New York Giants I was sitting in Cal's room helping him with a case of beer which he had ordered up from the hotel commissary. We were only into our second bottle when he remarked he had better get a hold of "The Belgian" because he knew how badly he was taking the afternoon's loss. He got on the phone to Lambeau and told him he had a case of beer in his room and invited him to come on

They're In The Movies Now. Otto Stiller started filming Packer games from the grandstand roof in 1923 with a hand-powered camera. Remember Eskimo Pies? *Lefebvre-Stiller photo.*

The Packer Legend

down and help drown his sorrows. Lambeau did so, and my recollection is that Curly and I each drank about two or three bottles of beer and went to the case for another when we found it empty. Cal had finished off about 18 of those 24 bottles all by himself.

Calhoun was always plugging Lambeau as a coaching genius wherever he went on tour, but many times the feature stories in the metropolitan papers turned out to be about George W. Calhoun. One of his jobs at home games in Green Bay was giving out the complimentary tickets to the press. He kept a very close track of what papers used material from his weekly newsletter, and those were the sports editors and writers who were favored with complimentary tickets. Cal always made the sportswriters pick up their tickets at the pass gate at the stadium, and that way he could make sure that it was the writers themselves who were using the free tickets. He guarded that pass gate so religiously that one of his nicknames became "Gates Ajar" Calhoun.

One of Cal's hobbies, so to speak, turned out

A Silver-Tongued Devil

The late Dave Yuenger, who covered the Packers for a number of years before becoming managing editor and then editor of the Green Bay *Press-Gazette*, kept a file of what he called "Calhounisms." They were a combination of mixed metaphors, fractured similes, twisted adages, and malapropisms used by George Whitney Calhoun in his everyday speech. For instance, when he was being badgered for press tickets, Cal would answer angrily: "There aren't any seats left; the place is filled to captivity."

Here are some other classic examples from Dave's files:

Regarding animals: 'We've got the bull right by the woods." Or: "Take the bull by the hands." He acted like "a lamb in sheep's clothing." Or it was a case of "a horse of one and a half dozen of another." Guys he didn't like were "like two snakes in a pod."

When he misplaced something, he "looked heads and tails for it," or it was "like looking for a needle in a hay rack," or "like looking for a weasel in a haystack."

Of a tough decision, he always said that "one head is better than two," or "I'm on pins and cushions," and "I couldn't make heads or shoulders of it." At times, he "kept going around in half-circles."

He referred to "Alcoholics Unanimous" and said a fellow was "as sober as a crutch." Good fortune was being "born under a silver spoon," or "riding on the gravel train."

Cal had a regular roster of cronies whom he called first thing every morning with the gossip of the day. Many of these corruptions of the language popped out during these conversations, and Yuenger, whose desk was nearby, would hasten to convert them to typewritten notes and put them in his file.

Cal was an excellent copy editor in his own right and would tell a reporter to "write a half a paragraph on that," or to "wrap your finger around your hand, don't forget this."

On days when things weren't going so good, he'd remark that "it's a long trail that has no winding," or that it was a "forlorn conclusion all along." The trouble was that there were "too many hands in the puddle," and that's what "broke the camel's straw." He often warned that "you can't have your cake and sleep in it too," or that "forewarned is foreskinned."

Sometimes he would admonish, "Don't sit there like a stump on a log," or "don't be so damned delicatessen about this." On other occasions, it was "easier than flying off a log," or he had "killed three bones with one stone."

He always wound up a conversation with one of his buddies with: "Okay, keep your ear peeled to the ground."

After his bitter break with Lambeau, he remarked to a friend, "I called him everything in the book except the Bible," and he said that from now on Lambeau would have to "pedal his own canoe." Then he added: "You can have those throatcutters who stab you in the back."

But in the end, he always predicted that "100 years from now we'll probably get through tomorrow all right."

to be extremely valuable in later years. He cut out the box scores and statistics of every game played in the NFL and pasted them in notebooks which he kept up to date every week. In the 1950s, a writer by the name of Roger Treat got the idea of compiling an encyclopedia of pro football, and Calhoun's files of all the NFL games became one of Treat's main sources of information.

Cal's long and intimate association with the Packers came to a tragic end, however. One morning as he was reading through the sports news which came over the *Associated Press* teletype machine, he read a story from Chicago to the effect that "General Manager Curly Lambeau of the Green Bay Packers announced today that George Strickler, formerly sports editor of the Chicago *Tribune*, has been named publicity director for the Packers in Green Bay. He will replace George W. Calhoun, who has retired."

That was the way Cal learned that his old pal Curly Lambeau had dumped him. He was a bitter enemy of Lambeau from that day forward, as were three other members of the old "Hungry Five": Lee Joannes, president of the club in the 1930s; Dr. W.W. Kelly; and attorney Jerry Clifford. Before he concluded his career in Green Bay, Curly managed to turn many former friends into enemies. Only Andy Turnbull remained as Curly's friend and supporter among the group who had seen the Packers through their early years.

After Calhoun retired from the Green Bay *Press-Gazette*, he continued to maintain his historical files on the Packers and again was of great assistance when the Pro Football Hall of Fame was being organized in Canton, Ohio.

It was in these retirement years when he told me on frequent occasions that he was working on a book on the history of the Packer and even told me that he had some proofs back from the printers which he was correcting. A frantic search of all of his papers and belongings after he died failed to reveal any trace of such a book. I think such a book was a dream which Cal had had for a long time but never realized. I hope that wherever he is in the "Valhalla of Pro Football" someone will give him a copy of this volume which I have dedicated to him.

If I have gone on an emotional binge in writing about George Whitney Calhoun, there is a point to my story.

The game of pro football as we know it today was created by dreamers like Curly Lambeau and George Calhoun who never took the time to question whether a little town like Green Bay could compete in a national football league. Remember this: They had no revenue even from radio in those early days, let alone today's TV bonanza. They lived on gate receipts and on their wits and their hype, if you will. Theirs was a constant battle to sell people on a game most of them had never seen before, a game where the athletes played for pay.

Curly and Cal knew back in the 1920s that they were selling entertainment as well as football. And if their hoopla seems a bit corny today, so be it. It sold tickets.

An Historian's Historian

Roger Treat, the compiler of *The Encyclopedia of Pro Football*, first published in 1952 then revised and reprinted in 1959, had much to say about George Whitney Calhoun.

"Without the monumental help from many sources, this volume could never have been completed. A frantic SOS was broadcast in all directions, endorsed by Commissioner Bert Bell of the NFL. The response was heartwarming. George Calhoun of Green Bay, Wisconsin, forwarded his precious and massive files and proved to be a true triple-threat on digging up facts which once seemed as inaccessible as the vital statistics on the population of Mars.

"The Green Bay Packers, Curly Lambeau and George Calhoun through the years have become synonymous.

"The dynamo of the Packers, other than Lambeau, was a man whose name is never printed in the programs, but who has been from the beginning, and still is, the senior advisor, the patriarchal statesman, the father confessor, the defender of the faith, the only official Monday morning quarterback and the historian of all things Packer. George Whitney Calhoun is his name and he is known wherever major league football has been played, from Boston to San Francisco. Even though Lambeau has moved on to other fields, Calhoun is still there on the telegraph desk of the *Press-Gazette* and the Packers would be lost without him."

GREEN BAY PRESS-GAZETTE

"EVERYBODY READS IT"

GREEN BAY, WIS., MONDAY EVENING, DECEMBER 9, 1929.

PACKERS WHIP BEARS; WIN NATIONAL TITLE

FOUR QUINTETS TIED FOR LEAD IN LOCAL LOOP

IOWA DENIED REINSTATEMENT IN BIG TEN

LIDBERG STARS AS BAYS TAKE GAME, 25 TO 0

THEY BROUGHT GREEN BAY ITS FIRST NATIONAL CHAMPIONSHIP

Northern Paper and Public Service Fives Win at "Y" Gym.

HAWKEYES END RELATIONS IN SPORT JAN. 1

No Comment Accompanies Resolution Passed By Board.

FACULTY BOARD OF SCHOOL TO DECIDE COURSE

Expect Hawkeyes to Follow One of Three Paths In Athletics.

Eddie Kotal Also In Limelight Catching Passes to Score.

FOSTER DECLARED ELIGIBLE TO PLAY ON BADGER QUINTET

Return of Veteran Center Gives Squad Two All-Conference Men.

Expect Lively Session at Gathering of Baseball Men

SCOTT ENTERS RING AGAINST VON PORAT IN "HEAVY" BATTLE

Winner of Bout Tonight Will Be In Line For Match With Jack Sharkey.

SIX SCHOOLS PLAN NEW SPORT CIRCUIT

New Rocky Mountain Conference Is Formed.

CHARGES AND ANSWERS

LOCAL "Y" BOYS TEAM TIES WITH FOND DU LAC

SOFT-HEARTED HOLD-UP MEN GIVE VICTIM $5

ROGERS HORNSBY WINS NATIONAL PLAYER AWARD

Week-End Sport

FAMOUS AUTO RACER DIES AT HOME ON WEST COAST

WINTER'S ICY HAND
WILL LITERALLY MELT AWAY IN THE RADIANT HEAT OF HURLBUT'S

SUNBEAM COAL

Chapter Three

THE

FIRST

TRIPLE

CHAMPS

The three league championships won by the Packers under Vince Lombardi, climaxed by Super Bowls I and II, have been publicized over and over as the ultimate sports achievement, but actually a triple championship was old hat to the Packers. They accomplished the same feat back in 1929, 1930, and 1931, and the record of those teams was even more spectacular than those of the late 1960s.

In 1929, the Packers were undefeated, posting 12 wins, no losses, and one tie; and in the three-year span, they compiled 34 wins against five losses and two ties.

Curly Lambeau had begun recruiting players from beyond the Green Bay area in the early 1920s. The first player of national reputation to join the Packers was Howard (Cub) Buck from the University of Wisconsin, a giant of a center

who anchored the Packer line from 1921 through 1925. The next year saw Jug Earp arriving from Monmouth College in Iowa to take over the center spot as Buck moved to tackle. Along with Earp came Howard (Whitey) Woodin, a guard from Marquette. In 1924, the Packers acquired the great punter and running back from Nebraska, Verne Lewellen. Carl Lidberg, a fullback from Minnesota, joined the team in 1926, and in 1927, two former Marquette stars, end Lavvie Dilweg and quarterback Red Dunn, put on the Packer colors.

Tom Nash, an end from Georgia, signed in 1928, and that was year that the little town of Green Bay first made its big splurge on the national sports scene when the Packers beat the New York Giants at the Polo Grounds, 7-0. Tim Mara had launched the Giants as a new member

GREEN BAY PACKERS 1929 © STILLER'S 1929 WORLD CHAMPIONS

1929 World Champions, Won 13, lost 0, tied 1. Left to right, back row: Cal Hubbard (T), Geneva, Hurdis McCrary (B), Georgia; Tom Nash (E), Georgia; Bernard Darling (C), Beloit; Claude Perry (T), Alabama; Red Smith (G), Notre Dame; Verne Lewellen (B), Nebraska; Roger Ashmore (T), Gonzaga; Johnny "Blood" McNally (B), St. John; Jim Bowdoin (G), Alabama; Lavvie Dilweg (E), Marquette; Jug Earp (C), Monmouth. Front row: Curly Lambeau (B), Notre Dame; Paul Minnick (G), Iowa; Bo Molenda (B), Michigan; Roy Baker (B), Southern California; Eddie Kotal (B), Lawrence; Red Dunn (B), Marquette; Dick O'Donnell (E), Minnesota; Mike Michalske (G), Penn State; Bill Kern (T), Pittsburgh; Whitey Woodin (G), Marquette; Carl Lidberg (B), Minnesota.

Lefebure-Stiller photo.

The Packer Legend

of the National Football League that year, and the Giants had beaten the Packers in Green Bay by the same score earlier in the season. But when the Packers took on the Gotham Giants in their home territory and stood off every challenge, it made headlines in all the metropolitan press.

The 1928 season, with a record of 7-4-3, was a preview of things to come.

Four all-time Packer greats joined the team in 1929: Cal Hubbard, Mike Michalske, Bo Molenda, and the immortal Johnny (Blood) McNally. Michalske, Hubbard, and Molenda all came from the New York Yankees, a team that had folded the previous season, and Blood, as McNally was better known, became available during the 1928 season when the Pottsville team folded.

The three former Yankees were all very happy to settle down in a town like Green Bay. Their previous team had been a traveling club put together by promoter Charley Pyle to showcase the talents of the great Red Grange. The Yankees had no home field and played all their games on the road. The year Michalske joined them out of Penn State, they played 36 games in one season. They would often play a game one afternoon, hop on a train, and travel to the next town where they would either play the next day or the day after.

In those days, football players carried all their own gear wherever they went, and their total outfit could be held in one handbag. There was very little provided in the way of dressing quarters. Michalske recalls that when they played in Pottsville, Pennsylvania, the team dressed in the fire station two blocks away from the stadium, then ran down to the field for the game and dragged their butts back afterwards.

When the Packers played the Stapletons over on Staten Island in metropolitan New York, they dressed in their hotel rooms in downtown New York, took a bus to the Staten Island ferry, then rode the boat over to the island where they proceeded on foot to the stadium. You can imagine the excitement that a football team in full uniform, minus their shoes of course, created on the Staten Island ferry.

Michalske and Hubbard had played side by side with the Yankees, and very soon they took over anchoring the left side of the Packer line. Dilweg was at left end. With Jug Earp at center, Woodin and Paul Minnick shared the right guard spot. Claude Perry was at right tackle, and Tom Nash at right end.

What About Sand?

Johnny Blood's real name was John McNally. He was the son of a wealthy milling family in New Richmond, Wisconsin.

At the time he was going to college, football players often picked up a little side money by playing for pro teams on Sundays. While strolling down the main street of their college town one Saturday night, Johnny and a buddy who were going to play for a pro team on Sunday were discussing what names to use as pros. At that point, Johnny looked up and noticed a theater marquee advertising the movie *Blood and Sand* starring Rudolph Valentino and Vilma Banky.

"That's it," said John. "You be Sand, and I'll be Blood."

And from that time on for the rest of his football career, John McNally was known as Johnny Blood.

GREEN BAY PACKERS 1930 WORLD CHAMPIONS STILLER PHOTO

1930 World Champions, Won 10, lost 3, tied 1. Left to right, back row: Bernard Darling, Beloit; Whitey Woodin, Marquette; Bo Molenda, Michigan; Claude Perry, Alabama; Tom Nash, Georgia; Lavvie Dilweg, Marquette; Cal Hubbard, Geneva; Elmer Sleight, Purdue; Verne Lewellen, Nebraska; Johnny "Blood" McNally, St. John; Jug Earp, Monmouth; Mike Michalske, Penn State; Curly Lambeau, Notre Dame. Front row: Jim Bowdoin, Alabama; Ken Radick, Marquette; Wuert Engelmann, South Dakota State; Hurdis McCrary, Georgia; Red Dunn, Marquette; Dave Zuidmulder, St. Ambrose; Merle Zuver, Nebraska; Paul Fitzgibbons, Creighton; Arnie Herber, Regis; Dick O'Donnell, Minnesota; Carl Lidberg, Minnesota.

Lefebvre-Stiller photo.

The Packer Legend

On defense, the Packers used a seven-man line in 1929. Fullbacks Lidberg or Molenda backed up the line, the halfbacks covered the outside, and Dunn went back to safety. Gradually, however, they experimented with a "roving center," and Michalske wound up the next year as a weak side linebacker.

Dunn was an experienced field general who had played with the Milwaukee Badgers and the

All-time All-Pro. Mike Michalske came to the Packers from the New York Yankees in 1929 after a college career at Penn State. He was known as "Iron Mike" because of his stamina in the two-way game. He now lives in De Pere.*Lefebvre-Stiller photo.*

The Packers employed the Notre Dame box in the backfield, which Lambeau had learned under Knute Rockne. Quarterback Red Dunn was behind the center. Bo Molenda and Carl Lidberg alternated at fullback, flanked right or left just behind the line. Verne Lewellen was at left half, and Johnny Blood was at right. Dunn could hand off to any one of the three backs or drop back to pass.

Early Field General. Red Dunn was a graduate of Marquette. He joined the Packers in 1927 and quarterbacked the team to their first three championships, 1929-1931, then retired after the 1931 season. *Lefebvre-Stiller photo.*

The Packer Legend

GREEN BAY PACKERS 1931 NATIONAL LEAGUE CHAMPIONS

1931 World Champions, Won 12, Lost 2, Tied 0. Left to right, back row: Curly Lambeau, Dick Stahlman, Johnny Blood, Elmer Sleight, Cal Hubbard, Tom Nash, Hurdis McCrary, Jug Earp, Arnie Herber. Middle row: Roger Grove, John Don Carlos, Hank Bruder, Milt Gantenbein, Bo Molenda, Rudy Comstock, Russ Saunders, Front row: Red Dunn, Nate Barrager, Jim Bowdoin, Wuert Engelmann, Lavvie Dilweg, Mike Michalske, Faye Wilson, Paul Fitzgibbons. Not present when picture was taken, Verne Lewellen, Ray Jenison, Bernard Darling, Frank Baker, Art Johnstone, Ken Raddick, Dave Zuidmulder, Whitey Woodin, Bill Davenport.

Lefebvre-Stiller photo.

The Packer Legend

Chicago Cardinals after graduating from Marquette. He, Lewellen, and Lidberg had already had two seasons together in the Packer backfield when Molenda and Blood came along.

Blood has to be one of the most colorful players to ever wear a Packer uniform. He had a well-deserved reputation as a lady's man, and he also liked alcoholic beverages. Lambeau put Blood into a room with Michalske whenever they were on the road, thinking that the older and more staid Michalske could keep Blood in line. Even

Incipient Congressman. Lavvie Dilweg was an All-American end at Marquette before joining the Packers in 1927. He made All-Pro in 1931. He practiced law in Green Bay after retiring from football and was elected to Congress from Wisconsin's Eighth District.*Lefebvre-Stiller photo.*

Mike, however, failed at that assignment.

I happened to be present one Friday evening in the New Yorker Hotel when the Packers had come to the "Big Apple" to play the Giants on Sunday. Blood had been out beyond the curfew hour and awoke Michalske upon returning to invite him to have a nightcap. Mike allowed as though he would, but he complained that there was no ice. Blood said that was no problem; he could take care of that. He disappeared for about a half hour, then reappeared, marching through the hotel lobby to the elevator carrying a cake

Early Triple Threat Back. Verne Lewellen came to the Packers from Nebraska in 1924. He was a great running back and passer as well as one of the finest punters in the game's history.*Lefebvre-Stiller photo.*

Jug for Juggernaut. That was Francis Earp's nickname. A graduate of Monmouth, he came to the Packers in 1922 and played center and guard during the championship era. He made his home in Green Bay, later becoming publicity director for the Packers. *Lefebvre-Stiller Photo.*

of ice, complete with tongs.

The next morning Blood was still in a state of inebriation, and Michalske suggested to him that he probably had the flu and would so inform Lambeau at practice. But Blood was not going to miss practice for a little thing like bottle flu.

That morning I was helping tag balls for the kickers who were practicing. Everyone stood around and watched as Blood tried to meet the ball with his foot during his turn. About the second try, he fell flat on his back, and Lambeau came storming over and fired him on the spot. He might have stayed fired, too, if Michalske and others on the team hadn't prevailed on Lambeau that evening to reinstate him. He went on to play a spectacular game against the Giants on Sunday.

Blood was one of the key elements in making the Packer passing game click, for he had the knack of coming down with the ball in a crowd. He left the Packers after the 1936 season and went to the Pittsburgh Steelers where he played three more years before becoming head coach there. He now resides in Palm Springs, Calif., and is in remarkably good health for a man of his years. He was recently honored at a sports award dinner in neighboring Appleton, and while I was renewing acquaintances with him there, I commented on his appearance and asked him if he exercised regularly. "No," he responded, then added, "But...I think about it a lot."

One of the most famous games in Packer history occurred late in that first championship season of 1929 when the Packers again engaged the New York Giants at the Polo Grounds. They beat them, 20-6, and only 11 men played the game on offense and defense for the Packers until the final minute of play when Lambeau sent Paul Minnick into the game to substitute for Jim Bowdoin. Curly wanted to give the rookie Minnick a little playing time, but Bowdoin was so angry at being replaced that he charged back into the game two plays later and kicked Minnick out.

Hubbard was a giant of a man among players of those days and would rank pretty well with the giant tackles of the present era. He had great upper body strength, as we describe it today, and could easily handle the opposing tackle and end when playing defense and often took on the whole side of the opposing line when playing offense. He was also a coach on the field, and he, Michalske, Dunn, and Blood frequently made up plays as they went along.

Red Grange had left the Yankees after the 1927 season and had joined the Chicago Bears. One of the largest crowds in Packer history up to that time turned out at the old City Stadium for the Bear game but were disappointed when Grange could not play because of an ankle sprain he had suffered the previous Sunday. Despite Grange's presence with the Bears, however, the Packers beat their long-time enemy three times

The Packer Legend

during that first championship season by scores of 23-0, 14-0, and 25-0.

The third Bear game was played in Chicago, and when the team arrived home that Sunday evening on the Chicago and Northwestern Railroad, hometown fans lined the tracks for the five miles between DePere and Green Bay with kerosene torches. Then the team was paraded from the station to the Beaumont Hotel for a giant victory celebration.

Michalske recalls that they were given a watch as a memento of their second championship in 1930, but he says that after the third championship in 1931, they were merely told it was nice to have them home. Mike says that Green Bay fans had already grown a little complacent about titles.

The Packers actually almost made it four in a row in 1932. They played two tough games against the Bears, tying the first one, 0-0, and winning the second, 2-0. They were undefeated when they again challenged the Giants in New York and lost, 6-0. They were still leading the

Giant of a Tackle. Cal Hubbard anchored the left side of the Packer line in the triple championship era, playing from 1929 to 1935. Cal was big enough that he could have matched up with linemen in the modern era. Hubbard was inducted into the Pro Hall of Fame in 1963. He was an original member of the Packer Hall of Fame, and he was an All-Pro selection three times, 1931-33. *Lefebvre-Stiller photo.*

Ridin' the Rails

Packer trivia buff Jimmy Ford tells the story about how Johnny Blood came to Green Bay when he was joining the Packers back in the 1920s.

Blood caught a freight train in his hometown of New Richmond, Wisconsin, and rode in a Soo Line boxcar to Amherst Junction, a whistle stop a few miles east of Stevens Point. Johnny had the presence of mind to ask the station master at New Richmond to have the Green Bay and Western combination passenger-freight train wait for him at Amherst, a standard procedure in those times.

When the G.B.&W. engineer didn't see anyone depart the Soo Line passenger car, he started up his locomotive and headed for Green Bay. Of course, he didn't know that Blood was riding free in a boxcar.

Blood made a run for the G.B.&W. train and caught onto the back platform of the last car, the baggage car. Sometime later the baggageman noticed him, invited him inside, and even shared his lunch bucket with him.

league until the last two games, however, when they lost to Portsmouth, 19-0, then were beaten out of the championship by the Bears in Chicago, 9-0. The Packers actually won more games than the Bears did but lost the title by percentage points. The Bears tied six games that season and ties counted in their favor under the scoring system then in use.

How then would the triple championship teams of Curly Lambeau compare with Vince Lombardi's three-time winners?

Obviously, there is no definitive answer since players went both ways in those early years versus the platoon football of today.

But I am certain there were a number of players on those teams who would be stars in today's game. Start with Blood and Lewellen. Very few punters have come along since who

Quarterback Delay. Red Dunn runs to daylight after faking a pitchout to Eddie Kotal, the Lawrence College (Wis.) grad who always played without a helmet. Blocking for Dunn are Jug Earp, Whitey Woodin, Roger Ashmore, and Tom Nash. It was a 1928 game against the Chicago Cardinals. The Packers shut down the Cards, 20-0. That year the Packers gained national attention when they invaded the Polo Grounds and beat the New York Giants.

Lefebure-Stiller photo.

could match Lewellen, and remember the ball he was using was much rounder than that of today. Michalske, who never weighed much over 200 pounds, would hold his own as a linebacker today, and Hubbard would stack up with the best tackles, offense or defense. Dilweg would probably be playing tight end in modern formations.

All that we can say is that they beat the best teams in the country for those three years, playing 14 games a season. Not bad by anyone's standards.

An Athletic Virtuoso

Richard (Red) Smith was one of the most versatile athletes ever to be connected with the Packers. He played professional football and baseball in the major leagues during the same time period, and later he coached and managed in both professional sports.

Smith hailed from a little town upriver from Green Bay, Combined Locks. He went to Lawrence College in Appleton two years before transferring to Notre Dame where he became a star lineman under Knute Rockne. He played guard for the Packers from 1927 through 1929, the latter being the first of their triple championship years.

Smith was playing professional baseball at the same time with the Milwaukee Brewers in the American Association. He also played for several other Triple A clubs until he became a catcher with the New York Giants.

After his playing career, Red managed the Green Bay Bluejays baseball team in the Class A Triple I League, and at the same time he was the line coach under Curly Lambeau from 1936-43. He went on up in professional baseball as an assistant under Charley Grimm with the Chicago Cubs, then managed the Brewers to the American Association pennant in both 1951 and 1952. He went with the Toledo club after the Boston Braves moved into Milwaukee, and eventually he went into private business in the Ohio city.

A mid-winter sports banquet in Appleton which annually fills a banquet hall with 1,200 people is named for Red. One year Walter (Red) Smith, the famous sports columnist who died in January of 1982, was an honored guest. Oddly enough, Red Smith the columnist is from Green Bay, and he attended Notre Dame at the same time Red Smith the athlete was there. The columnist told the banquet audience that despite both of them being in the same place at the same time, they never knew each other until later in their illustrious careers.

Richard (Red) Smith. The Combined Locks native both played and coached in major league football and baseball. He handled the Packer offensive line from 1936 through 1943 and at the same time managed the Green Bay entry in a Class A baseball league. *Post-Crescent photo.*

Andrew B. Turnbull

The business manager of the Green Bay *Press-Gazette* organized the backing of Green Bay businessmen and formed the unique community football corporation in 1923, serving as its first president. *Press-Gazette photo.*

Chapter Four

THE

HUNGRY

FIVE

When Lee Joannes was president of the Packer corporation, he held the Packer franchise in the National Football League in his personal possession as security for $6,000 he had loaned the corporation to bail it out of receivership. Today, that franchise has to be worth at least $25,000,000. Joannes went out and raised enough money from business friends to repay the loan and preserve the financial integrity of the football corporation.

Financial disaster had struck the Packers in the midst of the Great Depression when a set of bleachers at City Stadium collapsed during a game and one of the spectators was injured. He sued the corporation for damages and was awarded $5,000. At the same time, however, the insurance company with which the Packers carried their public liability policy went

bankrupt, and to add to the misery, it was a mutual insurance company. The Packers were assessed an additional $2,500 to settle up with the company's creditors.

Packer management decided to go to court and petition for the appointment of a "friendly" receiver for the Packer football corporation. Joannes was a good friend of Circuit Court Judge Henry Graass, who was also a faithful Packer fan, and Graass appointed Frank Jonet, a Green Bay accountant, as receiver for the club.

All of this occurred at a time when the National Football League was beginning to enjoy considerable improvement in its fortunes. Despite the lingering Depression, prosperity really began to blossom for the NFL in the 1930s. The league was divided into East and West divisions in 1933, setting up a play-off game for

City Stadium in the '30s. The stadium built by the Green Bay School Board with Packer help behind East High School was gradually improved and enlarged until it could seat some 20,000 fans in the mid-'30s. But a lot of fans still stood along the fence.
Lefebure photo.

the championship. That same year, George Marshall bought the Boston franchise; Art Rooney took over the Pittsburgh club; Bert Bell converted the Frankford Yellowjackets into the Philadelphia Eagles; and Charles Bidwell bought the Chicago Cardinals; all names which will go down in NFL history.

In 1934, the league instituted the college player draft with the idea of equalizing the talent among teams. Owners like Halas, Rooney, Mara, Marshall, and Bell realized that what made a successful league was balanced competition and that there had to be concessions made by the clubs in the large cities if franchises like Green Bay's were to be protected. George Halas was a loyal friend of the Packers in league affairs since the day he got the franchise back for Curly Lambeau, despite the fact that their rivalry on

The Deadly Weapon

The first forward pass ever thrown in a football game was thrown by Gus Dorais when he starred for Notre Dame in 1912.

Dorais and end Knute Rockne were relaxing on a beach that summer before practice started for the season. Naturally, they had a football along, and they started throwing it back and forth to each other. Suddenly, a light went on in Rockne's football brain. Rockne realized the total value of the forward pass as an offensive weapon. He and Dorais worked on their passing game in secret through the remainder of the summer, even keeping it a secret from their coach.

In a crucial game with Army that fall, the Fighting Irish were struggling along until Rockne came back to the huddle and informed Dorais that he could outrun the Army secondary. Dorais told him to head straight down the field and he would let go with a bomb.

Notre Dame went on to defeat Army handily, and the forward pass became part of the Notre Dame offensive arsenal from then on and soon spread to other teams.

Curly Lambeau brought the forward pass to Green Bay after playing one season under Rockne in 1918, and pioneered its use in professional football.

The Packer Legend

the field was one of the bitterest in the league.

At the same time, the league took other steps to equalize this competition, instituting the waiver rule to give the teams with the poorest records first crack at players that other teams released, and setting a limit on the number of players each team could have under contract. At the time the limit was set at 24.

The first College All-Star game was played in August of 1934, and to the surprise of everyone, the All-Stars tied the Chicago Bears, 0-0.

The Packer corporation began to prosper during the receivership and benefited from the increased popularity of professional football on a national scale. Probably the greatest thing that happened to the Packers during that period was the arrival on the Green Bay scene in the fall of 1935 of a fabulous football player by the name of Don Hutson. Hutson's exploits are detailed in a subsequent chapter, but suffice it to say that the Packers were able to work their way out of receivership in 1937.

Another world championship in 1936 was a major factor in that financial recovery. They won the Western Division title with a 10-1-1 record, then beat Boston in the play-offs, 21-6. The championship game was moved from Boston to the Polo Grounds in New York because Marshall was disgusted with the lack of fan support he was receiving in the Boston area. The next year he moved his club to the nation's capital, where it has remained since as the Washington Redskins.

Joannes was principally responsible for rescuing the Packer corporation from its Depression-era troubles. As mentioned above, he personally loaned the corporation $6,000 in order to settle the damage judgment. Then he set out once again with the help of other members of the "Hungry Five" and others to sell stock in the corporation. By 1937, enough capital money had been raised to justify the circuit court's ending of the receivership. The corporation was renamed the Green Bay Packers, Inc., but the basic principles of the original *Articles of Incorporation* were retained, preserving the non-profit status.

In 1939, the team began to divide its home games between Green Bay and Milwaukee, and the tapping of the much larger market surrounding the Milwaukee area has been one of the real secrets of the Packers' financial stability ever since. The Packer franchise includes not only the territory within a radius of 75 miles of Green Bay, as is the standard franchise provision, but also the Milwaukee area. This has had the effect over the years of dissuading others from trying to establish a competing professional football team in the Milwaukee market.

A great flap arose among Packer fans, however, when the Pack again won the Western championship that year, 1939, and Packer management, trying to build a following in Milwaukee, decided to play the championship game against the New York Giants in the Beer City. The Packers played their Milwaukee games at State Fair Park which was far from an ideal stadium, with permanent seats only on one side of the field and bleachers on the other. It turned out to be a wintry, blustery day, and all the New York sports writers wrote about was the wind whipping through the press box and threatening to topple it to the ground at any moment.

By 1941, the corporation was beginning to invest some of its cash reserves and put $5,000 into National Defense bonds. Another 1500 seats were added to City Stadium, and in that same year of 1941, the Packers met the Bears in a play-off game for the league championship. They lost that one, 33-14, but the Packer minutebook reveals that they took $10,000 of the profits from that game and put them into war-time Liberty Bonds.

The protection of that financial reserve has been a steadfast goal of Packer management over the years, starting with Lee Joannes, and

Deflation?

Undoubtedly it will never happen again, but during the Great Depression, the Packers actually reduced the price of their tickets.

At a meeting of the directors in August of 1932, it was decided that the price of season tickets would be reduced from $15 to $12, and box seats were cut from $25 to $20.

At the time, the Packers played six home games a season.

By the way, the Packers raised the prices of season tickets in the spring of 1982. Just another sign of the times.

continuing through his successors, Emil Fischer, Russ Bogda, and Dominic Olejniczak. They were determined to accumulate sufficient reserves to withstand any emergencies, and this reserve came into very good use during the war years.

In 1943, both the Packers and the National Football League faced a critical decision on whether to go ahead and play that season with

In the Name of Competition

There were three actions taken by the National Football League in its formative years which have contributed greatly to the ability of the Green Bay Packers to compete with much larger cities across the country.

The first of these was the institution of the college draft in 1934 and along with it the so-called reserve clause in player contracts.

Commissioner Bert Bell wrote about what this has done for professional football in a pamphlet he prepared in 1956.

Bell knew very well whereof he spoke. He was captain of the team at the University of Pennslyvania, then coached at Temple University. He was able to buy the Frankford franchise from the NFL at an auction after three wealthy owners had lost about $80,000 over the previous three years. He then moved it to Philadelphia.

Bell wrote: "In those days, there were four top teams and six poor teams in the league. The former were the New York Giants, Chicago Bears, Green Bay Packers and the Washington Redskins, formerly the Boston team. From 1933 to 1946 the championship was almost always won by one of these four top clubs. The other six teams usually won only two, three, four games a year. There was no real competition between the top teams and the poor teams because good college football players all wanted to play with the winning clubs irrespective of the amount of salary offered by the poorer clubs."

He recalled that in 1939 his Philadelphia team played Brooklyn to 100,000 empty seats in the Philadelphia municipal stadium. The advance sale of tickets had brought in only $1,100. Then it rained the day of the game, and the few spectators who made an appearance sat in the press box.

It was Bell who proposed the player selection system and the league approved his plan for equalizing the strength of the teams. Basically, through the draft, the team which finishes the season in last place in the league is the team which is given the first choice of players at the next annual selection meeting. The selection round proceeds until the league champion has made the last choice, then each team selects one player per round, continuing in the same order.

The reserve clause reserves to the club the player's services under a one-year contract with a one-year option in addition. If at the end of the year, a player does not sign a new contract and plays out the option, he then becomes a free agent.

Bell wrote that he was "convinced from his many years of experience that the player selection system and the reserve clause are absolutely vital to the existence of professional football as we know it today." He believed that the surest way to maintain keen competitive spirit permeating every club and every player is to continue the highly successful methods used to equalize player stength among the league teams.

The other great accomplishment of Bert Bell came after he became Commissioner of the NFL, and it is the one which is so extremely important to the Packer financial underpinnings today. That was the putting together of a league television package with the proceeds divided equally among the member clubs.

This did not come about easily. By the late fifties, most teams in the league had their own television contracts. In 1956, the Packers made a deal with the CBS network to televise 11 of their 12 games for a fee of $75,000 a year over three years. Obviously, what players were still available, or whether to postpone play until war's end. Both the league and the Packers decided to go ahead and play although the Packers estimated that they would face a loss of $25,000 to $30,000. It was their reserve which carried them through and on into the post-war years when professional football really came into its own.

for the Survival of the NFL

clubs in larger television markets had much more lucrative contracts.

Bell had helped the Packers put together their deal with CBS, but he was stymied in going any further with a league package by a decision of the Supreme Court of the United States in February of 1957, holding that professional football, unlike professional baseball, was subject to federal anti-trust laws.

Friends of professional football in the Congress, notably Rep. John Byrnes of Green Bay, took up the cudgel, however, and introduced legislation exempting professional football from the anti-trust laws in certain specific instances, notably, the televising of their games. The legislation was approved by Congress, and Bell proceeded to put together the league television package as we know it today. The Packers' revenue from this television contract has exceeded five million dollars a year in the last five years.

The new 5-year contracts negotiated in 1982 will bring the Packers an average of $13.6 million a year.

Three of the Hungry Five. Members of the Packer Executve Committee huddled with Commissioner Bert Bell when he visited Rockwood Lodge in the 1940s. Left to right: A. B. Turnbull, first president of the corporation; Lambeau; Pres. Emil Fischer; Bell, and Attorney Jerry Clifford. *Press-Gazette photo.*

The Packer Legend

Chapter Five

THE

HUTSON

PHENOMENON

No one player has ever dominated the National Football League so thoroughly and convincingly as did the immortal Don Hutson during the 11-year period he demoralized opponents' defenses from 1935 to 1945. An argument could be made for the great running back Jim Brown of the Cleveland Browns, but Brown never once led his team to an NFL title, whereas Hutson was more than instrumental in taking the Packers to three champioships.

Don Hutson had made his reputation as a pass receiver at Alabama, but he was a fragile looking individual, carrying only about 175 pounds on his six- foot frame. Curly Lambeau was able to sign him for the Packers because most other coaches in the league thought he was too small to play pro football. As the saying goes, appearances can be deceiving.

Hutson's first play in a Packer league game foretold the terror he would create in defensive backfields for the rest of his career. The Packers were facing the hated Chicago Bears in the opening game of the 1935 season at City Stadium in Green Bay. The Packers received the opening kick-off but only returned it to their own 16-yardline. On the first play from scrimmage, Arnie Herber faded into his own end zone and threw a pass down field as far as he could heave it. Beattie Feathers was playing safety for the Bears. Let him take the story from there, as he related it to me some years later.

"I saw Herber throw this pass down field, and I saw this lanky guy loping down toward me. I knew the ball was going way over my head, and I was sure it was way out of Hutson's reach. But all of a sudden, he turned on his speed, ran right

The Other End. Milt Gantenbein of Wisconsin paired with Don Hutson at end during the championship era. Here he makes big yardage against the Chicago Bears at City Stadium in the late 1930s. *Lefebvre photo.*

by me, took the pass in perfect stride, and went on for a touchdown.''

The Packers kicked the extra point, and that is the way the score stood after 60 minutes of play: Hutson 7, Bears 0.

Hutson repeated his spectacular performance against the Bears when the Packers went to play Chicago at Wrigley Field later that same season.

I was covering the game for the Green Bay *Press-Gazette* from the sidelines, and my wife was sitting with my parents up in the stands. With only about three minutes to play, the score was Bears 14, Packers 3, and figuring that the game was all but over, I started up into the stands to join my family. I got to the first level when I heard this roar and turned just in time to get a look at the field to see Hutson out in the flat. He had taken a pass from Herber and proceeded to elude all 11 Chicago Bears on his way to the goalline, making the score 14-10 with less than a minute to play.

The Packers then kicked off, and on their first play from scrimmage, the Bears gave the ball to Bronko Nagurski for a buck into the line to chew up the clock. It was a good call, but Packer tackle Ernie Smith met Nagurski head-on, straightened him up, and stripped him of the ball. Smith also recovered.

On the next play, Herber found Hutson in the corner of the end zone, unloaded a bomb, and the Packers won, 17-14.

The Hutson legend had been born.

He terrorized defensive backs merely stepping onto the field. Not only did he have the great change of pace, which Beattie Feathers first discovered, but he also had the greatest pair of hands of any end who ever played the game. On numerous occasions, Hutson was double-teamed by defensive backs. He would be surrounded by opponents and would still come down with the ball.

Hutson had two great passers throwing to him

during his Green Bay career.

Arnie Herber was a hometown product, a graduate of Green Bay West High School where he had starred in football, basketball, and track. He had attended Regis College for one year before coming home to try out for the Packers. Herber could throw a football almost the length of the field. In fact, on some occasions, the Packers would have Herber throw into the end zone instead of taking a chance on a punt on a slippery field, for in those days a pass on fourth down into the end zone came out to the 20-yardline.

Herber left the Packers after the 1941 season and was replaced by another famous passer, Cecil Isbell from Purdue, who teamed up with Hutson in the 1941 and 1942 seasons. Isbell joined the Packers in 1938 and succeeded Herber as a starter in the 1941. He led the league in passing in both 1941 and 1942.

The Packers finished 9-4 that first season, 1935, Hutson was with the team, then won the league championship in 1936. One of the key games that second season was a battle between the Packers and the New York Giants at the Polo Grounds late in the season. The Packers beat the Giants, 26-14, and went on to their fourth national crown.

They played the Boston Redskins in the world championship game that year, which was the only title game ever played on a neutral field, namely the Polo Grounds in New York, until the first Super Bowl in 1967, because Redskins owner George Marshall was in the process of moving his team to Washington due to poor attendance in the Massachusetts city.

Immediately after the kickoff, Packer Lou Gordon recovered a Boston fumble at mid-field. Herber dropped back and threw a 43-yard touchdown pass to Hutson, and that set the tempo of the game as the Packers completely dominated the Easterners. Final score: Packers 21, Redskins 6.

The Giants got their revenge for past Packer indignities, however, when they beat the Packers for the championship, 23-17, in 1938. But in 1939, in the NFL title game played at State Fair Park in Milwaukee, the Packers returned the favor by whitewashing the Giants, 27-0. Surprisingly, Hutson did not score in that game, spending most of the afternoon acting as a decoy for the other ends, with Herber throwing one touchdown pass to Milt Gantenbein in the first quarter and Cecil Isbell throwing to Joe Laws for a touchdown in the third quarter.

As the seasons rolled on, Hutson began piling up records for scoring and pass receiving which have yet to be equalled or even challenged. Any comparison to his feats must be tempered with one very important factor: the NFL season was

1936 Championship Team, Won 10, Lost 1, Tied 1. Front row, left to right: Tony Paulekas, Tiny Engebretsen, Lon Evans, Ade Schwammel, Champ Seibold, Frank Butler, George Sauer, Cal Clemens, Buckets Goldenberg. Middle row: Curly Lambeau, Bernie Scherer, Hank Bruder, Lou Gordon, George Svendsen, Walt Kiesling, Johnny Blood, Ernie Smith, Swede Johnson, Red Smith. Back row: Joe Laws, Arnie Herber, Herman Schneidman, Russ Letlow, Wayland Becker, Paul Miller, Clarke Hinkle, Don Hutson, Milt Gantenbein, Bobby Monnett.
Lefebure photo.

only 11 games long when Hutson played. Taking that point into consideration, one wonders what sort of marks he would have set if he had played 16-game seasons. Certainly, his achievements

Hutson's Records. Don Hutson still holds several NFL scoring and receiving records. The footballs he holds here and their corresponding digits indicate those records he held during his spectacular career with the Packers, 1935-1945. Hutson still holds several Packer records, many of which may never be broken. *Lefebvre photo.*

Records That May Never Be Broken

Don Hutson retired over 35 years ago in 1945, but a number of the league and Packer records he established still stand. This is a singularly fantastic feat considering the Packers only played 11 regular season games each year during his career.

Here's a recap of Hutson's records as they stood at the time of his retirement:

League Records

Scoring
Most seasons leading league	5

Touchdowns
Most seasons leading league	8
Most in career	105

(Now held by Jim Brown, 126.)

Pass Receiving
Most seasons leading league	8
Most consecutive seasons leading league	5

Packer Records

Scoring
Total points, career	823
Most points, season	138

(Now held by Paul Hornung, 176.)
Most points, game	31

(Now held by Paul Hornung, 33.)
Most points, one quarter	29
Most touchdowns, career	105

Pass Receiving
Most passes caught, career	488
Most passes caught, season	74
Most passes caught, game	14
Most TD passes caught, career	99
Most TD passes caught, season	17
Most TD passes caught, game	4
Most yards catching passes, career	8,010
Most yards catching passes, season	1,211

(Now held by James Lofton, 1,294.)
Most yards catching passes, game	237

(Now held by Bill Howton, 257.)

rank with those of all-time greats in any other sport.

When Don retired after the 1945 season, Curly Lambeau was up against it to structure a new offense. Hutson had dominated the attack that much during his 11-year tenure. Lambeau also lost his premier passers at about the same time.

Hutson helped Lambeau as an assistant coach for one season after he retired, but by this time he had established several profitable businesses in Green Bay, one a very popular bowling alley

The Great Arm. Arnie Herber was the other half of the famous "Herber to Hutson" passing combination which terrorized the National Football League and brought Green Bay two Championships in 1936 and 1939. Herber could throw a football nearly the entire length of the field and with pinpoint accuracy. He is a member of the Pro Hall of Fame and is also in the Packer Hall of Fame. *Lefebvre photo.*

They're All Champs. Four players from the championship era pose with Curly Lambeau and Red Smith at training camp in 1937. Arnie Herber and Mike Michalske are on the left, Milt Gantenbein and Hank Bruder on the right.
Lefebvre photo.

and bar and another a car dealership for the wartime Kaiser-Fraser line of automobiles. The demands these enterprises put on his time took Don away from football.

Hutson was smart enough to see the end coming for Kaiser-Fraser, however, and sold out his dealership shortly after the end of World War

Bull's-eye Herber

A sports feature company in California once made a movie of Arnie Herber's passing ability while the Packers were barnstorming in the West.

They hung a piece of plate glass from the goal post, and they told Arnie they wanted him to throw as many times as it was necessary for him to bust the glass. They said they would keep on shooting film until he was able to score.

"What would you do that for?" Herber retorted.

He then stationed himself about 60 yards away and proceeded to throw the ball and broke the glass panel into smithereens on his first attempt.

II. He parlayed it into a Cadillac-Chevrolet dealership in Racine, Wisconsin, an enterprise which became so profitable that he gradually cut off his business ties with Green Bay.

I had two memorable personal experiences with Don Hutson. The first involved teaching him to ski.

We had a small private ski club on the outskirts of Green Bay, and after he retired from football, Don became interested in learning winter sports. I guess he figured if he had to spend winters in Wisconsin, he might as well enjoy it. As you might imagine, a person of Hutson's athletic ability and body coordination picked up skiing very readily, and I always considered him one of my prize pupils.

Concerning the other experience, Hutson did me a personal favor which I will never forget.

After he gave up football and positioned himself behind a desk, Don began having terrible back trouble. He went to specialists all over the country without getting any relief. His personal physician from Racine was attending a medical meeting in Vienna, however, when he heard a presentation by an orthopedic surgeon from Vanderbilt University Medical School in Nashville, Tennessee, a surgeon who specialized

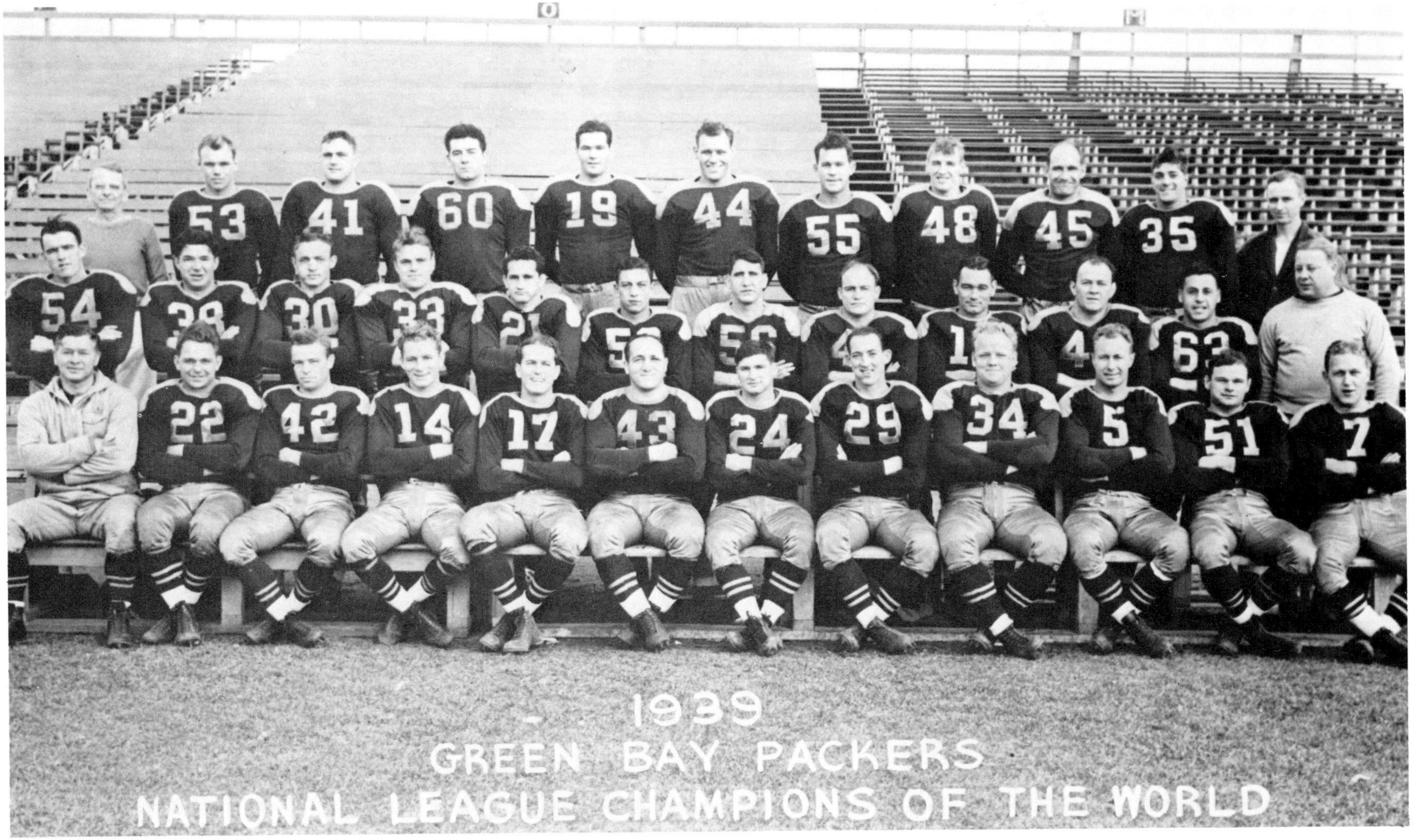

1939 — GREEN BAY PACKERS — NATIONAL LEAGUE CHAMPIONS OF THE WORLD

1939 Championship Team, Won 9, Lost 2. Front row, left to right: Coach Curly Lambeau; Milt Gantenbein, Wisconsin; John Wilson, Dubuque; Don Hutson, Alabama; Cecil Isbell, Purdue; Buckets Goldenberg, Wisconsin; Joe Laws, Iowa; Charley Brock, Nebraska; Tiny Engebretsen, Northwestern; Hank Bruder, Northwestern; Herman Schneidman, Iowa; Eddie Jankowski, Wisconsin. Middle row: Larry Craig, South Carolina; Arnie Herber, Regis; Clarke Hinkle, Bucknell; Dick Weisgerber, Wilmette; Pete Tinsley, Georgia; Larry Buhler, Minnesota; Clyde Goodnight, Tulsa; Russ Letlow, San Francisco; Lee Mulleneaux, Arizona State; Bill Lee, Alabama; Gus Zarnas, Ohio State; Asst. Coach Red Smith. Back row: Trainer Dave Woodward; George Svendsen, Minnesota; Paul Kell, Notre Dame; Charles Schultz, Minnesota; Carl Mulleneaux, Utah; Baby Ray, Vanderbilt; Allen Moore, Texas A&M; Harry Jacunski, Fordham; Ernie Smith, Southern California; Frank Balaz, Iowa; Trainer Bud Jorgenson.

Lefebvre photo.

The Packer Legend

in back problems. Don's doctor asked the other physician if he thought he could help Hutson, and he allowed as if he thought he could.

The solution was a simple one. The surgeon ordered Hutson to do 25 sit-ups every hour on the hour during his waking moments. He told Don that his back muscles, once used to the rigorous conditioning of a football player, had collapsed since he was no longer as physically active, and it was simply a matter of building up those muscles which support the spine.

I ran into Don one day at a marina up in nearby Door County, where he was docking his motor yacht. I saw him jump from the bow of the boat to the dock and fasten the bow line to

a cleat. I had known that he was having back trouble over a period of time, and I was amazed at his new-found agility. He told me of his experiences at Vanderbilt Hospital, and it was of intense interest to me because I was suffering from a very severe case of osteoarthritis in my hip joints. With Don's help, I arranged an appointment in Nashville, and the same surgeon set me out on a course which eventually led to full recovery from my arthritic condition.

Don Hutson today is leading the life of a retired gentleman in Palm Springs, California, but he still retains connections with the Packers as a long-time member of the Board of Directors, and now as a director emeritus.

Hard-hitting Fullback. That's Walt Schlinkman running for yardage against the Chicago Cardinals in a game in the late 40s. Other Packers visible include Clyde Goodnight, Nolan Luhn and Larry Craig. *Lefebvre photo.*

The Packer Legend

The Great Bronko Buster

A player acquisition Curly Lambeau made in 1932 contributed greatly to the championships won by the Packers in the late 1930s. His name was Clarke Hinkle, a fullback from Bucknell.

When Hinkle reported to the Packer training camp that summer, he started hearing about the great and formidable Bronko Nagurski, the intimidating fullback with the Chicago Bears. Nagurski hailed from International Falls, Minnesota, and he played football like a lumberjack.

Hinkle started psyching himself up for his first meeting with Nagurski, which occurred in the second game of the season with the Bears in Green Bay. Hinkle kicked off for the Packers, and Nagurski took the ball on his own five. He headed straight up field. Hinkle headed straight down field. Everyone in the stadium braced for the collision, a head-on at about the Bear 30.

For a few minutes both players lay sprawled out on the field. Then Hinkle stumbled to his feet and staggered over to the sidelines. Nagurski was still prone. The Bears carried him off the field.

Imagine then the build-up for their second meeting that season in the game in Chicago. Hinkle came out the winner again.

Nagurski backed up the Bear line on defense. He preferred to block a runner down with his head and shoulders rather than tackle him.

Late in the game Hinkle broke through a hole in the Bear line, only to be met by Nagurski. Bronko threw his whole body at Hinkle and knocked him back across the line of scrimmage, but Hinkle landed on his feet and proceeded to run over Nagurski's prostrate form. He negotiated the hole three times, once backward and twice forward, the last time across the goalline.

Hinkle was a great kicker, in addition to being a powerful runner. On the all-time scoring list, he is credited with 43 touchdowns, 31 PATs, and 28 field goals for a total of 373 points in 10 seasons, seventh on the all-time Packer scoring list.

One of the Greatest. Clarke Hinkle has been called the finest all-around player in Packer history. A punishing runner, he was a fine defensive back, better than average passer, and a great place kicker and punter. He ranks seventh on all-time Packer scoring list and fourth on the rushing list. *Lefebvre photo.*

Lambeau at the Peak. Curly was a natty dresser and a fine figure of a man as this photo of him in front of the Rockwood Lodge entrance demonstrates. But the boys at the Corner Drugstore said he had "Gone Hollywood," and Rockwood Lodge was one of the factors which helped to bring his downfall. *Lefebvre photo.*

The Packer Legend

Chapter Six

"...'TIL LAMBEAU

WENT

HOLLYWOOD."

The year 1945 marked the end of World War II and peace for the Western World, but it was just the start of the war in pro football.

The All-American Football Conference was organized in late 1945 and started the 1946 season with six teams. This meant that there were now 18 teams playing professional football, and all of a sudden pro football players and college graduates began to realize that they could command considerably larger salaries than had been the case previously in the National Football League. To make matters worse, the AAC put teams in the major cities along with teams from the NFL. Jimmy Crowley, once of Green Bay, was the principal owner of the Chicago Hornets, and Charlie Collins started a third team in New York City, the New York Bulldogs.

The pro football war had serious ramifications for the Packers. It began just at the time when Don Hutson had retired and Packer fortunes on the field began to deteriorate.

Curly Lambeau still had almost complete control of the Packer operations, but he was beginning to push his luck. He sold the Executive Committee on the idea of purchasing a large lodge and a considerable amount of acreage on the shore of Green Bay about 15 miles north of the city. Rockwood Lodge had been built by the Catholic Diocese as a recreation center but had not achieved the success that had been hoped, so the Packers were able to buy it for $32,000. They put another $8,000 into refitting the facilities and also bought six pre-fabricated houses. Curly's idea was to house the team there during the training season.

Early in 1947, Curly hired George Strickler,

a sports writer for the Chicago *Tribune*, to take over as publicity director for the Packers, replacing George W. Calhoun. This produced the first defection among the "Hungry Five." As I recalled in a previous chapter, Calhoun read about his replacement while tending the Associated Press teletype machine in the *Press-Gazette* office one morning. Needless to say, he was somewhat surprised and deeply hurt.

The Rockwood Lodge purchase began to anger Packer Executive Committee members and directors early that summer when it was found that there was such a shallow cover of topsoil on the practice field that players very quickly came down with shin splints, sore feet, and other maladies. Within a few weeks, it was necessary to bus them from the lodge all the way back into Green Bay to practice on their old training field.

Expenses for equipping and decorating the lodge also began to mount, and at one meeting of the Executive Committee, the financial committee threatened to resign over the bills which were being presented by Lambeau for decorating the cottage that he and his wife were occupying. The decorating had been done by *Marshall-Field* in Chicago. It was about this time that the Monday morning quarterbacks in Green Bay began to remark that Lambeau had "gone Hollywood."

During the last years of the war, Curly began to spend more and more winters in California. He married an attractive young blonde from the Los Angeles area and brought her back to Green

Bay for the summer and the football season. But by the next winter he divorced her, and by the time the team was moving into Rockwood Lodge, he married another woman from California who took over the decorating of their cottage at the lodge.

It was at this point that the Executive Committee began to be concerned about control of expenditures. In June of 1947, the committee decided that from that point on it would meet weekly on Monday noons to get a report from Lambeau as vice-president and general manager. The Executive Committee was also divided into five subcommittees which were given control over the supervision of finances and other business matters such as grounds, contracts, policing the stadium, and publicity.

At the annual stockholders meeting in July of 1947, two vice-presidents were authorized, and Lee Joannes was brought back into the picture as a vice-president along with Lambeau, with Emil Fischer succeeding Joannes as president. Fischer was a very successful businessman in Green Bay, the owner and operator of a large cold storage plant.

The team's showing on the field was not helping Lambeau's cause either. In both 1946 and 1947, the team finished with 6-5-1 records, and in 1948, they won only three games while losing nine.

By the end of the 1948 season, the poor record on the field was reflected on the team's profit and loss statement, and at a directors meeting in

Rockwood Lodge, Lambeau Folly. Curly got ambitious in the 1940s and purchased Rockwood Lodge, a former Catholic diocese summer retreat on the Green Bay shore north of the city. It was to be the team's headquarters during the training season, but the shallow turf over solid bedrock soon gave the players shin splints and they had to be bussed back to Green Bay for practice. *Lefebvre photo.*

The Packer Legend

1944 Championship Team, Won 8, Lost 2. Left to right, front row: Buckets Goldenberg, Paul Duhart, Ben Starrett, Pete Tinsley, Forrest McPherson, Larry Craig, Charley Brock, Lou Brock, Roy McKay, Joe Laws. Second row: Trainer Bud Jorgenson, Bill Kuusisto, Ray Wheba, Glenn Sorenson, Bob Flowers, Harry Jacunski, Ted Fritsch, Don Perkins, Charley Tollefson, Joel Mason, Gust Seaburg. Back row: Curly Lambeau, Don Hutson, Paul Berezney, Ade Schwammel, Irv Comp, Tiny Croft, Bob Kercher, Bob Kahler, Baby Ray, Mike Bucchianeri, Asst. Coach George Trafton. *Lefebvre photo.*

Turning the Cards' End. Jim Gillette takes off on a long gainer in a 1947 game against the Chicago Cardinals. He played only that one season. Jack Jacobs (No. 27) was the quarterback. *Lefebvre photo.*

Beating the Bears. Ed Cody breaks away on this end run in the opening game of the season in Green Bay in 1947. The Packers won, 29-20. That's Clyde Goodnight blocking (No. 23). *Lefebvre photo.*

The Packer Legend

December of 1948, the directors reviewed what they termed "the poor showing of the team and its finances." At the same meeting, Strickler was told bluntly to cease using the title of assistant general manager.

The situation continued to deteriorate during the 1949 season. At the stockholders meeting in August, another of the original "Hungry Five" left the fold when A. B. Turnbull resigned from the board. He had retired and was moving to California. A Green Bay attorney, Victor McCormick, who was a close friend of Lambeau's, was elected as a director to replace Turnbull. He also became an Executive Committee member at the same time.

The 1949 Packers won only two games while losing 10, and one of those victories came against the New York Bulldogs who were in their first season in the league.

By November, the financial situation became critical. At a special directors meeting, Lambeau was ordered to drop a number of players from the roster and renegotiate the salaries of all the other players. Strickler was fired as publicity director, and the directors decided to close Rockwood Lodge and put it up for sale.

In a desperation move, they decided to try a special exhibition game on Thanksgiving Day, hopefully to raise enough funds to pay off the immediate bills. It was to be a colorful and fun day. Don Hutson agreed to put on a uniform and receive some passes from Arnie Herber, and Verne Lewellen was recruited to show off his famous spiral punting style. There was a great deal of enthusiasm generated for the game, and tickets were selling hot and heavy until Thanksgiving morning when residents of Green Bay awakened to a heavy snowfall. The snow continued up until game time at 2:00 p.m. Despite the inclement weather, enough fans turned out to raise about $50,000, with which the Packers could pay off some of their most pressing debts.

The Executive Committee decided at this point that the only way to rescue the corporation from its financial bind was to conduct another sale of stock, so a special committee of directors was appointed to frame a recommendation for such a sale.

Attorney McCormick was chairman of the committee, and Lambeau was one of its members. At its first meeting, Lambeau told the group that he knew of four investors who would each put up $50,000 for stock in the Packers if the corporation was converted to a profit rather than a non-profit corporation. It was easily surmised that McCormick was one of the four. He had inherited a great deal of wealth from an uncle some years before. The other five members of the committee out-voted McCormick and Lambeau on this proposition. They steadfastly insisted that the character of the Packer football corporation must be maintained as originally conceived as a community nonprofit corporation.

A climactic meeting of the Board of Directors was held on November 30, 1949, when the committee reported to the directors and recommended that the number of shares of capital stock in the corporation be increased to 200,000 and that a stock sale be held early in 1950.

At the same meeting, Lambeau's contract extension came up for discussion, and it was moved and seconded that his contract be extended two years. Three members of the original "Hungry Five" led the opposition and moved for a secret ballot on the extension. That motion was narrowly defeated, however, on a 12-9 vote, and the motion to extend Lambeau's contract was then approved by a vote of 18-3. The no votes came from George W. Calhoun, Attorney Jerry Clifford, and Dr. W. W. Kelley. The only member of the original "Hungry Five" voting for Lambeau was Lee Joannes, who did so reluctantly.

Lambeau, as it turned out, had won an empty victory. He had been confirmed for another two years as coach and general manager, but what Lambeau really wanted was the conversion of the corporation to a profit-making entity in which he and a few friends could in effect appropriate the franchise. The four men that he had mentioned at the committee meeting were ready, willing, and able to subscribe the entire 200,000 shares of capital stock and take over ownership of the franchise.

Thus, for these reasons, it came as a complete surprise to Packer fans when the announcement came from Chicago in January of 1950 that Lambeau had terminated his long association with the Packers to become vice-president and head coach of the Chicago Cardinals. But it was no surprise to members of the Packer Board and Executive Committee, who knew that the real disagreement between Lambeau and the Packers had come over the ownership issue rather than his team's performance on the field.

Lambeau coached the Cardinals for two losing

The Grey Ghost of Gonzaga

All-time Packer great Tony Canadeo, who has contributed immeasureably to the Packer organization both as a player and a corporate officer, was long-known as the "Grey Ghost of Gonzaga", and yet Tony never had the good fortune to play on a championship team.

Tony acquired his nickname in college. He was prematurely grey. Drafted in the seventh round in 1941, he played for Curly Lambeau for three seasons until he was called into military service in 1944, and that year the Packers won the league title.

Tony returned to the Packers in 1946 and finished his career under Coach Gene Ronzani in 1952. He ranks third on the all-time ground gaining list behind Jim Taylor and John Brockington and is 17th on the all-time scoring list with 31 touchdowns for 186 points.

In 1943 and 1949, Tony made the All-Pro Team. Also in 1949, he became only the third back in NFL history to rush for over 1,000 yards with 1,052, but despite his performance, the team's record in Curly Lambeau's last season was a miserable 2-10.

The NFL gave Tony the ultimate recognition in 1974 when he was inducted

into the Hall of Fame in Canton, Ohio.

Tony was elected to the Packer Board of Directors in 1955, to the Executive Committee in 1958, and as Vice-President in May of 1982.

seasons in 1950 and 1951, then moved on to the Washington Redskins where he again coached for two years, 1952-53. Finally, in that latter year, he had a winning season with a record of 6-5-1. Lambeau then coached the College All-Stars for his old friend Arch Ward of the Chicago *Tribune* for several summers before finally retiring to his summer home in Door County, Wisconsin, spending his winters in California. He died suddenly of a massive heart attack on June 1, 1965, while operating a riding mower, cutting the lawn of a friend in Door County. He was 67.

Thus ended the career of certainly one of the most colorful characters in the formative years of professional football in this country.

As a coach, Lambeau had a knack for choosing good ballplayers and for motivating them to give their best efforts as a team. Above all, Lambeau was a showman. Early on he recognized that

A Financial Blessing

Ownership of Rockwood Lodge, which had become an albatross around Curly Lambeau's neck in his last years as Packer coach and general manager, turned out to be a bonanza for the Packers in early 1950.

In the middle of the winter when the corporation was badly in debt, Rockwood Lodge burned to the ground and the Packers collected $75,000 in insurance proceeds. They had put the property up for sale earlier but had found no takers.

There was a lot of friendly kidding in the community of Packer board members as to which one had put the torch to the lodge.

professional football was as much an entertainment medium as it was a sports event. He was one of the originators of the forward passing game, recognizing that it was the most exciting phase of offensive football.

Lambeau was a colorful character himself, with a fine head of steely gray hair and the features of a rugged athlete. He was a classy dresser and was particularly in his element when surrounded by beautiful women.

In the end, however, it was this very showmanship which did him in. As the boys at the Corner Drug Store used to say, "Everything went down hill after Lambeau went Hollywood."

Lambeau's Last Staff. These were Curly Lambeau's assistants in his last season coaching the Packers in 1949. Left to right: Tom Stidham, Bob Snyder, Charley Brock and Don Hutson, with Curly at the projector. *Lefebvre photo.*

The Packer Legend

GREEN BAY PRESS-GAZETTE

30 PAGES.　　　　　　　　　　　GREEN BAY, WIS., FRIDAY EVENING, DECEMBER 9, 1949　　ASSOCIATED PRESS UNITED PRESS　　PRICE 5c

Pro Football Leagues Announce Merger

Rep. Thomas Gets 6-18 Months, Quits Congress

13 Teams, Including Packers, In Set-Up

Wife Discloses She Will Run To Replace Him

Former Prober Draws Term for Padding His Office Payroll

WASHINGTON—Rep. J. Parnell Thomas got six to 18 months in jail and a $10,000 fine today for cheating the government by "padding" his office payroll.

Immediately after the sentence was pronounced Thomas' wife was announced:

"I intend to seek the congressional seat about to be vacated by my husband."

Mrs. Thomas told reporters her husband's resignation is in the mails.

Thomas is 54. His wife is a little younger.

Federal Judge Alexander Holtzoff gave an ear-burning lecture to Thomas along with the jail term, and the fine.

Did Much Good Work

Judge Charges Woman Tried To Tamper With Larson Jury

Note Dropped at Hotel; Steinle Postpones Action Until After Trial Is Concluded

LA CROSSE, Wis.—A woman hotel employee was declared by Circuit Judge Roland J. Steinle today to have made "a willful attempt to influence the jury" in the Arnold Larson murder trial.

Judge Steinle said he would "dispose of the situation" after the trial. The case is expected to go to the jury late today.

Urges Slash in Federal Budget

Byrd Proposes Plan for $7.5 Billion Reduction To Prevent Tax Raise

WASHINGTON—Sen. Byrd (D-Va) today sought to lead the nation away from the "economic primrose path of indefinite deficit financing" with a plan calling for a $7,500,000,000 slash in federal spending.

A towering mass of flame lights up the scene at the Panhandle Eastern pipeline's compressor plant at Centralia, Mo., after a natural gas line blew out and caught fire. The flow of gas was interrupted to cities in Illinois, Indiana and Michigan. Nine workmen escaped injury, but damage was estimated at near $100,000. (AP Wirephoto)

City One of Three Coldest in U.S. Today; Warmer Forecast

Shares Dubious 'Honor' With Marshfield and Wausau; Minimum of 20 Degrees Seen Tonight

Green Bay, Wausau, and Marshfield, with nine below weather this morning, were the coldest spots in the nation.

Clamp Lid on Slav Mission

Soviet-Ruled Police in Reich Hold Unit Under House Arrest 16 Hours

BERLIN—Soviet-controlled German police today released members of the Yugoslav military mission and consulate staff after holding them under house arrest for more than 16 hours on charges of trying to "interfere with lawful order."

Lewis Demands On Hard Coal Men Revealed

NEW YORK—The United Mine Workers have asked anthracite coal operators for a 100 per cent increase in welfare payments and a basic wage increase of 95 cents to $1 a day, it was announced today.

Higher Pay Scale Will Boost Cartage Rates

MILWAUKEE—The

New Yorkers Hear 'Save Water' Refrain Constantly in Drive

NEW YORK—New York today is a city with very little water in reserve.

Fischer To Be President of National Division; Three A-A Clubs Are Added

PHILADELPHIA—The National Football League and the All-American Conference merged today to end a four-year football war.

Announcement of the merger was made at a press conference summoned by Bert Bell, commissioner of the National Football league, and J. Arthur Friedlund, representing the AAC.

The new league is to be known as the National-American Football league. It is to be divided into two divisions — the National and the American.

Thirteen teams will comprise the new league. This includes all ten NFL teams and the Baltimore Colts, Cleveland Browns, and San Francisco Forty-Niners of the AAC.

Emil R. Fischer of the Green Bay Packers will be president of the National division and Daniel Sherby of the Cleveland Browns of the American division.

Bell will remain as commissioner of the combined league.

The only team to lose its identity completely in the merger is the Chicago Hornets of the old AAC. The Buffalo Bills are merging with Cleveland, with the new club to have its home in the Ohio city.

The Los Angeles Rams of the National and the Los Angeles Dons of the AAC will consolidate their interests.

EMIL R. FISCHER

Means a Lot To Green Bay, Fischer Says

"All these rumors that Green Bay was going to be dropped out of the league ought to be laid to rest now."

This was the comment of Emil R. Fischer, president of the Green Bay Packers, when he was informed of the official announcement late this afternoon that the National-American conference had come to agreement after nearly four years of undeclared warfare.

Couple Tells Of Finding Devroy in Car

District Attorney Is Silent on Names

British Laborites Win By-Election

BRADFORD—The British Labor party scored a victory over Winston Churchill's Conservative today in a parliamentary by-election that had been billed as a barometer of the party's general strength.

Yugoslavia Court Convicts 10 Russians of Espionage

SARAJEVO, Yugoslavia—The Sarajevo county court returned a verdict today against all 10 Soviet citizens on trial for espionage.

Today's Weather

Published by U. S. Weather Bureau.

High Thursday, 16. Low last night, 9 below zero.

For Green Bay and vicinity: Intermittent light snow and warmer tonight and Saturday. Lowest temperature tonight near 9° degrees, and highest Saturday near 28. Moderate southerly winds increasing to fresh Saturday.

Today's Chuckle

PART II

THE

LEAN

YEARS

1950 - 1958

Gene Ronzani. The former Marquette quarterback and long-time Chicago Bear back came to the Packers as head coach in 1950, but Lambeau had left them with few quality ball players and no money. *Lefebvre photo.*

The Packer Legend

Chapter Seven

RESCUE

AND

RONZANI

When Curly Lambeau announced at the league meeting in January of 1950 that he was leaving the Packers to become head coach of the Chicago Cardinals, he not only left the team without a head coach, he also left few quality football players and debts of about $75,000. But the Packers had faced adversity before. They were far from being washed up.

The war between the National Football League and the All-American Conference had been settled in late 1949, and Baltimore, Cleveland, and San Francisco joined the 10 teams in the NFL to make up a new 13-team league which was divided into National and American Conferences. The Packers remained in the National Conference with their old rivals the Bears and Detroit, along with the Baltimore Colts, Los Angeles Rams, New York Yanks, and the San Francisco 49ers.

Once again the old warhorse, Lee Joannes, played a key role in the revival of Packer fortunes. He told the Executive Committee on February 6, 1950, that he had talked with Gene Ronzani, an assistant coach and former quarterback with the Chicago Bears, and Ronzani was available to succeed Lambeau as head coach. Ronzani was a native of Iron Mountain, Michigan, and a graduate of Marquette University in Milwaukee. When several members of the committee questioned Joannes on whether any other prospective coaches were available, Joannes retorted in his typical Belgian style, "We're not taking a chance on Ronzani, he's taking a chance on us. Hell, he doesn't even know if he is going to get paid."

Ronzani was introduced as the new head coach

at a special stockholders meeting called that month, at which the stockholders also authorized the sale of additional stock in the corporation at $25 per share under the same terms and conditions as had previously existed. A limit of 200 shares was imposed on any single owner, a move intended to prevent any one person or corporation from ever acquiring control of the organization. Joannes was named chairman of the stock sale committee, the same job which he had performed once before back in the 1930s. Mayor Dominic Olejniczak was his co-chairman, Olejniczak having been elected to the board that year.

Joannes had served as president from 1930 until 1947 when he stepped aside in favor of Emil Fischer, but when the Packers were in dire touble it was Joannes who returned to lead the stock

sale drive which was to raise $125,000. With these funds the corporation was able to pay off all of its debts and still have about $50,000 in working capital for the 1950 season.

Ronzani's first team went 3-9 in 1950, but his victories included a dramatic 31-21 victory over the Chicago Bears in Green Bay which endeared him to Packer fans right off the bat. He was 3-9 again in 1951 but was in the thick of the championship race in 1952 until the last three games of the season when the team collapsed on the road, particularly in their last two games on the West Coast against Los Angeles and San Francisco, finishing 6-6 for the year.

Ronzani was working with a scarcity of talent, and during the 1952 season he was the inventor of what is now known as the shotgun formation, used so successfully in recent years by Coach

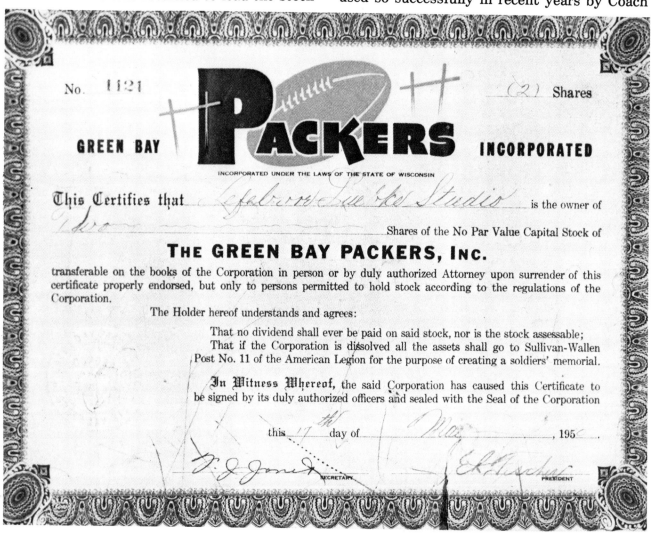

Another Stock Sale. The Packers went back to their fans for financial help after Lambeau left and raised $125,000 by selling shares of stock for $25 apiece during the year 1950. It paid off their debts and gave them working capital which became the seed money for the successful operation they are today. *Lefebvre photo.*

The Packer Legend

All-Time Packer Greats. Babe Parilli, Tobin Rote, Tony Canadeo and Fred Cone present an autographed football to a young fan, Larry Bero.

Press-Gazette photo.

Tom Landry of Dallas, and imitated by others. Ronzani had Tobin Rote, a big, rugged running back with a strong arm, as his quarterback, but he had practically no running game whatsoever and not much of an offensive line. So he stationed Rote about 10 yards back from the center and let him either pass, if he could find an open receiver, or run for his life. In the majority of cases, Rote wound up doing the latter. Rote proved what he could do with a good line in front of him and capable receivers when he went to the Detroit Lions and took the Lions to the 1957 World Championship, defeating the Cleveland Browns, 59-14. Rote had taken over as quarterback for Detroit's Bobby Layne who broke a leg in a game early in the season.

Things went from bad to worse for Ronzani in 1953, however. The only two games the Packers won were against Baltimore, which had become the swing team in the merger of the two leagues and was a patsy for every other team in the league. By the time the team was about to make its annual trip to California for the last two games it was badly demoralized, and Ronzani resigned and turned the reigns over to one of his assistant coaches, Hugh Devore.

Ronzani left the Packers with one asset which was to prove vitally important in their later success under Vince Lombardi. He hired a young graduate of Notre Dame by the name of Jack Vainisi as the team's first talent scout. Vainisi had been an all-city guard in high school in Chicago, and his family lived across the street from a hotel where many Bear players resided. He got to know Ronzani there when Ronzani was playing for the Bears, and later they renewed

The Packer Legend

One Tough Cookie. Tobin Rote was one of the mainstays of the Packer teams in the Ronzani and Blackbourn regimes. As No. 1 quarterback, he spent most of his time running for his life.*Lefebvre photo.*

their acquaintance when Ronzani went to Notre Dame as an assistant coach while Vainisi was playing there. He told Vainisi that if he ever got a head coaching job in professional football, he wanted him on his staff.

Vainisi was back-packing through Europe with a pal after his graduation from Notre Dame in 1950 when he got word from Ronzani that he wanted him on his staff in Green Bay.

There were few talent scouts in professional football in those days, but Vainisi struck up a friendship with the premier scout in the business at the time, Eddie Kotal of the Los Angeles Rams. Kotal was a graduate of Lawrence College

in Appleton and had played with the Packers back in the 1920s. He took Vainisi under his wing.

Draft choices which Vainisi scouted out under Ronzani and later under his successor, Lisle Blackbourn, became the nucleus of the great teams which Vince Lombardi fielded in the 1960s.

There is an incident I recall about Eddie Kotal which is probably worth mentioning at this point. When Kotal played with the Packers from 1925-1929, one of his distinguishing traits was the fact that he almost always refused to wear a helmet. He had curly blond hair, which was rather long for players of that era, and he could be spotted anywhere on the field because he was playing without headgear.

One year the Packers were scheduled to play the Staten Island Stapletons in New York. George Calhoun got the bright idea of suggesting to Curly Lambeau that he contact Jim Crowley, then the head coach at Fordham University, and see if Crowley would play some of the late season

Still a Record Holder. Al Carmichael returned a kickoff 106 yards for a touchdown against the Bears Oct. 7, 1956, but the Packers lost, 37-21. His record still stands. *Lefebvre photo.*

The Packer Legend

games with the Packers after his college schedule was over. Crowley said that it might be possible and that he would try to make it. So Calhoun told the New York press that Crowley was going to play halfback for the Packers in their game with Stapleton, and of course, it made headlines in all of the metropolitan papers. It was a natural since Crowley was a Green Bay native where he starred at East High School and later was a member of the Four Horsemen of Notre Dame.

When game time came, however, Crowley failed to show, so the Packers put Crowley's game jersey on Eddie Kotal. Eddie scored two touchdowns in that game, and the next day the headlines read, "Crowley scores twice for Packers." That day he wore a helmet.

One of Vainisi's first draft choices in 1952 was Vito (Babe) Parilli, quarterback from Kentucky. Parilli later became part of the Lombardi story along with a nucleus of other great players Vainisi selected for Green Bay.

I always felt badly about Ronzani's unsuccessful career with the Packers because he was a fine gentleman and continued to be one of the Packers' great supporters in the years after he had given up coaching. His family continued to reside in Iron Mountain while he was coaching in Green Bay, and he made

Stellar Defender. Bobby Dillon was an All-Pro three times and played in two Pro Bowls. What made his performance so impressive was the fact that he had sight only in one eye. *Lefebvre photo.*

Pass Receiving Great. Bill Howton ranks right up there with Don Hutson in several of the all-time rercord lists of Packer receivers. But Vince Lombardi traded him before the 1959 season when he asked for too much money. *Lefebvre photo.*

frequent trips to the Upper Peninsula to go trout fishing, which he loved. He would always bring back a supply of Italian sausage for members of the Executive Committee, a favor which I badly missed after his leaving.

Ronzani lived in Milwaukee in the years after he retired from football and became a salesman for a steel supply company which was organized by a number of his former Chicago Bear colleagues. But he was always noticeably in attendance at Packer home games in both Green

Bay and Milwaukee.

Gene always attended the Packer homecoming games when alumni were introduced between halves and at other functions when the Packers were seeking public support. He coached the team at a very inopportune point in Packer history when they were short of both players and money. They were in the transition period from the long Lambeau era toward an entirely new future in a greatly expanded and fabulously profitable National Football League. Ronzani's four years as head coach were a stepping stone toward that future.

Star Player and Coach. Dave (Hawg) Hanner played defensive tackle, 1952-64, made the Pro Bowl, 1954-55, then became a defensive coach when he retired in 1965. He was fired by Starr after the 1979 season, then rehired as a scout. *Lefebvre photo.*

The Father of the 60s Dynasty

In the early days of professional football, teams did not have an entire staff of scouts out looking over the college seniors who would be eligible for the next NFL draft.

Curly Lambeau was a full-time talent scout for the Packers in addition to being head coach, general manager, and vice-president of the corporation. Curly really spent full-time on the job, too, prospecting for players during the off season as well as in the fall.

College coaches weren't much help in those days as there was more or less an unwritten law that college football was in direct competition with the pro game. That is one reason why Gene Ronzani hired Jack Vainisi as a full-time talent scout for the Packers.

Vainisi had gone to Notre Dame to play football until a congenital heart problem stopped his career in the bud, but he became a manager for the Fighting Irish football team. The contacts he made in that position led Ronzani to believe that Vainisi could be a great help to the Packers in establishing relations with various college coaches around the country.

Today, Vainisi is given the major credit for drafting and acquiring through trade many of the players that made Vince Lombardi famous. Included in his selections and trades were Paul Hornung, Bart Starr, Boyd Dowler, Bill Forester, Hank Gremminger, Dave Hanner, Gary Knafelc, Jerry Kramer, Ron Kramer, Max McGee, Norm Masters, Ray Nitschke, Jim Ringo, Bob Skoronski, and Jess Whittenton.

Vainisi's career was cut short by a fatal heart attack, but he will always be remembered as one of the men who helped build the Packer powerhouses of the 1960s.

The Golden Boy Signs. One of the highlights of the Blackbourn regime was the signing of Paul Hornung of Notre Dame, the team's bonus choice in the 1957 draft. He was selected by Jack Vainisi, left, the team's first, and at that time, the only talent scout. Executive Committee members Bernard Darling, Les Kelly, Russ Bogda, and Lee Joannes watch Hornung sign. *Lefebvre photo.*

Lisle Blackbourn. The Packers tried the college ranks for a head coach after Gene Ronzani resigned, hiring Lisle Blackbourn away from Marquette University in Milwaukee, where he had a fine record, but like Ronzani, he lasted only four years.
Lefebvre photo.

Chapter Eight

THEN LIZ

AND SCOOTER

The Packers operated without a general manager during the four years Gene Ronzani was head coach. The officers and Executive Committee had vowed after the last years of Curly Lambeau's reign as vice-president and general manager as well as head coach that they would never turn over that much authority again to one single person. But it also had become apparent that the Executive Committee, operating as part-time volunteers, could not handle all the administrative chores of the organization, particularly as pro football was growing in many ways, including fan support.

The directors appointed a study committee under Jerry Atkinson, general manager of the city's largest department store, to investigate and recommend changes in the management structure. The committee suggested that the size

of the Executive Committee be reduced from 13 to seven persons to make it more manageable and that the Executive Committee hire a business manager on a full-time basis to take over the administrative workload.

That manager became Verne Lewellen, a Packer great during the triple championship era, a lawyer who had served Brown County, Wisconsin, as District Attorney, and subsequently became a corporate official with the Standard Oil Company in Green Bay. Lewellen took over as business manager in early 1954, and his first job became that of recruiting a head coach to succeed Ronzani. Hugh Devore, who had taken over the team in the last two games of the 1953 season and who was well liked by Packer management, turned down the opportunity to continue as head coach and returned to his alma mater, Notre Dame.

At this point, the Executive Committee decided to try the college ranks for a new head coach, and upon Lewellen's recommendation after a considerable search, they chose Lisle Blackbourn, head coach at Marquette University in Milwaukee and formerly a very successful high school coach in Wisconsin.

Blackbourn suffered from the same problems that Ronzani inherited from Lambeau, primarily a lack of overall talent on the Packer squad. He won four and lost eight in his first season, 1954, and improved on that with a 6-6 record in 1955, but in 1956, he was back to a 4-8 losing season.

Blackbourn's final season as head coach in 1957 was notable in a number of ways.

The brand new city stadium was dedicated during the opening game of the 1957 season, attended by then Vice-President Richard Nixon and the reigning Miss America, Marilyn VanDerBur. Blackbourn's Packers beat the Chicago Bears in that dedication game, 21-17.

Blackbourn had reacquired Babe Parilli as his quarterback after having traded him to Cleveland in 1954, and Parilli was the hero of this opening game. He threw touchdown passes to Billy Howton and Gary Knafelc, but the Packers still trailed the defending Western Conference champs, 17-14, late in the game. The crucial play came when the Bears faced a fourth and one situation at midfield and went for a first down. Packer defenders swarmed all over them and held. When the Packers took over, Parilli threw to Howton for 41 yards to the eight, then to Knafelc for the winning touchdown.

It was in 1957 also that the Packers received the bonus choice in the player draft, and Blackbourn, on advice from Jack Vainisi, took the "Golden Boy" from Notre Dame, Paul Hornung, who was also the Heisman Trophy winner. For the regular first round pick, he took the great offensive end, Ron Kramer of Michigan.

Blackbourn also acquired fullback Jim Taylor in a trade with the Pittsburgh Steelers. As it turned out, Hornung and Taylor became Blackbourn's undoing, and ironically, they went on to become two key performers in Lombardi's triple championship years.

Late in the 1957 season, when the Packers had won only one more game after their opening victory against the Bears, Blackbourn was questioned at an Executive Committee meeting as to why he wasn't playing Hornung and Taylor

more. It had long been and still is the policy of the Executive Committee not to interfere in any way in the coaching of the football team, but the committee does retain overall supervision of the total amount of money which is allocated to the coach for player personnel. In this instance, one Committee member, Fred Leicht, felt that they were owed some explanation about why two very high-priced ballplayers were sitting on the bench. He commented to Blackbourn that the coach had asked the committee for funds over and above the normal range of player salaries to acquire Hornung and Taylor. Blackbourn retorted angrily that it was none of the Committee's business. The unfortunate part of the exchange was the fact that Leicht was probably the most respected of all the members of the committee and a very mild-mannered gentleman. The rest of the Committee took obvious umbrage at Blackbourn's handling of the situation.

The only other game that Blackbourn won that year was against Pittsburgh, which at that time was one of the weaker teams in the league. The team lost to Detroit in its third from last game, then collapsed again in the two games on the West Coast. Relations between Blackbourn and the Committee had deteriorated considerably after the exchange of angry words over Hornung and Taylor, so Blackbourn's contract was not renewed at the end of the 1957 season.

The noble experiment of dipping into the college ranks had not worked out. Committee members concluded that handling the more mature athletes on professional football teams was a different ballgame than handling high school or college players, and they felt that Blackbourn's greatest lack was an inability to communicate with and motivate his players.

Blackbourn returned to Marquette where he renewed a successful career in college coaching until Marquette abandoned football several years later. Shades of the Dan Devine story in years to come.

One other valuable asset that Blackbourn left the Packers for future years was the choice he made in the 17th round of the 1956 draft when he took a quarterback from Alabama by the name of Bryant (Bart) Starr. Starr had sustained a back injury in his senior year of college which explained why he was still available in the 17th round. The choice did not create any great excitement among Packer fans at the time. But a number of Blackbourn's draft choices in those 1956 and 1957 seasons became key performers

The Blackbourn Era. Head Coach Lisle Blackbourn huddled with Publicity Director Jug Earp, Business Manager Verne Lewellen, Coach Ray McLean, Talent Scout Jack Vainisi and Coach Red Hearden in 1957. It was Blackbourn's last season. *Lefebvre photo.*

in the great championship days under the legendary Vince Lombardi.

Ray McLean was probably one of the most popular assistants on Lisle Blackbourn's coaching staff. Ray had been a dynamic running back with the Chicago Bears in the 1940s, where he acquired the nickname of "Scooter."

The Packer Executive Committee decided to give McLean a shot at the head coaching job, succeeding Blackbourn. The decision to go with McLean was an exceedingly popular one, not

Record Holder. Fred Cone's kicking records are still recorded on the Packer all-time lists. In addition he was a standout fullback. He played from 1951 through 1957. *Lefebvre photo.*

The Kentucky Babe. Vito Parilli was the Packers' first draft choice in 1952, was traded to Cleveland in 1954, then brought back to Green Bay in 1956. He has been an assistant coach with several other NFL teams since retiring. *Lefebvre photo.*

only with the fans but also with the players; and maybe the latter proved to be McLean's undoing.

McLean inherited a dispirited team that had several players who were very high-spirited off the field if not on it. Except for the two years, 1952 and 1955, when the Pack broke even with 6-6 records, Green Bay fans had not enjoyed a winning season since 1947 when Curly Lambeau was still around, and even then, they had only gone 6-5-1. Over that 10-year span, they won a total of 36 games against 83 losses and one tie. No one suspected at the beginning of the 1958 campaign that the Packers had yet to hit bottom.

During McLean's short term at the helm, Paul Hornung thoroughly demonstrated how he had acquired the nickname "Golden Boy" as he made the rounds of certain nightly haunts in and around Green Bay. It was factually true that he

All-Time Loser. Ray (Scooter) McLean was at the same time the most popular Packer coach and the losingest one. Brought to the Packer staff in 1951 by fellow Bear, Gene Ronzani, he was an assistant through 1957 when he took over as head coach and posted a 1-10-1 record. *Lefebvre photo.*

had to beat the girls off with a baseball bat. The women literally flocked to him.

Hornung had plenty of company in his nightly exploits in the persons of players like Max McGee, Ron Kramer, Dan Currie, Bill Quinlan, Fuzzy Thurston, and Jerry Kramer. Every one of them liked to have his fun, even it did mean breaking training. If they had spent as much time concentrating on their play on the field as they did practicing their moves with the ladies, the Packers under McLean might have enjoyed a reasonable amount of success.

I remember a meeting of the Executive Committee about half way through the summer training season when McLean told us he was having disciplinary problems with a number of the players. He said that he had fined five of them for violating curfew, but he added that he was not going to disclose this fact to the press and public. I disagreed with McLean's decision on this and told him that I thought publicizing the incident would have a positive effect on the team as a whole, more so than keeping it quiet. I argued the point to no avail. It was kept hushed up, and McLean's disciplinary problems with certain players continued to multiply as the season went on. To make matters worse, those problems showed up in the team's performance on the field.

It was a totally disastrous season. The Chicago Bears pounded the Pack, 34-20, in the opener at home, then McLean was able to eke out a tie with the Detroit Lions in the second game, 13-13. Baltimore came away with a one-touchdown win, 24-17, in Milwaukee the following week. The Washington Redskins were poor hosts as they put it to the Packers, 37-20, but McLean was able to slip by the Philadelphia Eagles, 38-35, in a game that featured little defense.

From then on, however, it was strictly downhill. The Packers were annihilated by the Colts, 56-0, and never came closer to winning than the 24-14 spread by which the Lions beat them in their second meeting. The Packers wound up with a record of 1-10-1.

McLean was a real gentleman and resigned shortly after the season ended. He went to Detroit as an assistant coach the next year, and his career there ended even more tragically than it did in Green Bay. He contracted terminal cancer and died some years later.

Ray will always be remembered by Packer fans as one of the finer gentlemen who ever coached the team.

The reader is reminded at this point that many of the players who performed on the team which had the worst record in Packer history made up the nucleus of the team which Vince Lombardi inherited the following season. Here, for instance, is a list of the players on that McLean team: Bart Starr, Jim Taylor, Paul Hornung, Max McGee, Ron Kramer, Gary Knafelc, Boyd Dowler, Jim Ringo, Jerry Kramer, Dave Hanner, Nate Borden, Ray Nitschke, Dan Currie, Tom Bettis, Bill Forester, Hank Gremminger, Bobby Dillon, and Jesse Whittenton. All these players were starters in Lombardi's first league game in 1959.

And that begins the fabulous story of Vince Lombardi.

Broadcasting's Predecessor. Packer fans gathered in Legion Park to watch an out-of-town game re-enacted on the Playograph Board. The game was re-created from telegraph reports sent from the town where the Packers were playing that day. In bad weather, they moved the board into Turner Hall, an auditorium downtown. It was a lovely way to spend a Sunday afternoon when the Packers weren't playing at home.

Lefebure-Stiller photo.

The Packer Legend

Chapter Nine

PACKERS HIT

THE AIRWAVES

It is a Sunday afternoon in October of 1923, and the Packers are playing the Chicago Bears in Chicago.

Some 500 Packer fans are jammed into the gymnasium of Turner Hall in downtown Green Bay. On the stage is a large replica of a football gridiron, and a life-size football moves up and down the field to visually portray the play-by-play account of the game which is being broadcast over the public address system by Jim Coffeen, a man who knows football since he was a member of Curly Lambeau's 1919 team and who has been associated with the Packers in one way or another ever since. The play-by-play is being sent by telegraph from Wrigley Field in Chicago to Turner Hall in Green Bay, and Coffeen is recreating the game from those brief wireless reports.

That scene in Turner Hall was a microcosm of televised National Football League games today with their millions of viewers all across the country. But that is where it all began for the Packers.

Coffeen was also the field announcer when Pete Platten, who owned a radio shop in Green Bay, installed a public address system in the brand new city stadium which the Board of Education had built behind East High School in 1924. The stadium was for the joint use of East High and the Packers because the Packers came up with the seed money to get it started. Platten laughs today as he recalls the mechanical problems he faced with a public address system in those days. The speakers were powered by 6-volt wet-cell batteries, and every game day Platten would have to pick up a dozen of those batteries from

Original Voice of the Packers. Russ Winnie of WTMJ in Milwaukee handled the Packer radio broadcasts when they first started broadcasting their games in 1943. He was known as "The Voice of the Packers" until he was succeeded by Bob Heiss.

a local garage and carry them with the speakers out to the stadium to be hung on support brackets and connected up to the wiring system.

Platten and Coffeen operated from a table next to the Packer bench at the 50-yardline, but in those days the microphone would not transmit the human voice through cable for more than 10 or 12 feet. So one of Coffeen's helpers would follow the ball up and down the field flashing cards to him showing the down and the yardage, and again, Coffeen would recreate the situation from the numbers on those cards. By the next year, Platten invented a transformer which would capture the range of the human voice and transmit it through a longer cable to the amplifier. Coffeen was then able to follow the action up and down the field and describe it over the public address system from the point of play.

Platten installed the entire system for free in exchange for being allowed to put up a sign over the press box advertising the Platten Radio Company. He did receive the momentous sum of $25 a game, however, from Pres. Lee Joannes of the Packers for advertising Joannes Brothers Wholesale Grocery Company over the public address system. Platten even lost that income, however, when the NFL in later years banned the broadcasting of commercials over the public address system.

The first radio broadcasts of Packer games were also done for free over station WHBY in Green Bay and WTMJ in Milwaukee in 1931. Each station carried only the games in their own city, however, since there was no interconnection between stations in those days.

The first commercial braodcast of Packer games came in 1943 when station WTMJ paid the Packers $7,500 for the rights to broadcast its games. Russ Winnie became "the voice of the Packers" and traveled with the team, broadcasting all of its games.

The price of radio rights gradually increased until in 1952 the Packers took bids for those rights. The Wisconsin Network, a combination of state stations which was broadcasting University of Wisconsin football games, matched the bid from WTMJ of $20,000 and was awarded the rights on the strength of the fact that their announcer was Earl Gillespie. He had created a great following among Green Bay sports fans when he was the sports announcer on station WJPG, owned by the *Press-Gazette* in Green Bay. Gillespie had moved to station WEMP in Milwaukee, and that being one of the Wisconsin

Network stations, he became available to become the new voice of the Packers.

The personality of the announcer was an important factor in those early radio broadcasts because in radio the play-by-play man was an out-and-out supporter of the home team, broadcasting all the games at home and away. Bob Heiss of WTMJ succeeded Russ Winnie as the voice of the Packers. Two other announcers who had made their names on station WJPG in Green Bay followed Gillespie. They were Tony Flynn and Blaine Walsh. Another ex-Green Bay announcer now handles the radio broadcasts. Jim Irwin broke into the business with WLUK-TV in Green Bay. He is currently assisted by color man Max McGee, the former Packer All-Pro receiver.

The first televising of Packer games came in 1953 when the Dumont Network paid the Packers $5,000 for each of three games which they televised that year. The Lions game in Detroit on Thanksgiving Day was also televised for the first time that year, with the Packers getting $15,000 as their share of those rights.

It was also in 1953 that the TV Quarterback Club was organized by station WBAY in Green Bay with Bob Houle as host. The Quarterback Club meeting was televised live every Monday evening from WBAY auditorium.

In 1955, the radio rights were granted to the Miller Brewing Company of Milwaukee for $20,000, but the brewery said they were not interested in televising any games because the expense of transmitting the telecast from other cities back to Wisconsin was exorbitant.

The first package of television games came the next year when CBS paid the Packers $75,000 to televise all of their games. At this point, however, with the very rapid growth of the television industry, it was becoming quite apparent to Packer management that they ranked at the bottom of the league in capacity to realize substantial income from television rights. The Green Bay TV market consisted of the Milwaukee metropolitan area, other cities in Wisconsin like Green Bay and the Fox Cities, and then a vast expanse of forest lands to the north all the way to Lake Superior which was sparsely populated. This was complicated by the fact that in those days telecasts were blacked out in the home city where the games were being played, meaning that when the Packers played in Milwaukee, that metropolitan population was subtracted from the potential audience.

The Packer Legend

And Now a Word From The Lip

It was mere coincidence that Earl Gillespie followed his boyhood neighbor, Tony Canadeo, to Green Bay, but it turned out to be a fortunate coincidence for Earl.

Tony's mother used to do all her shopping for bakeries at the shop where Earl's mother worked in Chicago. Tony had gone on to star in football at Gonzaga University on the West Coast, then was drafted by the Green Bay Packers.

Gillespie came to Green Bay as an aspiring young baseball player in the Milwaukee Brewers' farm system. Playing first base on the Green Bay Bluejays, he earned the nickname of "The Lip" with his constant chatter. John Walter, former sports editor of the Green Bay *Press-Gazette* and then manager of radio station WJPG, got the idea that the talkative Gillespie might make a pretty fair sports announcer and gave him that opportunity.

I vividly remember Gillespie walking around downtown Green Bay during his lunch hour practicing play-by-play announcing of a hypothetical baseball game, or football or basketball for that matter.

Walter's confidence was rewarded. Gillespie became a top-notch sports announcer on WJPG, then graduated to a spot on the staff of station WEMP in Milwaukee, which was a heavily sports-oriented station.

As a matter of fact, it was Gillespie's availability through WEMP which won the Packer radio broadcast rights away from station WTMJ in Milwaukee for the Wisconsin Network, a group of state stations put together by Walter and Hugh Boice of WEMP.

So in 1952 Gillespie became the radio voice of the Packers and held that position through 1956.

I recently asked Earl what the Packers had meant to him in his broadcasting career. He told me:

"It was the culmination of a dream I had harbored since my very first day in radio with WJPG in 1947. The late Gene Ronzani,

then head coach of the Packers, told me in 1950 to take a job offer from WEMP in Milwaukee if I wanted to someday do the Packer broadcasts.

"The Packer assignment in the fall of 1952 was actually my first major league job. Despite other career highlights such as 'Voice of the Milwaukee Braves,' World Series broadcasts, Marquette University and Wisconsin Badger football, College All-Star football games, and NFL title games on radio, those five years as 'Voice of the Packers' shall always remain among my most cherished memories.

"The Wisconsin Network lost the broadcast rights to the Packer games after the 1956 season, a sad moment for me. You can imagine my elation when the late Vince Lombardi selected me to be the TV voice of the Packers on CBS in 1964. I'm proud of the fact that today I am the only person active in the media who has covered the Packers from Curly Lambeau to Bart Starr. And that's a lot of years of ups and downs, thrills, great players, championships, and best of all, warm, personal, and lasting friendships."

that television rights should be sold as a package by the league and the proceeds divided equally among the member clubs. Considering the fact that teams like the New York Giants, Chicago Bears, and Los Angeles Rams already had lucrative contracts for televising their games in their large metropolitan markets, it is most remarkable that Bell was able to prevail upon owners like George Halas, Tim Mara, and Dan Reeves into giving up their contracts for the sake of the betterment of the league. Bell was adamant, pointing out that if this disparity in revenues was not corrected, competition within the league would gradually shrink, to be dominated by a few wealthy clubs, and teams like Green Bay were bound to disappear. This was a critical matter for the Green Bay Packer football corporation, and it was the great friendships which the Packers had developed over the years with people like Halas, Mara, and Art Rooney in Pittsburgh that swung the tide in favor of the league approach to TV revenue.

In recent years, the Packers have received over $5,000,000 a year from that television package. CBS had most of the NFL teams signed up when the package was put together, and this coincided

Current Packer Voice. Jim Irwin started his broadcasting career in Green Bay, then became the play-by-play announcer on the Packer network.

There had been talk within league circles of putting together a league television package, but this was prevented by a ruling of the United States Supreme Court in 1957 holding that professional football, unlike professional baseball, was subject to the federal anti-trust laws, and therefore any combination put together by the league for packaging television rights would be in restraint of trade. Commissioner Bert Bell, with a great deal of help from league cities and particularly congressmen from those league cities, went to Congress seeking legislation exempting professional football from the Sherman and Clayton anti-trust laws. Representative John W. Byrnes of Green Bay was most instrumental in shepherding the legislation through Congress, and after being debated in committee for several sessions, it finally was adopted in 1961.

With the legal complications out of the way, Bell went to work persuading the member clubs

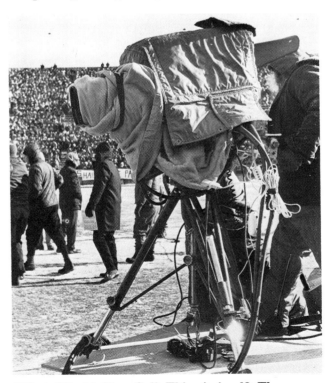

What Would You Call This Animal? They were trying to keep this television camera from freezing up during the Ice Bowl Game in Green Bay Dec. 31, 1967. *Green Bay Press-Gazette photo.*

Bob Heiss and Charley Grimm. Heiss succeeded Winnie as the Packer radio announcer when Winnie became general manager of WTMJ. Here he interviews Jolly Charley Grimm, who was then managing the Brewers in the American Association.

All-Stars 7, Packers 0. The Packers lost the first time they played in the College All-Star Game. Jimmy Ford of Durkee Mailbag fame says it was due to the new uniforms Curly Lambeau had ordered. It was a hot muggy night in Chicago's Soldiers Field, and the new jerseys didn't breathe, wilting the Packers. *Lefebvre photo.*

Still the Golden Boy. Paul Hornung became a broadcast color man when he retired from football as a player. Here he interviews Coach Bart Starr when the Packers played in Dallas in 1975. *Vern Biever photo.*

with the merger of the National and American Football Leagues. NBC had the rights to most of the AFL teams. At a later date, ABC joined the package with its Monday Night Football, introducing Howard Cosell to professional football fans.

The new television contract negotiated in 1982 with the three networks totals over $2 billion and will mean about $13.5 million to each club for the next five years.

When CBS first started televising Packer games, they emulated radio by engaging a so-called hometown announcer who did all of the Packer games. Ray Scott was that voice for some 10 years, assisted by ex-pro players like Johnny Lujack and George Connors, and finally by Tony Canadeo, the Grey Ghost of Gonzaga himself.

In 1966, however, CBS abruptly changed this system and assigned various broadcasting teams to NFL games on a rotating basis. CBS said it was doing so for the sake of objectivity on the part of the game announcers, but it was really an expense reduction move since now it required only one team of announcers per game instead of two. Previously in a game in Green Bay, for example, there would be one announce team for the Packers and a separate team for the Bears.

In recent years television revenues about matched income from the sale of tickets at football games as far as the Packers were concerned. So it is obvious that television revenues are the prime factor in enabling the Packer football corporation to compete in the National Football League.

The Packer Legend

Best Not Play Packer Trivia

When Radio Station WNFL asked Jimmy Ford to sponsor their post-game broadcasts after Packer games, he replied that he would buy the time if he could do the show himself.

Jim, a hometown athlete of some note in years gone by, is known throughout the area as "The Durkee Man," and he had an idea for a radio program he would call "Durkee's Mail Bag." He went on the air with it in the mid-1960s, and he's been doing the show after every game ever since.

The format is simple: ask Packer fans to write in, say hello, comment on the team, or better yet, ask questions. Jim had begun to accumulate a file of Packer trivia, stories he had heard from veteran players he knew or which he had dug out of the microfilm files of the Green Bay *Press-Gazette* at the library.

At first, he had to fake the questions so that his sidekick on the program, Arnie Herber, could read the answers Jim had already prepared for him. In subsequent years, Ted Fritsch, Charley Brock, and Mike Michalske joined him on the show.

By now the Durkee Mail Bag files are filled with newspaper clippings, old Packer programs, and microfilm printouts of old newspaper files. Here are some of the stories Jim told me when I interviewed him for this book:

A young fellow from Kewaunee by the name of Ike Karel was on the University of Wisconsin team in 1895 and used to pass through Green Bay on his way home to visit. He had heard that Green Bay had a city team which was claiming to be the best in Wisconsin, so Karel stopped off to watch them practice one day. He issued a challenge to them to play the University of Wisconsin for the state title.

The team gathered that night at their usual watering hole, John Gross' tavern in downtown Green Bay, and they composed a reply to the challenge which said in effect, "Go get yourselves a reputation before challenging us to a game."

Nothing came of the challenge, but Karel

Jim Ford

stopped by again after the Wisconsin season was over to bat the breeze with the Green Bay players who were practicing in a vacant lot on the West Side at the corner of Oakland and Dousman Streets. They asked Karel if he would teach them a few plays the university used so they could try them out for a game against Marinette the next Sunday. Karel spent Friday and Saturday with the team, and at the end of practice Saturday he stood up on a large boulder at the corner of the lot and told the team, "I sure wish we had you guys down at Madison. We'd beat anyone we played. You're going to have a world beating team here some day."

Karel went on to get a law degree at Wisconsin, and he became a circuit judge. He obviously had a special ability to foresee the future.

* * * * *

Jim ferreted out the reason why the Packers lost their pro league franchise after

With the Man from Durkee's

the 1921 season, their first in the league.

They played the Chicago Supremes in a post-season game in Chicago and used two Notre Dame college players in the contest. George Halas tells in his autobiography that the league decided to make an example of Curly Lambeau and the Packers.

But the league relented that next spring, and Lambeau was able to borrow $250 from his friend Don Murphy to renew the franchise. Murphy loaned him the money on the condition that he could play in the opening game that season, so Muprhy was in the lineup when the Packers kicked off. That one play became his entire pro football career.

* * * * *

Jim has a movie film Otto Stiller took of Louis Duggan's special seat for Packer games in the 1920s. Duggan parked his moving van just outside the fence at City Stadium and installed an over-stuffed chair on top of the van, where he had a perfect view of the field. But Duggan was no interloper. He bought two tickets to every game.

* * * * *

As the Packers readied for the 1923 season, the *Press-Gazette* headlined the news that they had signed an All-American end from Princeton. Dollie Gray played the first two games that season before Lambeau became suspicious. He was an imposter, but the Packer press book still lists on the all-time player list one "D. Gray, No College."

* * * * *

Jim has a clipping from the front page of the Chicago *Tribune*, picturing a personal note from George Halas to the Packers for $1,500. Seems only 5,000 fans turned out for a game in a snowstorm in Chicago and all the cash Halas could give the Packers was $1,000. The note represented the balance of their $2,500 guarantee. The note is now exhibited in the Pro Football Hall of Fame in Canton, Ohio.

* * * * *

Jim knew Arnie Herber from when they grew up together, and he tells the story about Herber's unusually small hands. Herber learned in high school that he could throw the ball longer and more accurately if he palmed it, with the laces in his palm instead of at his finger tips as most passers do. He developed a passing motion which was more of a push than a snap, but with it he became the finest long bomb passer the game has ever known.

Jim also tells that Don Hutson had flat feet and that he had to have his feet taped in a special way for football. That explains his peculiar loping running style which completely baffled opponents. He never seemed to be running as fast as he really was.

* * * * *

And finally Jim tells about these Packer firsts:

The first team to have cheerleaders. East and West High cheerleaders turned out for several games in 1931, but they didn't go over very big.

The first team to fly to a game by airplane, in the early 1940s.

The first team to have a public address system, in 1923, as related in another chapter.

The first team to have a Quarterback Club, one organized by Charley Brock and the Packer Alumni Association in the 1950s.

And the first team to have a mascot, a dog named Olive.

"How did he get the name Olive," I had to ask.

"Because he liked Durkee olives," he said.

The Old and the New. The Packers played in the Bellevue baseball park in the early 1920s while the new City Stadium was being built behind East High School. *Lefebvre-Stiller photo.* Lambeau Field is the fine new modern bowl which is now the home of the Packers, seating 56,500 fans with parking for 6,000 cars surrounding it. The county's Veterans Memorial Arena is next door, housing the Packer Hall of Fame. *Lefebvre photo.*

The Packer Legend

Chapter Ten

PLAYGROUNDS

FOR BIG BOYS

Lambeau field in Green Bay, the home of the Packers and one of the finest professional football facilities of its kind in the country, stands as a monument to the steadfast loyalty of Packer fans and the entire Green Bay community to their beloved football team. The story of the building of this stadium is part of the remarkable history of this team.

The old wooden stands at City Stadium behind East High School on the banks of the East River in Green Bay were deteriorating badly in those final years in the early 1950s. Every year the stadium subcommittee chaired by Fred Leicht would make an inspection of the underpinnings of the stadium and would have to order substantial replacement of the wooden members which supported the 23,500 seats.

Built as it was on the banks of the East River,

the site also provided very poor footings for the erection of any substantial stadium structure.

Not only were the stands inadequate but there were practically no modern facilities available at the stadium. Both the Packers and the visiting team dressed in the locker room at East High School. Early on the teams would gather in a circle at opposite ends of the field for their halftime rest and regrouping talks.

The playing field at old City Stadium was separated from the stands by a cinder track which East High used during track season. A wooden fence divided the playing field from the track and the front rows of the stands, and fans entering the park through the main gate promenaded down this track to get to their seats.

On beautiful fall football days in Green Bay, the female fans took advantage of this promenade to show off their finest fall costumes, and there was considedrable competition among the ladies to appear at their very best. This is where the latest styles in fur coats and jackets were displayed. It was also an era when women wore hats, and the fall haberdashery finery was very much in evidence at Packer home games.

Women faced one severe handicap, however, in attending Packer games in those days. There were, as I mentioned already, no toilet facilities for female fans. The men felt free to relieve themselves under the stands between halves, and despite the fact that these seats provided an open view below the stands, women were very cautious not to look around between periods of play. This also meant that the ladies of necessity had to refrain from the intake of any liquid refreshments for periods of several hours before game time.

The ladies also faced other hazards at the old stadium. The foot rests under the seats consisted of one 2X12 plank, and the rest of the footing was open to the ground. On frequent occasions, women dropped their handbags or even items of apparel down through these openings. The Packers would station security guards under the stands to retrieve any such items and take them to the lost and found counter where they could be repossessed.

Peter Platten, one of the original radio dealers in Green Bay, donated his services to install and man the public address system at the old stadium. He operated from a little cubbyhole in the press box. Before and during the games, he would have to go down under the stands to inspect his wiring and sometimes repair connections. He told me the story that the security guards under the stadium stands used to have Xs marked under certain seats, which indicated the seat locations of the female fans with the finest displays of legs.

Peter had a brother named Emmett who gained a reputation as one of the most boisterous Packer fans in the city. At his own expense, he would buy air time on a local radio station to conduct a pre-game show before the broadcast of Packer games. Platten was a man of intense loyalty to the team but one who also had a very short fuse.

Emmett had a front row seat, and only a three-foot high fence separated the playing field from the cinder track and stands. On one occasion, he became particularly upset over a Bear player whom he claimed was always offside. The player in question was Bill Hewitt, probably one of the finer defensive ends that ever played for George Halas. He was so fast off the ball that on frequent occasions it appeared he was offside. Between plays, Platten leaped over the fence, charged onto the field, and slugged Hewitt in the jaw. Hewitt was so stunned at the sudden attack that he stood there in complete consternation, while Platten marched heroically back to his seat.

When the Executive Committee began considering possibilities of constructing a new stadium, it was estimated that the additional seats which were contemplated could well be occupied totally by female fans who would flock to a new stadium offering them toilet facilities.

Interior Shot of Stadium. This was the interior of Bellevue Park with its covered grandstand. The Bears beat the Pack, 3-0, in this game in 1923. That's Curly Lambeau playing safety at left. *Lefebvre-Stiller photo.*

The Packer Legend

Some of the members of the Committee projected a need for a stadium in the neighborhood of 32,500 seats. This astonished and even frightened some of the older members of the Packer Board. I well remember getting a telegram from Andy Turnbull in California in which he warned me that erecting a stadium of 32,500 seats would mean the bankruptcy of the Packers because we would never be able to sell out that many seats on a season ticket basis.

The question of where to site the new stadium, however, was even more difficult than the matter of capacity. There was a great deal of tradition wound up in the old stadium on the East Side. It was practically the birthplace of the team back in 1919, but as I mentioned before, it provided poor footings for a stadium of any size.

A groundswell of support grew up for building the stadium in a city park on the West Side called Perkins Park which the city then owned but which was undeveloped. It was on the extreme western limits of the city and was adjacent to the main traffic artery, U.S. Highway 41, which runs north through the Fox River Valley up into Northern Michigan.

When this groundswell of support for a stadium on the west side reared its ugly head, however, a comparable uprising of support came from the east side of the city to retain the stadium in its then present location.

The Executive Committee found itself caught in the middle of this neighborhood argument until Fred Leicht had the brilliant idea of engaging an outside engineering firm to make an impartial study of possible sites in the city for the new stadium. The Osborn Engineering Company of Cleveland, Ohio, came highly recommended, and the Packers entered into a contract with them to conduct such a study.

The results of that study were a pure bonanza

Old City Stadium at Its Peak. The stadium behind East High School had been expanded to seat 23,500 fans in the mid-1950s. It had served its purpose but a new stadium was badly needed, and there was no more room to expand at the old site. *Lefebvre photo.*

The Packer Legend

Nixon Dedicates New Stadium. Vice-Pres. Richard Nixon was met at the airport by Mayor Otto Rachals, left, Sheriff Artley Skenandore, and Rep. John W. Byrnes, on the right. *Lefebvre photo.*

for the Packers and the city of Green Bay. The Osborn company came up with a totally new site on the far southwestern outskirts of the city, which was then almost exclusively farm land, but it was also adjacent to what was to become the outer beltline, Highway 41, around the city on the west side. It was a site which also had very fine access into the city.

Not only was this site ideally located but it consisted of a sloping piece of ground which was made up of very firm hard clay soil, and the Osborn company recommended moving large quantities of this earth from one side of the hill to the other in order to form a natural earthen bowl. The engineers pointed out that at least the lower half of the seats then could be constructed below ground level without the need for expensive supports. It also would allow fans to enter the stadium through vomitories at about midpoint, and thus they would not have to climb up or down more than half the total rows of seats.

The obvious advantages of the plan won immediate support from the entire Packer organization and from city officials in Green Bay. It had been the concept from the beginning that the city would construct the stadium and the Packers would enter into a 20-year lease which would guarantee repayment of at least 50 percent of the servicing cost of the bond issue which would provide the construction funds. Remember that the old City Stadium was owned by the city school board as an adjunct to East High School, so it was contemplated that the

new stadium would also be available for high school games and other public events. This necessitated a referendum, however, to approve the issuance of bonds. The total cost of the project thus became a political as well as an economic matter. Architects were hired to design the stadium in line with the recommendations of the Osborn company, and bids were solicited for its construction.

In order to hold down the cost, however, the county highway department agreed to perform the ground moving phase of the construction at a nominal cost, and the city public works department agreed to undertake such work as sewer and water and surfacing of parking lots.

When all the bids came in and all these contributions were put together, the total cost came to $969,000. City officials and Packer officials were overjoyed at being able to go to referendum with a figure under a million dollars.

This is where the support of the average resident of Green Bay became so very important. Led by the local newspaper, the *Press-Gazette*, and with a broad-based committee of citizens organized to get out a yes vote, all facets of the building of the stadium and its financing were placed before the voting public. Old friends like Gene Ronzani and George Halas of the Chicago Bears came to the Packers' support. In a mammoth pep rally at the Columbus Club on the weekend before the vote, Halas came to Green

Dedication of New Stadium. Nixon officiated at the dedication ceremonies Sept. 30, 1957. Left to right: Rep. John W. Byrnes, Gov. Vernon Thomson, Miss America Marilyn VanDerBur, Nixon, and Packer Pres. Dominic Olejniczak. *Press-Gazette photo.*

The Packer Legend

Bay and bluntly told Packer fans that the only way they could continue to compete in the National Football League was to build the new facility.

The yes vote carried by over a 2-1 margin. Construction of the stadium began in 1956, and the stadium was dedicated at a game with the Bears in September of 1957, with Vice-President Richard Nixon in attendance. There had been a weekend of festivities in Green Bay including a giant parade at which Miss America, Marilyn VanDerBur, was the grand marshall.

And the Packers beat the Bears, 21-17.

About this time, the new Air Force Academy was being built at Colorado Springs, Colorado, and included in the facilities there was a football stadium of approximately the same capacity of Green Bay's. The cost of that stadium was $15,000,000.

Lambeau Field, as it was later named in memory of the Packers' co-founder, was built exclusively as a football stadium, and it is one of the finest facilities of its kind in the country

Bears in Parade. The Chicago Bears had a float in the dedication parade, but they lost the subsequent football game as the Packers won their first contest in the new stadium, 21-17. *Lefebvre photo.*

for its size. Every seat in the stadium has an unobstructed view of the field, and the fact that there is no running track between the field and the stadium means that the front row seats are in close proximity to the playing field.

Among the improvements made by the Packers in subsequent years was the installation of aluminum seating to replace the original wooden seats, which were always subject to deterioration and resultant splintering. The lighting system for night football and the public address system have also been upgraded to the finest quality available in recent years, and a new million dollar scoreboard was erected several years ago.

It wasn't long before the 32,500 seats were being sold out regularly on a season ticket basis, and the stadium was subsequently expanded a number of times. In 1960, additional seats were added on the sidelines, bringing the total capacity to 38,670. In 1963, following Vince Lombardi's first championship, a number of temporary bleachers were added in the end zones, increasing the capacity to 42,200. Then in 1966, the temporary bleachers were replaced by permanent seating in the end zones, boosting the capacity to 50,860, and the entire bowl was finally completed in 1970 bringing the capacity to its present size of 56,150. All seats are currently sold out by March of any given year, and there are over 9,000 prospective buyers on the waiting list.

In each case, the Packers donated the

Elaborate Press Box. This is the four-story press box atop City Stadium. It is equipped with an elevator. Media people are served a hot lunch and other refreshments. *Lefebvre photo.*

The Packer Legend

construction cost to the city, and during these years and up to the present time, the corporation has continued to make additional improvements to the facility. A very fine Packer headquarters building was constructed in 1960, providing training quarters for the team as well as offices for the coaches, administrative staff, and the ticket office.

This headquarters building has been expanded on several occasions until it now provides the ultimate in an exercise room, training quarters, locker rooms, classrooms, and so forth.

The press box has also been expanded and several years ago an elevator was installed to facilitate carrying the heavy television camera equipment to the upper stories of the press box as well as the media people themselves.

One of the great assets of the site was the fact that adequate parking space was available. The huge lot surrounding the stadium provides parking right at the site for some 6,000 cars.

Starting in 1961, the Packers also acquired property across Oneida Street to the east for a number of practice fields. One of these fields has now been covered with artificial turf to acquaint the players with that surface in advance of playing on artificial turf in other cities.

During the training season, the team is housed in dormitories at St. Norbert College in nearby DePere, a four-mile trip by auto or bus. The total complex is by far one of the finest such facilities in the entire NFL, and in assessing its quality, you have to think back to the overwhelming vote of approval by the citizens of Green Bay to build the kind of facility which would keep Green Bay competitive in the NFL.

For Charity's Sake

The two charity games in which the Packers have participated in Green Bay and Milwaukee have raised almost $3 million for the sponsors to date.

In 1951 the Tripoli Shrine Temple in Milwaukee began sponsoring a pre-season game there in which the Shrine, the Packers, and the visiting team split the gate receipts three ways after expenses are taken off the top.

For quite a few years, the Chicago Bears were the opponent, and the gate gradually built to the point where it has been a sell-out in recent years. The $1.4 million raised through the game so far has gone to support Shrine Hospitals for Crippled Children and Shrine Burn Centers.

The Bishop's Charity Game in Green Bay was initiated in 1961, with a committee appointed by the Bishop of the Green Bay Diocese handling all arrangements.

In both cases, the sponsors handle everything; printing their own programs, selling the tickets, arranging for advertising and promotion, etc. They also guarantee the visiting team a minimum take plus expenses. Proceeds go to the Bishop's Charity Fund. Proceeds of this game are also approaching $1.5 million to date.

Bishop and Chairman. Bishop Aloysius Wycislo and long-time chairman Gene Sladky are honored before the annual charity game in Green Bay. *Lefebvre photo.*

Old Timers Suit Up. Packer stars of yesteryear put their uniforms back on to help the team raise money on Thanksgiving Day, 1949. Left to right, back row: Tiny Engebretsen, 1934-41; Herb Nichols, 1919-20; Curly Lambeau, 1921-30; Jug Earp, 1922-32; Lavvie Dilweg, 1927-34; Verne Lewellen, 1924-32; Johnny Blood, 1928-36; Front row: Charley Brock, 1939-47; Don Hutson, 1935-45; Arnie Herber, 1931-41; and Joe Laws, 1934-45.

Press-Gazette photo.

Packer Band Director. Wilner Burke took over directorship of the Packer band when it was the city band back in 1923, and he still wields the baton at all home games. *Lefebvre photo.*

The Packer Legend

Chapter Eleven

MUSIC,

MAESTRO,

PLEASE!

The Packer band has been a do-it-yourself project from the very beginning, and it still is that way.

When I called band director Wilner Burke for an appointment to talk to him about the band's history, he said that I had gotten him in from the garage where he was repairing and painting the boxes in which the band's uniforms would be stored during the off-season.

The first Packer band was the result of a conversation at George DeLair's restaurant on Washington Street in downtown Green Bay. George and some of his cohorts like Ed Schuster rounded up a number of musicians to play during the Packer games out at old Hagemeister Park. This was in 1921, only two years after the Packers came into being, and certainly the Packer band today can state with pride that it

is the oldest such organization in professional football.

Many members of that original group, who called themselves the Lumberjacks, were members of the Green Bay City Band, and in 1923 the City Band actually took over playing for the Packer games, both in Green Bay and Milwaukee. Burke was a member of that band, and he remembers very well traveling to Milwaukee by truck and sitting on two-by-four seats for that several hour trip each way.

About that same time, a Milwaukeean by the name of Eric Karll wrote and composed the Green Bay Packer song, and soon thereafter it was being played by the band at the start of all Packer home games, certainly another first in professional football.

The words of the chorus go like this:

Lumberjack Band. An early Packer institution which has continued to this day is the Packer band, originally a group of Legionnaires and other volunteers who followed the team to Chicago by train and paraded around the field between halves, dodging debris thrown by Bear fans.

Lefebure-Stiller photo.

The Packer Legend

Go, you Packers, go and get 'em,
Go, you fighting fools, upset 'em,
Smash their line with all your might,
A touchdown Packers, fight, fight, fight,
Fight on, you Blue and Gold, you glory,
Win this game the same old story.
Fight, you Packers,
Fight and bring the bacon home to Old
  Green Bay.

I don't suppose there are very many Packer fans who can recite the opening verses of the song, but just in case you want to know them, here is the way they go:

Hail, hail the gang's all here to yell for you.
And keep you going in your winning ways.

Hail, hail the gang's all here to tell you too,
That win or lose,
We'll always sing your praises, Packers.

As an aside at this point, the Packers decided to print sheet music to the Packer song back in 1953 and had 10,000 copies printed. I think there must be at least 8,000 or 9,000 still available at the Packer office and the Packer Hall of Fame.

Burke went to Pres. Lee Joannes in 1939 and asked him if the Packers would purchase new uniforms for the City Band for they were getting decrepit. Joannes responded that he and Curly Lambeau wanted to start their own band and asked Burke if he would become the director and organize this group. Burke readily agreed and enlisted about 30 of the best players from the

In Their Own Bandshell. The Packers built a shell for the band at Old City Stadium in the 1940s, the better for the crowd to hear the music. By this time, they were complete with drum majors and baton twirling majorettes.
Lefebvre photo.

The Packer Legend

Still the Lumberjack Band. The uniforms in this era still echoed the original theme of the band when they dressed up in lumberjack outfits and invaded Chicago for the Bear game. The coats and pants were Kelly green, the shirts bright red.

Lefebure photo.

The Packer Legend

Headdresses Now. The uniforms are the same, but the majorettes are now sporting Indian headdresses. Many of the band members put in more than 25 years of service. *Lefebvre photo.*

City Band to form the official Green Bay Packer Band.

The band continued to carry out the Lumberjack theme, and their uniforms were made up of bright green pants, caps, and ties with flaming red shirts and heavy waist-length coats, the kind that lumberjacks wore in the north woods. Burke remembers that the uniforms arrived at Frank Krueger's men's store only the day before the first game that fall of 1939, and the entire band gathered at the store that Saturday evening to try on their new attire. There was one complication: the red suspenders had not arrived. Burke recalls that they scurried all over town to get enough heavy duty safety pins to hold their pants up.

The Packers paid for the band's appearances in Green Bay and Milwaukee, but the band used to pass the bucket through the crowd asking for donations to send them to the Bear game in Chicago. Burke remembers that a round-trip ticket on the train in those days cost $3.00.

The band was placed in seats in Wrigley Field which were as distant from the main body of fans as the Bears could place them. Burke said hardly anybody in the stands could hear their music, so he decided during halftime the band would march onto the field and play the Packer fight song. By the time they got through playing, the field was littered with bottles thrown at them by unruly Bear fans. In future years, however, the Bears welcomed the band, realizing it was an added attraction.

The band had much better accommodations at

New Stadium, New Uniforms. Vince Lombardi dressed the band up in new uniforms in the 1960s. He said the band was "going big time" to match the fine new stadium. *Lefebure photo.*

The Packer Legend

City Stadium in Green Bay. A band shell was erected for it at the north corner of the field.

In the early 1940s, the band had become a marching band, and it put on whatever show there was before the games and during halftime. Drum majors and majorettes were added, and a succession of top-notch twirlers performed in later years.

Remember that these were radio years and not nearly as much emphasis was placed on the halftime show as there is today.

One of those drum majors, Don Marcoullier, came from DePere. He was to go on to become the bandmaster of the University of Wisconsin Band, and now is the bandmaster of Drake University in Iowa. Another real show stopper was drum major Bruce Stengel of Lena, Wisconsin, who is now a famous heart surgeon in Milwaukee.

Vince Lombardi changed the whole tone of the Packer band not long after he took over as head coach and general manager. He figured that the Lumberjack era was over as far as Packer football was concerned, and he wanted to give the Packers a new look that was as big-time as any of the other league cities. He instructed Burke to order entirely new uniforms and to put together a group of majorettes who would perform before the games and during halftimes. Thus were born the Golden Girls.

Halftime entertainment also became a much more important attraction now that the games were being televised, and Burke was asked by Lombardi to take over scheduling of the half-time entertainment.

Back in the radio days, Burke had used all kinds of different approaches to the halftime entertainment, which was of course limited to the fans in the stands. Several times a season, he would have a kids football game between halves. Burke would referee these games and sometimes came out of them in worse shape than the participants. He recalls one time when a pass hit him in the arm, breaking his watch and inflicting a cut in his wrist, bleeding to the extent that he had to go to the emergency room at the hospital for stitches.

With the dawn of the television era, however, the kids football games were replaced by marching bands from nearby high schools and colleges, and today Burke spends a considerable amount of time scouting the best marching bands to play between halves at Packer games.

The Golden Girls have also been revamped under the direction of Shirley Van, a professional dance instructor in Green Bay, and are now known as the Packerettes, performing intricate dance routines during time outs and television commercials.

Many of the members of the band have served a number of years under Burke's direction. Burke lists 11 members who have served 25 or more years, although Burke himself is the only one who can date his service back to the original band in 1923.

When five of the members were honored for their lengthy service during a half-time ceremony in a game in late 1981, Burke totalled up the years of service for the five men and it came to 157 years.

The Packer Band is thus part and parcel of the unique and colorful history of the Packer organization.

Serenading Vince. Three of Vince Lombardi's favorites, Fuzzy Thurston, Paul Hornung, and Max McGee, sang him a special song at a banquet in his honor when he retired. *Vern Biever photo.*

Lombardi Gets 5-Year Pact as Packer GM, Coach

New York Assistant Unanimous Selection

By ART DALEY

Brooklyn-born Vince Lombardi held the sports wonder of the world in the palm of his hand today.

He is the new general manager and head coach of the Packers ... He was given a "completely free hand" by Green Bay Packers Inc., at a momentous meeting Wednesday afternoon.

Lombardi, 45, will come to our town Monday to sign a five-year contract . . . Under Packer policy, no financial figures were told.

Offensive backfield coach of the New York Giants for the last five years, Lombardi suc-

ceeds General Manager Verne Lewellen and Coach Scooter McLean.

Lewellen is still on duty. His status undoubtedly will be clarified after Lombardi works into his dual role. McLean resigned after one season as head

coach Dec. 16.

The selection of Lombardi as the Packers' fifth head coach in their 40-year history—the fourth in the last 10 seasons, was announced by Packer President Dominic Olejniczak at 1 o'clock Wednesday afternoon in the presence of members of the Packers executive committee and the press, radio and television.

The announcement officially ended five frustrating weeks in which Packerland broiled under the heat of rumors, crabbing and discomfort resulting mostly from a lack of leadership following the worst season in Packer history—not to mention 10 years of losing.

The matter was settled quickly Wednesday. The executive committee asked the board of directors for authorization to conclude a deal for a new head coach and/or general manager. The board members, called in from cities throughout the state, voted 26-1 to give the committee that authority. The purpose was to spare prospects from being worked over by the larger group.

Lombardi steps into the sports phenomena known as

PRESS-GAZETTE Sports

Green Bay, Wis., Thurs. Evening, Jan. 29, 1959

ants," he said via telephone from New York today, adding:

"I'll be in there Monday to sign the contract and stay a few days. I'll have to get back here (New York) to close out some odds and ends. I expect to start in about the second week in February."

The length of Lombardi's contract was not announced at yesterday's press parley but the new coach revealed in New York that it was for five years.

Lombardi said he's "anxious to review the game pictures. I know a few things about the club and I know that there is a fine nucleus of veterans but I'll get a better idea of the personnel from the pictures. It will help me know what we can do on offense and defense. I plan to use the T-formation with some flanking variations."

Lombardi said he had "enough football background generally and in particularly with the Giants to handle the general manager position. Of course, I'll have someone to take care of the details."

A veteran of 20 years of coaching, Lombardi said "I'm extremely happy to get this opportunity in Green Bay but I'm unhappy about leaving the Giants and their entire organization. The Maras are wonderful people and I'll miss them all."

Lombardi has put in 20 years of coaching but his only head coaching assignments have been in high school and now in the pros . . . He never played pro football. "At 180 and a guard I was a little light," Lombardi laughed.

Lombardi broke into coaching as a means of working himself through law school at his alma mater, Fordham, taking a position as head football coach at St. Cecilia High in Englewood, N. J. in 1939. Success with the T-formation there gave him national recognition — not to mention six state titles and a string of 36 straight wins, and spelled the end of his law plans.

He installed the T for the freshmen at Fordham under Ed Danowski in 1947 and the following year coached the varsity offense.

Lombardi started a five-year career at Army in 1949, working on Army's T-attack. "I had never met Coach Blaik before he hired me," Vince recalled, adding: "I had an enjoyable time at the Point and I loved every minute of it." Army had an unbeaten season in Lombardi's first year.

"Style I Like — Daring"

Lombardi went to the Giants in 1954 — the year Jim Lee Howell took over as head coach from Steve Owen. "I like daring," Lombardi was Jim Lee's No. 1 aide and the new Packers' basic formation is the T with split-T line spacing. In passing situations he can throw

Shaw Wants To Be Traded; Packers, Giants Interested

George Shaw, the Baltimore Colts No. 2 quarterback behind John Unitas, wants to be traded.

That's the surprise story in Baltimore today. Shaw has asked Coach Weeb Ewbank to be traded so that he can play as a regular.

Reportedly, the Packers and Giants—involved in the switch of Vince Lombardi from the Giants to the Packers as head coach — are interested in the hard-riding red-headed QB.

Lombardi, reached in New York today, said "I know about Shaw but I am going to give our boys a look before doing any trading."

Vince was referring to the Packers' present quarterbacks — Bart Starr, Babe Parilli and Joe Francis. The new coach expects to "get an idea of their play — plus what I've seen myself, from the pictures." All three played in an exhibition against the Giants in Boston last August.

Shaw is considered the league's top benched first-team quarterback. When Unitas was injured in the

GEORGE SHAW, BALTIMORE QUARTERBACK

Packer game in Baltimore last fall he continued the rout and then led the Colts to two key victories in the next three games.

Ewbank discussed trade — and admitted that Shaw's name was mentioned — with Packer President Dominic Olejniczak at last week's league meeting in Philadelphia. Olejniczak said at the time that "we discussed trade but any trading will be done by the head coach."

The Giants reportedly offered the Colts their first draft choice in 1960 and 1961 for their first and second choices in 1960 for Shaw.

Brown, Halas Hail Lombardi Selection as 'Excellent Choice'

Vince 'Tough To Lick But a Sport,' Paul

By LEE REMMEL

Fabled Paul Brown, a longtime opponent, feels the Packers "made a very wise decision" in naming Vince Lombardi as general manager and head coach.

National Football League pioneer George Halas, owner-coach of the Chicago Bears, is in complete agreement. "I think that it was an excellent choice," he declared.

Brown, contacted by telephone, said, "I think the Packer committee has made a very wise decision. They have taken a man who is right currently in the swim from a successful operation and should give him a running go at it."

"He's A Good One"

Paul, who has formed his opinion of the new Packer head man the hard way in annual

and not always successful combat with the New York Giants, added, "I think he's a good one. We've competed against him for some period of years. He's tough to lick but a sport.

"I think he's been a vital cog in the Giants' success," Brown continued. "My feeling would be that he would do a good job. It's also an opportunity which I would say he has earned.

"I certainly wish this fellow well," Brown concluded. "He's a good one."

From Chicago, Halas characterized Lombardi as "sharp, smart, alert and a fine football man. What's more, he's an excellent student of football. He applies himself to the game and the game alone.

"It's a feather in the hat of Green Bay to get a man who is being considered for the West Point job." Halas pointed out. Lombardi, assistant to Col. Earl (Red) Blaik before joining the Giants in 1954, had been prominently mentioned for the Army post following Blaik's recent resignation.

"He was quite a factor in having the Giants become known as a Cinderella team last fall when they won the Eastern Division championship." George also noted. "They did quite a job in beating the Browns twice in a row to win

Rog Herold Takes Over But Knights Lose 66-63

Scores Last 10 Points in Loss To Illinois Tech

By LEN WAGNER

Roger Herold, older brother of the departed Gary, made a valiant effort to fill the mighty shoes of his "little" brother at Van Dyke gym Wednesday night but despite his efforts, the St. Norbert Green Knights dropped a slam-bang decision to Illinois Tech, 66-63.

Rog, a freshman who at 5-10 is only two inches taller than brother Gary, drilled home St. Norbert's last 10 points of the game with six free throws and two baskets in three shots. But that one misfire meant the game.

With only 28 seconds remaining, the Knights trailed by a mere 62-61 and had the ball out of bounds. Splitting the defense, Herold drove for the basket and shot one from his hip that sprang off the rim into the waiting hands of Techawk Don Neal. Rog immediately fouled him, but Neal cashed both free throws.

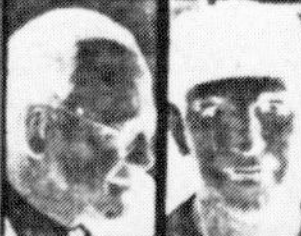

But Herold wasn't through yet. Breaking fast, the Knights crossed the center line and Herold fired a long jumper that again cut the score to one point with five seconds left. Roy Smits made a desperate attempt to intercept the toss but the ball went out of bounds. A second later Tech's John Olin was hacked and he sank two free throws after time had run out for the final count.

The loss, due in great part to Olin's 28 points, dropped the Knights below the .500 level to 6-7 for the season. They will have a chance to even it Saturday night when powerful Lewis invades Van Dyke gym. Tech evened its record at 6-6.

Herold, who wound up with 12 points in playing about half the game, was aided, to no avail, in the Green and Gold cause by Bill Feller's 19 points and Jerry Lamers' 16. Lamers' total leaves him just five points behind Gary Herold's third place standing in the Knight career scoring records.

Except for the shooting percentages, St. Norbert outplayed the Techawks but couldn't quite cope with the consistent Olin. Tech shot 36 per cent while St. Norbert, showing the lack of practice in the past two weeks, hit only 30 per cent. Olin banged home 11 of 30 shots, mostly the long push or jump variety.

St. Norbert outrebounded their guests, 33-31, and lost the ball only 10 times to Tech's 15. And, although Tech fouled 20 times to St. Norbert's 18, Lamers picked up his fourth foul early in the second half and was forced to sit out six minutes.

Tech took advantage of the absence of the Knights' steadying hand to pull from a nine point deficit, 39-30, at his departure to a 45-44 lead by the time he returned. The last eight minutes found almost hand-to-hand combat as the lead see-sawed five times and was tied three times before Tech took a 57-55 lead. This was widened to 62-57 before Herold went into action.

Bobcats in 18-2 Rout Of Mosinee

Dougherty, Katalin, Dier in Hat Tricks

By LEE REMMEL

The Bobcats, methodical marauders after a slow start, ended Green Bay's 13-year victory drought against Mosinee in the grand manner Wednesday night.

They established a new team and Arena scoring record with an 18-2 rout of the Wisconsin Amateur Hockey League's undefeated leaders, out of their depth in combat with this community's Mid - America League standard bearers before 2,025 onlookers.

In effect, it served the Bobcats as a full dress warmup for their imminent series with the Fort Frances, Ontario, Canadians, their guests Friday and Saturday nights. The victory, which ended a two-game losing streak, pegged the home forces' overall record at 12-10.

Though it took the Bobcats nearly seven minutes to uncork, it became apparent early that the visiting Papermakers were overmatched. The 'Cats banged the Mosinee net with five goals in the first period and ran up a prohibitive 9-0 lead before permitting the first Paper goal at 14:24 of the second period.

The Papers paid dearly for their temerity. Stung by this affront, the Bobcats stormed back to score in 43 seconds, Andy Cicoria doing the honors, and punched home another goal 48 seconds later.

As a matter of fact, they padded their lead to 15-1 before allowing the invaders their final tally at 7:39 of the

TURN TO PAGE 32, COLUMN 4

Meet the GM-Coach — Here are three phases in the big day of the new general manager and head coach of the Packers — all snapped in New York. He's shown above left in the traditional packing for travel scene and at right answering one of numerous telephone calls shortly after his appointment Wednesday afternoon. Below, gets the "good luck" signal from Jack Mara, president of the New York Giants. Vince had been backfield coach of the Giants for the past five years. (AP Photofax)

Sports Cocktails: 'You'll Like Him'

Lombardi 'A Terrific Selection,' Bell Says

By ART DALEY
Press-Gazette Sports Editor

Commissioner Bert Bell was highly enthusiastic and excited over the Packers' hiring of Vince Lombardi as head coach and general manager.

"Two or three other clubs wanted him as head coach in the last four years. Why, he's a terrific selection," Bell boomed over the telephone from league headquarters in Philadelphia today.

"And then they wanted him at West Point, you know," Bert said, adding: "I don't think you could have made a better selection."

Referring to hiring a coach new to pro football, Bell said "Lombardi knows the ropes; he knows administration; he knows the pro business; he knows coaching; he

1958 campaign and retired from the sport after two weeks due to injuries.

"Vince liked the looks of Green Bay when we were out here in 1957 and I'm sure he was interested then," big league meeting in Philadelphia last week, although he had been under consideration. "We reached an agreement Monday and Wednesday I was told that I had been approved, unanimously by the club." Vince said he was making "a complete break and I'm moving to Green Bay — lock, stock and barrel."

Newspaper, radio and TV are taking special note of the secrecy practiced by the Packers' officials during the hiring period. It was revealed yesterday, for instance, that Earl Evashevski, Iowa coach, actually came to Green Bay on Sunday afternoon, drove around town with Packer President Dominic Olejniczak and then left by plane. . . And

"He's a good selection and he'll read smart. Vince won't take any nonsense. If anybody's late for a scheduled meeting or practice he'll cajack down. He's very methodical and a good organizer.

"You'll like how he's around. And he's all business."

Skibinski, who missed the 1957 season here with a broken ankle, put it this way:

"I think they got a good man. I wasn't there very long but he sure handled us fellas on offense. He ran the show.

"He'd get on us pretty good and holler a little but he always had a smile on his face.

"When he gives it that 'let's go' on the field that's exactly what he means. He's a go-getter himself and that's the

PART III

THE

LOMBARDI

LEGACY

1959 - 1967

Vincent T. Lombardi

The Packer Legend

Chapter Twelve

"WHO

THE HELL

IS

VINCE LOMBARDI?"

When Packer president, Dominic Olejniczak, told the Executive Committee that he was recommending Vince Lombardi as the new head coach and general manager, I was the director who asked: "Who the hell is Vince Lombardi?"

Astonishing as it may seem today, Lombardi was not all that well-known when he was chosen as the fifth head coach of the Packers in their first 40 years of operation.

In his 20 years of coaching, his only previous head coaching job was at the high school level. As an assistant under Col. Earl Blaik at West Point, then under Jim Lee Howell with the New York Giants, Lombardi had won a solid reputation among football men, but he had finessed the publicity to his two bosses.

Even as a 180-pound guard at Fordham, playing in the line which acquired the title

"Seven Blocks of Granite," Lombardi did not get all that much ink, and his success as head coach at St. Cecelia High School in Englewood, New Jersey, made him a local hero but still did not attract much attention outside the area.

Lombardi took the coaching job at the Catholic high school in Englewood to help finance his way through law school at Fordham, but his record of 36 straight victories and six state titles ended his career in law. From there, Lombardi went to West Point as the offensive backfield coach under Blaik, and Army had an unbeaten season his first year on the staff. After five years at West Point, he joined the New York Giants staff during Howell's first year as head coach, continuing to coach the offensive backfield and masterminding the offensive strategy for the Giants.

Lombardi Conditioning. The Packer team gets its first exposure to Vince Lombardi. That's a young Bart Starr on the right. Because of this conditioning regimen, Lombardi teams were still going strong in the fourth quarter when other teams were wearing out. *Vern Biever photo.*

The announcement of Lombardi's hiring ended five weeks of frustrating, rumor-filled agony among Packer fans. After Ray McLean resigned in mid-December, the Packers announced that the Board of Directors had adopted a reoganization plan for the management of corporate affairs, which included paring the Executive Committee down from 13 to seven, authorizing the Executive Committee to hire a general manager to conduct the team's affairs, and significantly, setting up monthly rather than weekly meetings of the Committee. The decision about a general manager heightened the speculation as to who would become not only the head coach but also the general manager, the supposition being that the Packers would hire two men for the two jobs.

One of the notable applicants for the general manager job was none other than Curly Lambeau, who gave up his residence in California in January of 1959 to return to Green Bay as a full-time resident. He made it plain that he was applying for the general manager job.

Names of many prominent coaches were kicked around in the Packer rumor mill as the weeks went by without decision. They included Forrest Evashevski, popular coach at the University of Iowa; Hampton Poole, former head coach of the Los Angeles Rams who was then with the Hamilton Tiger Cats in the Canadian Football League; Jim Trimble, another CFL head coach; and Blanton Collier, head coach at the University of Kentucky.

The NFL draft came and went without the naming of a head coach. Jack Vainisi, the team's talent scout, did the picking during the draft.

When the selection came, however, it came in rapid fire order. On Wednesday, January 28, 1959, Olejniczak called a special meeting of the Board of Directors and requested that they give the Executive Committee authority to hire a head coach and general manager. He said that the candidate he had in mind was currently employed and that he did not wish to embarrass that person by way of an open discussion of possible candidates. The directors gave the committee that authority, and later that afternoon Olejniczak put Lombardi's name before the Executive Committee. He remarked that he had asked George Halas' opinion of Lombardi, and Halas had said, "I shouldn't tell you this, Ole, but he's a good one. I shouldn't tell you this because you're liable to kick the crap out of us."

Lombardi flew into Green Bay the next Monday to meet with the Board of Directors at the Hotel Northland, and the first thing he said when introduced by Olejniczak was: "I want it understood that I am in complete command here."

Lombardi moved swiftly to fill out his coaching staff, hiring Phil Bengtson of the San Francisco 49ers as defensive coach and Red Cochran of the Detroit Lions as offensive co-ordinator.

Lombardi said from the start that it was defense that wins football games, and he immediately took the trade route to shore up the Packer defensive team. When star end Bill Howton came to him and demanded more money, Lombardi quickly traded him to Cleveland for defensive end Bill Quinlan and halfback-receiver Lew Carpenter. He also traded for defensive tackle Henry Jordan and offensive guard Fuzzy Thurston, a draftee of the Philadelphia Eagles who had been cut by them, then served a year each for the Bears and the Baltimore Colts. Under Lombardi, Thurston became a whole new football player as one of Bart Starr's "guardian angels." Lombardi also brought along with him from the New York Giants the great defensive back Emlen Tunnell.

Came the opening of training camp early that summer, and the players met Lombardi for the

The Lombardi Sweep. Jerry Kramer (64) and Fuzzy Thurston (63) lead Jimmy Taylor around end in the famous Packer sweep. Bart Starr has handed off to Taylor as Lombardi watches approvingly. *Vern Biever photo.*

The Packer Legend

Riding the Sled. Lombardi's voice could be heard all over the neighborhood as he rode herd over his troops. Lombardi opted for short practices, running them for not more than an hour to an hour and a half. He drove his players as hard as he drove himself in his effort to achieve success. *Vern Biever photo.*

first time. It was a landmark meeting. In the first five minutes, the players began to understand what life under Vince Lombardi would be like. As the great defensive end Willie Davis put it: "He treated us all alike...like dogs."

Lombardi confined his practice sessions to not much more than an hour to an hour and 15 minutes, an hour and 20 minutes at the most, but every player knew exactly what he would be doing every minute of those workouts. They opened with exercises like the players had never experienced before, including Lombardi's famous "grass drill."

Lombardi made personnel decisions which were long overdue. Paul Hornung had been a quarterback at Notre Dame, and Lisle Blackbourn and Ray McLean had continued playing him at quarterback with the Packers, where he failed to impress. Hornung did not have all that great a passing arm, so Lombardi switched him to halfback to take advantage of his running ability, creating one of the most

dangerous option backs in the league.

Blackbourn had told the Executive Committee that he wasn't playing Jim Taylor because he couldn't learn the signals. Well, Lombardi found a way to get the signals into Taylor's head, and he started in Lombardi's famous three-back backfield when the Packers opened the season in Green Bay. As Paul Harvey says, you know the rest of the story. Taylor became one of the most devastating fullbacks in the NFL, recalling the likes of Jim Thorpe, Bronko Nagurski, and Jim Brown. What Lombardi realized was that Taylor did not need all that many signals; all he needed was to be handed the ball and told whether to go right or left. Taylor made his own holes and delighted in running over linebackers and defensive backs. His theory was that the shortest distance to the goal line was a straight line, and if anybody was in the way, he merely bulled his way over them.

Another of Lombardi's famous innovations also helped to make Taylor and Hornung into the terrific backs that they became. Lombardi's

What Did They Do That For? Vince obviously is puzzled over a play the team hadn't rehearsed on the practice field. *Vern Biever photo.*

phrase was, "Run to daylight," by which he meant that the ball carrier had to run with his eyes open, see which way the offensive linemen were blocking the defenders, and seize the opportunity to squirt through the hole. Thus, under Lombardi's system, the offensive ground plays were not so structured that the back had to hit the right hole regardless of whether there was daylight there or not. They merely looked for the daylight, then streaked through it.

When Lombardi's first team opened the league season, the backfield consisted of Hornung, the rejuvenated quarterback from Notre Dame; Taylor, the fullback who couldn't learn the signals; and Don McIlhenny, a scatback whom Blackbourn had obtained from Detroit in the trade for Tobin Rote. At the helm was Lamar McHan, whom Lombardi had acquired from the Chicago Cardinals.

McHan looked really good early in the season, winning the Packers first three games, but in reality, it was the defense that Lombardi and Bengtson had built that was winning those contests. The Pack beat the Bears in the opener, 9-6; then took the hapless Lions, 28-10; then San Francisco, 21-20. After that it was downhill for McHan. With three losses to match those wins, Lombardi decided it was time to go with Bart Starr as his No. 1 quarterback.

Starr had been around for three seasons already and hadn't shown much. The fact that Lombardi put all of his confidence in Starr made a new ballplayer out of him. He took command of the offense and began to run the team like the field general that Lombardi realized he could become.

Gary Knafelc told the story later about how Starr took charge in the huddle. If you know Bart like I do, you know that he hardly ever uttered a cuss word in his life, but at one point in a game when he had been trapped and thrown for a loss, he got the team in the huddle and said, "Gee, fellas, gosh darn it, let's cut this out and get going." They got going.

That first season Lombardi lifted the Packers to a 7-5 record and was unanimously voted Coach of the Year in the NFL.

In his second season in 1960, the Packers captured the Western Division title by winning their last three games and going 8-4 on the year, then lost to Philadelphia in the championship game. It was a bitterly fought contest, and it was a bitter defeat for Lombardi and his spirited team that by then had the bit in their teeth and

liked the idea of winning. They were behind most of the game but kept fighting back until in the last few seconds Jim Taylor was stopped by linebacker Chuck Bednarik on the Philadelphia eight, inches short of a first down. It was a fourth down gamble, and the Eagles took over the ball,

Here Today Gone Tomorrow

It's interesting to conjecture how Vince Lombardi would get along with today's pro football players with their agents, tax accountants, and lawyers and salaries up in the six-figure category.

Some indication comes from the experience of Jim Ringo, the All-Pro center who appeared in Lombardi's office one day with his agent.

"Let me get this straight," said Lombardi, "you're his agent?"

"Just a minute," Lombardi said as he went into an adjoining office.

He came back about five minutes later and said to the agent, "I'm sorry, you're talking to the wrong man. Jim Ringo is the property of the Philadelphia Eagles."

1961 Championship Team, Won 11, Lost 3. Left to right, front row: Herb Adderly (B), Michigan State; Ben Davidson (T), Washington; Elijah Pitts (B), Phillip Smith; Les Folkins (E), Washington; Ron Kostelnik (T), Cincinnati; Nelson Toburen (LB), Wichita. Second row: Ken Iman (C), SE Missouri; Willie Wood (B), Southern California; Hank Gremminger (B), Baylor; Tom Moore (B), Vanderbilt; Jerry Kramer (G), Idaho; Fuzzy Thurston (G), Valparaiso; Jess Whittenton (B), Texas Western; John Symank (B), Florida; Tom Bettis (LB), Purdue. Third row: Trainer Bud Jorgenson; Bob Skoronski (T), Indiana; Bart Starr (QB), Alabama; Gary Knafelc (E), Colorado; Jim Ringo (C), Syracuse; Norm Masters (T), Michigan State; Dan Currie (LB), Michigan State; Willie Davis (DE), Grambling; John Roach (QB), SMU; Lew Carpenter (B), Arkansas; equipment manager Dad Braisher. Top row: Bill Quinlan (E), Michigan State; Forrest Gregg (T), SMU; Emlen Tunnell (B), Iowa; Ray Nitschke (LB), Illinois; Dave Hanner (T), Arkansas; Henry Jordan (T), Virginia; Boyd Dowler (E), Colorado; Jim Taylor (B), LSU; Ron Kramer (E), Michigan; Bill Forester (LB), SMU; Paul Hornung (B), Notre Dame; Max McGee (E), Tulane.

Lefebvre photo.

The Packer Legend

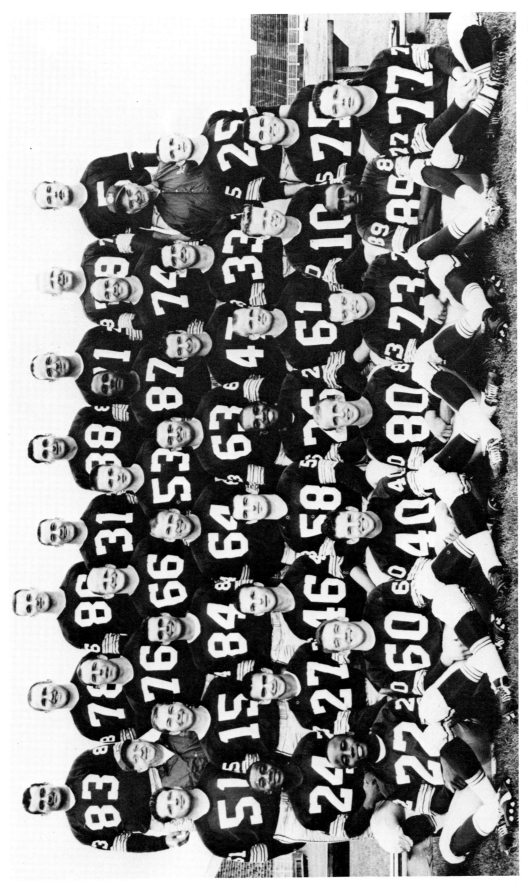

1962 Championship Team. Won 13, Lost 1. The team Vince Lombardi called his all-time greatest. Left to right, front row: Elijah Pitts, Ed Blaine, Earl Gros, Gary Barnes, Oscar Donahue, Ron Kostelnik. Second row: Willie Wood, John Symank, Hank Gremminger, Dan Currie, Herb Adderley, Nelson Toburen, John Roach, Forrest Gregg. Third row: Jim Ringo, Bart Starr, Gary Knafelc, Jerry Kramer, Fuzzy Thurston, Jess Whittenton, Lew Carpenter, Tom Moore. Fourth row: Equipment manager Dad Braisher, Bob Skoronski, Ray Nitschke, Ken Iman, Willie Davis, Henry Jordan, trainer Bud Jorgenson, Bill Quinlan, Norm Masters, Boyd Dowler, Jim Taylor, Ron Kramer, Bill Forrester, Dave Hanner, Paul Hornung. *Lefebvre photo.*

ran out the clock and won, 17-13. That was the first and last time a Lombardi team was ever beaten in a playoff game. They went on from there to win nine straight.

In 1961, they were 11-3 in the regular season, then clobbered the New York Giants in the championship game in Green Bay, 37-0. Hornung scored a record 19 points in that game, a record which has only been tied in later years.

This was the game about which columnist Red Smith, a Green Bay native, wrote one of the finest pieces ever penned about a pro football game. Let me quote the first two paragraphs:

"Back around 1634 when the big outdoor game in these parts was lacrosse, a victory for the Menominees over the Sacs was celebrated by tribal dancing, drinking, and yelling all night like one in despair. After three centuries and more, things haven't changed a lick, except that pro football has moved in as the most popular spectator sport.

"While wierd tribal cries and mystic incantations rose and froze above an open air hogan on snowy plains, the mighty Packers simply slathered New York's helpless Giants yesterday to give their untamed electorate its first National League championship in 17 years, and the best excuse for the New Year's Day wobblies since squaws learned to squeeze the juice from corn."

The most remarkable fact about that season was that Hornung, Boyd Dowler, and Ray

Papa Bear and Lombardi. The Chicago Bears owner and founder George Halas and Vince Lombardi were close personal friends and mutual admirers of each other off the field but were bitter rivals on the gridiron. Halas was one of the people who recommended Lombardi to the Packer Pres. Dominic Olejniczak. *Vern Biever photo.*

Want Any More? Packer All-Pro linebacker Ray Nitschke looms over a fallen foe who made the tragic mistake of trying to take him on one-on-one. Nitschke is a member of the Pro Hall of Fame and the Packer Hall of Fame. *Vern Biever photo.*

Nitschke had been called into military service. They were given weekend passes so they could join the team for a brief practice on Saturday, then play the game on Sunday.

It was a repeat performance in New York the next year. The '62 Packers had gone 13-1 before entering Yankee Stadium for a grudge match with the Giants. Sam Huff, the great middle linebacker, had been humbled in that 37-0 game in Green Bay the year before and had sworn revenge on Packer running backs.

The game was played in New York in even worse conditions than those in Green Bay the year before. The wind-chill factor was 41° below zero as the winds swirled around Yankee Stadium whose turf had been frozen into a skating rink during the night. So the Packers decided to run the ball straight ahead right at Sam Huff, and if guards Fuzzy Thurston or Jerry Kramer hadn't taken care of him by the time the ball carrier arrived, Taylor and Hornung alternated at running over Huff's frame. At game's end, he crawled off the field on hands and knees. The score was 16-7. The only touchdown

The Packer Legend

the Giants got came on a blocked punt, as their offense, built around Y.A. Tittle, Alex Webster, Frank Gifford, Phil King, Kyle Rote and Del Shofner, came away empty-handed. Taylor scored the only Packer touchdown after gaining 85 yards in 31 carries, and Kramer kicked three field goals in five attempts on that icy field, the margin of victory.

The Packers went 11-2-1 in 1963 but finished second in the NFC. They came in second again in 1964 with an 8-5-1 record, but then came the triple championship years.

In 1965, their record was 10-3-1, and they beat the Cleveland Browns in the championship game played in Green Bay, 23-12.

The 1966 and 1967 seasons produced the great grudge matches for the NFL championships with the Dallas Cowboys.

After going 12-2 in 1966, the Packers went to Dallas and beat the Cowboys for the championship in a high scoring game, 34-27, and in 1967 after a regular season record of 9-4-1, they met the Cowboys in Green Bay in the famous Ice Bowl Game for the championship. The story of that game is a chapter in itself.

In Lombardi's career with the Packers, they never finished lower than second place, and his

Kramer Takes a Breather. Jerry's career was almost ended by injuries several times, but he always bounced back. *Vern Biever photo.*

Championship Kick. Jerry Kramer kicks one of his three field goals as the Packers defeated the New York Giants in Yankee Stadium for their second straight championship in 1962. That's Starr holding. The score was 16-7. *Vern Biever photo.*

The Packer Legend

A Bespeckled Gregg. Lombardi called Forrest Gregg the finest football player he ever coached. Gregg took the Cincinnati Bengals to the Super Bowl as their head coach in 1982. *Vern Biever photo.*

teams became the standard of football excellence. Over a nine-year span as head coach, Lombardi's teams racked up 98 victories against 30 losses and four ties for a remarkable winning percentage of .766. Even more noteworthy, however, is the record of Lombardi-coached teams in post-season play. In 10 division playoffs and world championship games, the Packers emerged victorious nine times.

The success of the Lombardi teams is rivaled by few others in NFL history. They were a dynasty, as teams that are continuous winners over prolonged periods of time are termed. The Packers of the 1960s were to the NFL what the New York Yankees were to baseball from 1949-64, what the Boston Celtics were to the NBA from 1956-69, and what UCLA was to

Willie Takes to the Air. Willie Wood won a starting job as a free agent with his leaping ability. Here he tried to block a field goal attempt.

Vern Biever photo.

The Packer Legend

Punishing Victory. Jimmy Taylor practically had to be carried off the field after the Packers beat the New York Giants for the 1962 title on a frozen field and in a swirling, bitter-cold wind in Yankee Stadium, but you should have seen Giant linebacker Sam Huff after Taylor and Paul Hornung were finished doing their thing on him.   *Vern Biever photo.*

New Training Quarters. Vince tells Jim Ringo, Boyd Dowler, Ron Kramer, Bart Starr, and Jim Taylor how he talked a carpet salesman into donating wall-to-wall carpeting for the new Packer training quarters. The salesman met more than his match in Lombardi.   *Vern Biever photo.*

The Packer Legend

college basketball from 1964-1977.

The closest any other team came to matching the feats of Lombardi's Green Bay Packers happened back in the early years of the NFL.

From 1923-32, one franchise posted 96 wins against 28 losses and 11 ties for a winning percentage of .774, and that team was Curly Lambeau's Green Bay Packers.

1965 Title Team. Won 10, Lost 3, Tied 1. Left to right, front row: D. Robinson, D. Chandler, L. Aldridge, D. Hart, H. Gremminger, R. Kostelnik, W. Wood, H. Adderley, B. Jeter, M. Fleming. Second row: Trainer B. Jorgenson, L. Voss, C. Dale, B. Starr, E. Pitts, B. Anderson, Z. Bratkowski, D. Grimm, T. Moore, B. Long, T. Brown, eqpt. mgr. D. Braisher. Third row: Trainer D. Gentile, B. Curry, T. Crutcher, J. Coffee, L. Caffey, H. Jordan, J. Kramer, F. Thurston, B. Skoronski, W. Davis, R. Nitschke, asst. eqpt. mgr. B. Noel. Fourth row: A. Jacobs, R. Marshall, D. Claridge, K. Bowman, B. Dowler, F. Gregg, S. Wright, J. Taylor, P. Hornung, M. McGee.

Lefebvre photo.

Lombardi's First Staff. This is the staff Vince Lombardi assembled in his first year at Green Bay. Left to right: Tom Fears, Phil Bengtson, Norb Hecker, Lombardi, Red Cochran, and Bill Austin. All except Cochran went on to become head coaches in the NFL at one time or another.

Press-Gazette photo.

The Packer Legend

Lombardi's Last Ride. Tackle Forrest Gregg and guard Jerry Kramer carried Lombardi off the field after winning Super Bowl II at the Orange Bowl in Miami. It was the last Packer game Vince coached. The Packers outclassed the Oakland Raiders, 33-14. After sitting out one year as the Packers general manager, Lombardi accepted an offer to coach the Washington Redskins. *Vern Biever photo.*

The Packer Legend

The "Golden Boy"

The Packers were the next to last team in the league to receive the bonus choice in the draft, a publicity gimmick instituted in 1947, but when they finally received theirs in 1957, they made good use of it. They chose Paul Hornung, the Notre Dame quarterback who was the Heisman Trophy winner that year.

Dubbed the "Golden Boy" because of his head of wavy blond hair, Hornung stirred a lot of excitement among Packer fans, but he spent his first two seasons bench-warming a good deal of the time, playing third fiddle to Babe Parilli and Bart Starr.

When Vince Lombardi converted Hornung into a halfback, teamed him with Jim Taylor, and took advantage of his running ability to make him into an option back, Hornung suddenly came into his own.

Surprisingly, Hornung does not appear in any of the records for ground gaining in the Packer statistics. Those belong to Jim Taylor. But Hornung was dynamite when the Packers neared the goalline. He could smell the end zone, and with his "guardian angels," guards Jerry Kramer and Fuzzy Thurston, tackle Forrest Gregg, tight end Ron Kramer, and fullback Taylor blocking for him, Hornung posted scoring records which still stand in the league book as well as those of the Packers.

Hornung added to his scoring potential

Mutual Admiration Society. Paul Hornung and Vince Lombardi became very close personal friends. Vince said the hardest thing he ever did was put Hornung on the expansion draft list after his career with the Packers was over.

Vern Biever photo.

The Packer Legend

From Notre Dame

by kicking points after touchdown and field goals. He holds the all-time NFL record for most points scored in one season, 176 in 1960, Lombardi's second year. He was named to the All-Pro team in 1960 and 1961, and also played in the Pro Bowl Game both those years. He led the league in scoring three years in a row, 1959-61.

In the 1961 title game against the Giants in Green Bay, Hornung, who was on a weekend pass from the Army, scored 19 points, another all-time league record. He had been drafted for a year of military service. Then in the return match with the Giants in 1962, he and Taylor took turns humbling the Giant defense, best in the league up to then, and humiliating linebacker Sam Huff.

Hornung's career was rudely interrupted again in 1963 when he and Alex Karras of Detroit were suspended for the season by NFL Commissioner Pete Rozelle for having bet on NFL games. The evidence was somewhat circumstantial, and they denied betting on their own games. But Rozelle wanted to make an example of them, and suspending the league's leading scorer was a stark way of getting his message across.

Hornung returned to action in 1964, but the year's layoff had taken its toll. He had

The Guardian Angels. Fuzzy Thurston takes to the air as he and Jerry Kramer lead the blocking for Hornung. The Packers of the 1960s were known for the "end sweep," sometimes called the "Lombardi sweep." In the play, both guards pulled out of the line and sprinted for the outside with the running back following close behind. Although opposing defenses knew it was coming, there was very little they could do to stop it. The play worked consistently. *Vern Biever photo.*

particular trouble getting back into the groove with his kicking. In the first game against Baltimore, he missed four out of five field goals as the Packers eked out a 20-17 win, and for the season he made only 12 out of 38 attempts.

A humorous story made the rounds of the bars in Green Bay that season.

A fan supposedly stopped Paul on the street and asked, "Hi, Paul, how you doing?"

"I can't kick," Hornung allegedly replied.

Lombardi brought Don Chandler in as his kicker the next season. Chandler had played for the Giants when Lombardi was an assistant coach there. But Hornung still had

his nose for the goalline. In the return match with Baltimore, Hornung scored five touchdowns as the Packers won going away, 42-27.

And in the championship game against Cleveland in Green Bay, Hornung and Taylor gained 205 yards between them, and Hornung put the game away late in the third period when the Packers marched 90 yards down the field, and Hornung scored on a 13-yard sweep.

Hornung suffered a pinched nerve in his neck late in that 1965 season, and the injury finally ended his career. He was bothered with it constantly during the 1966 season, in which he carried the ball only 46 times.

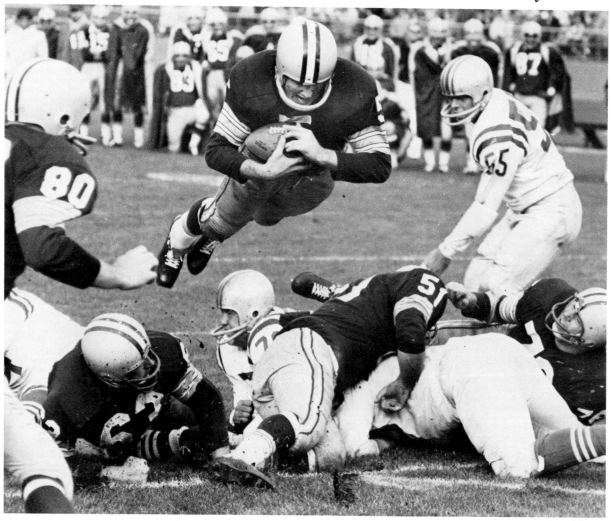

Nose For The End Zone. Hornung scores one of his many touchdowns. Note how the Packer line has flattened every defensive player in Hornung's way. Hornung scored 62 touchdowns in his nine-year career. Only Don Hutson and Jim Taylor scored more six-pointers. *Vern Biever photo.*

The Packer Legend

He was still on the squad for the first Super Bowl game, but Elijah Pitts had replaced him at running back by then and scored two touchdowns as the Packers beat the Kansas City Chiefs, 37-10.

Columnist Red Smith best summed up Hornung's career in this paragraph:

"One night in Vince's home - it was New Year's Eve after the title game with the Giants - the coach was pouring drinks for friends and there was a great big grin pasted on his face that wouldn't come off. He kept looking across the room at the laughing Hornung and saying this was a guy who could shake you off your trolley or lift you out of this world, a guy who probably was neither the greatest athlete nor the greatest football player in the world but who had that special ability to rise to the occasion and be the greatest of the great when the challenge was the sternest. And that grin never did come off."

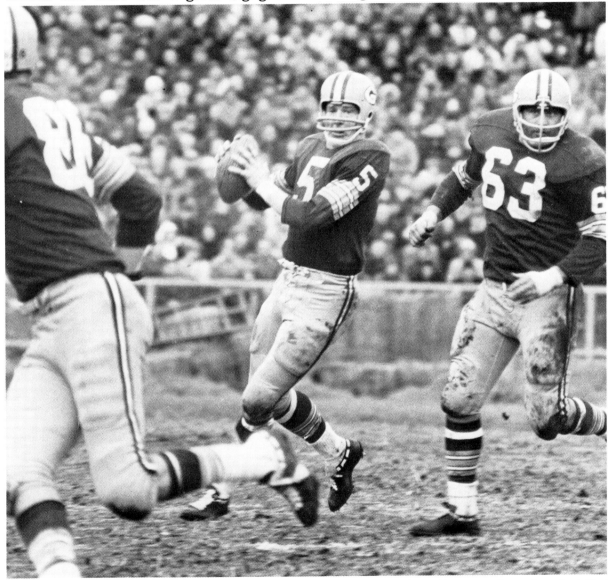

Option Halfback. Hornung was a quarterback at his alma mater, Notre Dame, and continued at that position for his first two seasons with the Packers under coaches Lisle Blackbourn and Ray McLean. Lombardi realized Hornung didn't have a "pro" arm, so he moved him to halfback and made him on of the most dangerous backs in NFL history. *Vern Biever photo.*

The Packer Legend

A
PACKER
ALBUM

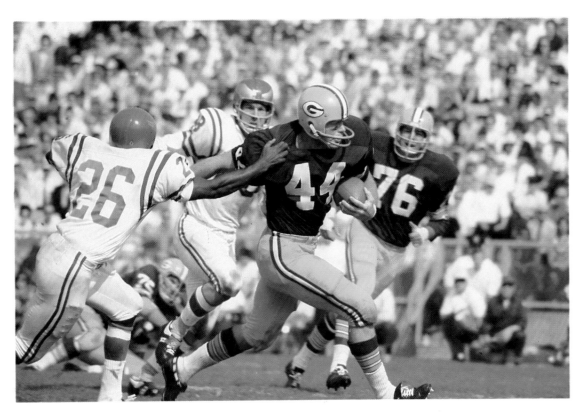

Donny Anderson (44) from Texas Tech was Lombardi's first high priced draft selection as a junior eligible in 1965. That's Bob Skoronski blocking for him.

Herb Adderley arrived from Michigan State in 1961 and became one of the all-time great cornerbacks in the NFL. He was inducted into the Pro Football Hall of Fame in 1960.

General Manager Lombardi watched the games from a cubicle in the press box after he retired as head coach. He kept a vigil light in the box with him for good measure.

Willie Davis was acquired by Lombardi in a trade in 1960 and combined with Henry Jordan to give the Pack a great pass rushing duo. He's a member of the Pro Football Hall of Fame.

The Packer Legend

Bart Starr gets a pass off under a great rush by the San Francisco 49ers. Taking beatings such as this finally forced him into retirement.

Jim Taylor sees plenty of daylight ahead as Packer blockers eliminate the Viking front line and linebackers. That's Ron Kramer working on Roy Winston (55).

Fuzzy Thurston (63) was one of Paul Hornung's "Guardian Angels" along with Jerry Kramer. Thurston looks for someone to mow down as Hornung takes off on a long gainer.

Don Chandler kicks one of his many field goals in this game against the Philadelphia Eagles in Green Bay with Bart Starr holding.

The Packer Legend

Tom Brown (40) returns an interception down the sidelines against the Eagles while Dave Robinson (89) takes off for some downfield blocking.

That's Marvelous Marv Fleming taking a pass from Starr for a big gainer against the Eagles in Green Bay. Watching (75) is Forrest Gregg.

The Packer Legend

Paul Hornung scores one of his many touchdowns against the Minnesota Vikings, all of whom have been eliminated from the play. Bob Skoronski escorts him across the goal.

Phil Bengtson, defensive coordinator under Lombardi, confers with linebacker Ray Nitschke on the sidelines during a pause in the action on the field.

The Packer Legend

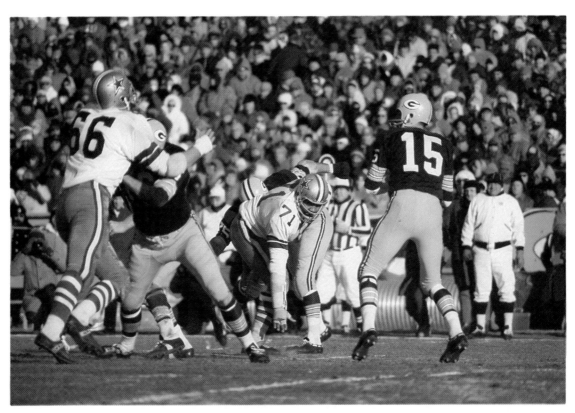

Starr begins to move the Packers downfield in the final minutes of the championship game against the Dallas Cowboys in Green Bay, Dec. 31, 1967.

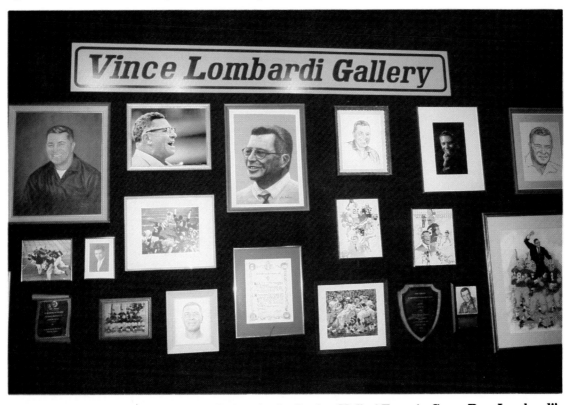

This is part of the Vince Lombardi Gallery in the Packer Hall of Fame in Green Bay. Lombardi's extensive collection of football memorabilia is on exhibit there.

Packer fans came dressed in snowmobile suits, sleeping bags, blankets, and face masks for the Ice Bowl Game with Dallas, Dec. 31, 1967. The Packers won 21-17.

MacArthur Lane (36) combined with Brockington in a big back backfield under Coach Devine, and the Packers won their division his first year, 1972.

Fans celebrated Green Bay's 11th league championship by tearing down the goal posts at Lambeau Field. They had endured an afternoon of 20° below zero cold.

Ray Nitschke was a great favorite with Packer fans during his 15-year career. The pom-pom girls send the middle linebacker out on the field with appropriate applause.

John Brockington ran for over 1,000 yards in each of his first three seasons but failed to keep up the good work after Dan Devine gave him a no-cut contract.

Jim Carter, who succeeded Nitschke as middle linebacker, scores a sack against Bear quarterback Bobby Douglas. Douglas later was on the Packer squad for one year.

The Packer Legend

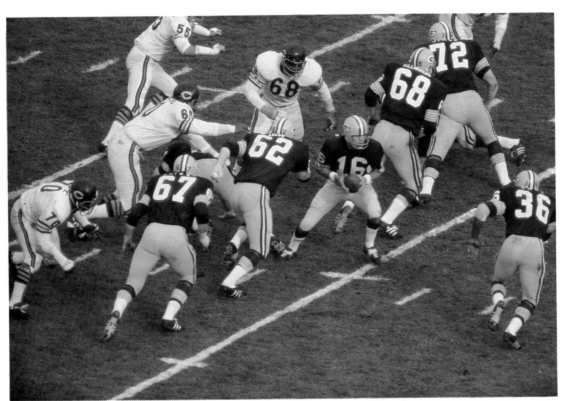

Here's the start of the Packer sweep with Scott Hunter handing off to MacArthur Lane. The blockers are Malcolm Snider (67), Bill Lueck (62), Gale Gillingham (68) and Bill Himes (72).

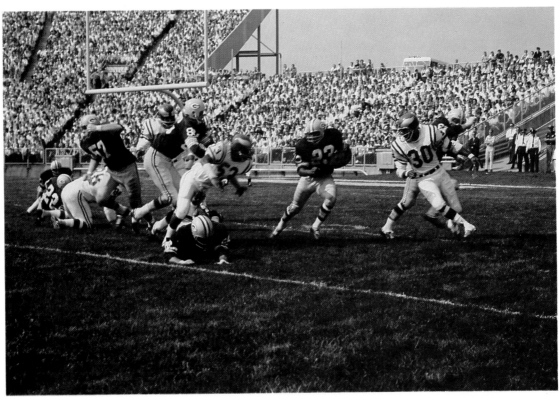

Travis Williams had a couple of fine seasons as a scat back in the late 1960s. Here he sees daylight against Philadelphia in a game in Green Bay.

The Packer band has been performing at home games since 1923, with Wilner Burke as director that entire span of years. They appear here at City Stadium.

Tailgate parties go on in the parking lot at City Stadium in Green Bay from August into December. This group was tending to its grilling in a late season game.

Barty Smith became the workhorse of the Packer backfield after he recovered from injuries he received in the All-Star game in 1974. That's Forrest Gregg blocking for him against the Eagles.

Gerry Ellis has become a real find as a free agent, leading the Packers in ground gaining the last two seasons. It takes more than one tackler to bring him down.

The Packer Legend

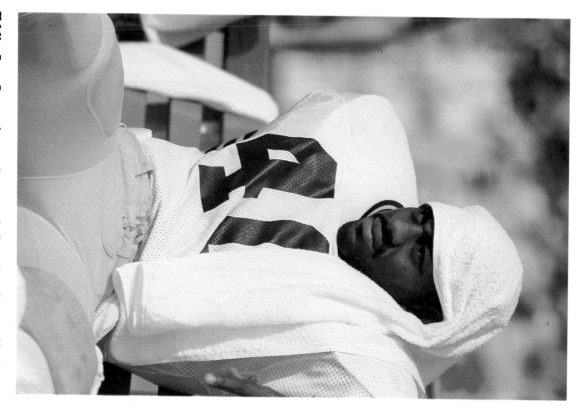

Eddie Lee Ivery is a picture of despair after suffering a disabling knee injury in Soldiers Field against the Bears for the second time in his short career.

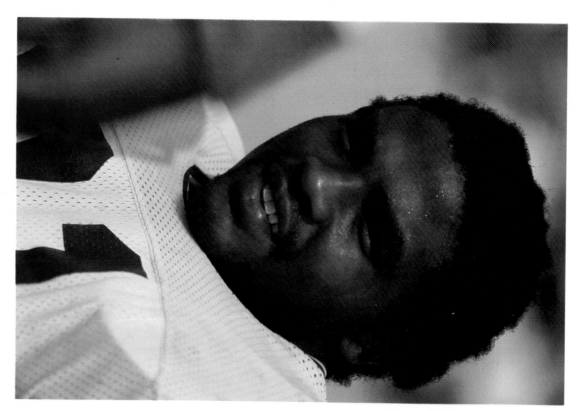

Gerry Ellis is not only a fine football player, he's a very handsome fellow. The Packers picked him up as a free agent after Los Angeles had let him go early in the 1980 season.

David Whitehurst took over as No. 1 quarterback during Lynn Dickey's long recovery from a broken leg. He confers on the sidelines with Bart Starr and Zeke Bratkowski, themselves former Packer quarterbacks.

Looking to the future are Rich Campbell (19), James Lofton (80), and Lynn Dickey (12). Campbell is understudying Dickey as the quarterback of the future.

John Hadl was a marked man when he came to the Packers in 1974. Dan Devine had traded away five top draft choices to get him, and he never did perform well for Green Bay.

Defensive coach Fred von Appen yells at his charges while riding the blocking sled on the Oneida Street practice grounds.

Championship Sneak. Chuck Mercein signals the touchdown which beat Dallas for the National Football League title in the famous Ice Bowl Game, Dec. 31, 1967. Mercein was supposed to get the ball on the play in the last 16 seconds of the game, but Starr kept it and scored behind Jerry Kramer's (64) block. Starr had gone to the sidelines during a time-out prior to the play and suggested the play to Lombardi. The coach had only one question: Was Kramer's footing good enough to make the block? Starr said it was, then he and the Packers made history, defeating the Cowboys, 21-17, then winning Super Bowl II for their third straight NFL championship. *John Biever photo.*

Chapter Thirteen

ONLY

IN

GREEN BAY

The temperature was 44° below zero when our vacation group awoke at the Powderhorn ski area in Upper Michigan that Sunday morning, December 31, 1967.

The pilot called from Neenah to see if we were still going to the National Football League championship game in Green Bay that afternoon.

"Well, of course, we are," replied our host, Don Schalk, a salesman for the Kimberly-Clark Corporation from whom my newspaper bought most of its newsprint supplies. "Be here by 10:30, and we'll meet you at the airport," Don continued.

A group of us were being entertained by Kimberly-Clark at a ski resort during the Christmas holidays, and I had been able to round up enough tickets so that all of us could attend

the game. When the rest of the group was apprised of the weather conditions, however, some doubt arose in their minds, particularly a couple from Washington D.C. As a matter of fact, the wife was from southern Alabama. We assured them, however, that we did this all the time in Green Bay and that we were certain that on a beautiful sunny day as we expected the temperature would warm up considerably by game time. I did not mention that I had called Green Bay and learned that the temperature was expected to warm up to 13° below zero at kickoff time.

Our next problem was getting to the airport, which was only a few miles away. We had rented cars while at the ski resort, and one attempt at starting the engines told us that it was an impossible situation; they were frozen solid. Our

The One Man Difference

Paul Hornung played nine years for the Packers from 1957-1962 and 1964-1966. He missed the 1963 season, having been suspended by Commissioner Pete Rozelle for gambling on college football games.

The one year he didn't play the Packers finished second to the Chicago Bears for the division title. The Bears had a record of 11-1-2, and the Packers were only a half game back at 11-2-1. The only two setbacks the Pack suffered came at the hands of the Bears, 10-3 in Green Bay and 26-7 in Chicago.

Both teams had essentially the same personnel in 1963 as they had in the previous two seasons when the Packers ran over the Bears four times: 24-0 and 31-28 in 1961, and 49-0 and 38-7 in 1962. The missing element in 1963 was Paul Hornung. His value to the Packers was proven in 1964 when the Pack stuck it to the Bears twice, 23-12 and 17-3.

It's easy to conjecture about the 1963 season. If Hornung had been playing, maybe the Packers would have won their third straight title that year. One win over the Bears would have put them in the title game against Y.A. Tittle and the New York Giants for the third consecutive year. Chances are the Packers would have defeated the Giants again. If they had, the Packers would have three triple championships instead of the remarkable two that do have.

Hornung's value to the Packers during his career can never be underestimated. Until Vince Lombardi converted him to a running back, his impact on the Packers was practically nil, but after that move?

Hornung had a remarkable career. He scored 62 touchdowns, kicked 190 PATs, and booted 66 field goals for a total scoring mark of 760 points. That placed him second to Don Hutson, who had 823, on the all-time scoring list. With his average of 84.44 points per season, it is quite likely that he would have outscored Hutson if he had played that 1963 season and had an average year.

One man can make a difference, even in the National Football League.

host was an enterprising fellow, however. While we were eating breakfast, he spied a Greyhound bus arriving in the parking lot with a load of skiers. He talked the driver into taking us to the airport, and the company jet picked us up promptly at 10:30.

When we arrived in Green Bay, my wife and I made a quick trip home and brought back snowmobile suits, sleeping bags, blankets, and the other accoutrements which are normal for attending Packer home games in late season. We bundled up the lady from Alabama in a sleeping bag and practically carried her into the stadium to our seats. We also brought several thermos bottles of coffee laced with brandy and other beverages designed to keep the blood flowing at such temperatures.

This then is the football game that became known as the Ice Bowl Game and was probably the greatest football game played during the Lombardi regime or in the entire history of the

Cold Lips. The Packer band kept playing until their instruments froze up. It was hard to keep anything warm that day. Several players suffered minor cases of frostbite, and dozens of fans had to receive medical attention because of the extreme bitter cold. The temperature was -13° at game time. *Vern Biever photo.*

Off to an Early Lead. Boyd Dowler caught two touchdown passes from Bart Starr in the first half of the championship playoff against Dallas in Green Bay, Dec. 31, 1967, but that early lead disappeared in the sub-zero cold of Lambeau Field later in the game. *Press-Gazette photo.*

Start of Winning TD Drive. Chuck Mercein, whom the Packers had signed as a free agent in mid-season, picked up valuable yardage as the Packers started goalward, behind 17-14, and with only minutes to play in the 1967 Championship game. It was Mercein who later bulled his way to the Dallas three yardline. *Press-Gazette photo.*

The Packer Legend

Packers for that matter.

Let me set the stage:

The Packers had won the league championship in 1965 and 1966 and were trying for a third straight title. In 1965, they had beaten Cleveland in Green Bay, 23-12, in the midst of a four-inch snowfall. In 1966, they had taken it to Dallas on their home field in the Cotton Bowl and had beaten the Cowboys, 34-27, with Bart Starr having one of his finest hours, passing for four touchdowns.

This then was a bitter showdown with Dallas, and everyone in the stadium, all 50,861 of them, thought that the Cowboys would collapse in the sub-zero weather.

The game began to look like a rout in the early going as Starr mounted an 82-yard touchdown drive in the first quarter, topped by a touchdown pass to Boyd Dowler, repeating with another touchdown pass to Dowler in the second quarter.

All of a sudden, however, the weather factor intervened and even-upped the game. Late in the second quarter, Starr fumbled when he was heavily rushed attempting to pass. Dallas lineman George Andrie picked up the ball and ran it in for a touchdown. Not long after that, Willie Wood fumbled a punt on the Packer 17 yardline, Dallas recovered, and Danny Villanueva kicked a Cowboy field goal to make the score 14-10 at halftime.

So the score remained until the dramatic fourth quarter. Then Dallas took the lead, 17-14, on an option pass from halfback Dan Reeves to wide receiver Lance Rentzel for a 50-yard completion and a touchdown.

There was 4:54 left on the clock when the Packer defense got the ball back for Bart Starr and the offense on the Packers' own 32-yardline. The field was frozen solid by then, and the temperatures had dropped to more than 20° below. It seemed inconceivable that the Packers could score in the amount of time left under those conditions.

Starr went to work with his typical methodical precision. Donny Anderson gained six yards off tackle, and Chuck Mercein eight up the middle. Mercein, a castoff from the New York Giants, had been picked up by the Packers on waivers only weeks before. Starr then threw to Dowler for 13 yards and a first down on the Dallas 45, but every fan in the stadium groaned as Anderson lost eight yards trying to circle end on the next play. Starr returned to the air, throwing to Anderson on a halfback delay,

putting the ball on the Dallas 39 yardline at the two minute warning.

On the resumption of play, Starr threw to Anderson again, using the same play for nine yards, then to Mercein who bulled his way to the Dallas 11. Then came a typical Starr call. After having thrown three consecutive passes to backs coming out of the backfield, he handed it to Mercein on a fullback delay and Mercein scratched his way to the three.

Now came the tough yards. Anderson made two off tackle and a first down, but with the ball of the one yardline, Anderson was held for no gain on first down. He slipped and fell trying to run the Packers' famous sweep on second down. There were 16 seconds left.

Starr took the last time-out and went to the sidelines to confer with Lombardi. A field goal was just a chip shot and would tie the game and send it into overtime. Starr suggested to Lombardi that they use the same short-yardage play that had gained two to three yards on a number of occasions previously during the game, the fullback sliding off right guard Jerry Kramer. Only Starr suggested that he keep the ball instead and follow Kramer's block, hopefully into the end zone.

Lombardi asked him one question. Did Jerry Kramer have good footing for his block? Starr told Lombardi that Kramer said that he did, and Lombardi said okay, go for it.

The rest is history. Starr kept the ball, leaned in behind Kramer's block, and planted the ball just over the goalline.

Starr doesn't know to this day whether they would have had time to get off a field goal attempt without being able to stop the clock with a time-out. He said they had practiced for just such an eventuality and that they would have had time to kick the ball, but the question is whether they could have gotten lined up in time to get off the snap.

Vince Lombardi always said that football was a game of inches.

In the dressing room after the game, he admitted that such a gamble was not his style. Facetiously he said he had pitied those 50,000 fans in the stadium and didn't want to put them through an overtime game.

"All the world loves a grambler", Lombardi laughed, "except when he loses."

Lombardi seldom lost because he knew he had the kind of people who could gain 13 inches when he needed them the worst.

Steaming Fans Let Loose. Packer fans weren't too frozen to keep them from streaming onto the field and assaulting the goal posts after their team had won another National League title, defeating Dallas 21-17. *Press Gazette photo.*

Super Bowl Trophy. This is the trophy the Packers won in Super Bowl II by defeating the Oakland Raiders in the Orange Bowl, 33-14. It is displayed at the Packer offices. The Super Bowl I trophy is in the Packer Hall of Fame. *Lefebvre photo.*

Chapter Fourteen

THE

SUPER

YEARS

Vince Lombardi was accustomed to psychological pressure all during his coaching career, but nothing he had ever known before prepared him for the emotional experience of Super Bowl I. Not only was the upcoming game against the Kansas City Chiefs the biggest challenge he and his Packer team had ever faced, it was also a challenge to the old established National Football League whose best team was meeting the champion of the upstart American Football League for the first time.

The AFL was the league which had disrupted the entire player personnel picture of pro football when it started in 1960. When the subject of a possible championship meeting first came up, Pete Roselle, the NFL's commissioner, told the rival league, "First, you have to get yourselves a football."

By 1966, the AFL not only had gotten a football but had become a conference in the National Football League with some very good football teams, the best of which that year was the Kansas City Chiefs.

The game attracted media attention in this country like few other sports events ever had before. Newspaper, magazine, television, and radio people converged on Los Angeles to cover the game from every aspect. Some billed it as a "David versus Goliath" affair or "the new kid on the block versus the old establishment." No one connected with the game was safe from media pressure except maybe Lombardi and his Packers, but the Packers, Lombardi in particular, faced a different sort of pressure.

Practically every coach in the NFL contacted Vince at least once during the two-week period he was preparing the Packers for the Super Bowl and informed him in no uncertain terms that they expected the Packers to demolish the Chiefs for the reputation of the senior league.

I experienced Vince's reaction to this pressure one evening when I stopped by his house on a personal mission.

The City Council of Menasha, a neighboring city to Green Bay, had passed a resolution congratulating Vince and the Packers on winning the NFC title and wishing them well in the Super Bowl. One of the printers, Bill Erickson, at our newspaper, the Appleton *Post-Crescent*, was a Menasha councilman, and he asked me to deliver the framed resolution to Vince personally.

When Marie Lombardi answered the front door, she apologized for Vince, saying he was engaged in his daily massage treatment for his gums. That toothy smile for which Lombardi was so famous was actually the result of receding gums, an affliction which effects many middle-aged men and women. I could hear the vibrator humming in the background, but soon it stopped and out came Vince wearing a freshly polished grin.

As we chatted over a cocktail, Vince began telling me about the enormous pressure which was being applied to him by the entire league. As a matter of fact, the phone rang while we were conversing, and it was George Halas calling from Chicago with the same message.

Players who participated in that first Super Bowl have recalled that Vince was like a maniac as he drove them in practice for the game. He sequestered them in an outlying motel in the Los Angeles area, and he went back to some of the

Spectacular Score. Boyd Dowler takes to the air to score the deciding touchdown in the Packer's victory in Dallas to win the 1966 title, 34-27, and advance into Super Bowl I. *Vern Biever photo.*

basic drills of the pre-season training camp in his efforts to concentrate the players' total attention on the upcoming game. That included the famous grass drill which Lombardi invented and which was an excruciating test of physical stamina. By the time the game rolled around, Lombardi had the Pack tuned to precision.

The Chiefs showed they were a good football team in the first half of Super Bowl I, out-gaining the Packers on the ground and going into the locker room at halftime behind only 14-10.

Aging Max McGee came in off the bench in the first quarter when Boyd Dowler was injured on the Packer' first offensive play. He caught a spectacular 37-yard pass from Bart Starr for the Packers' first score, bobbling the ball as he raced into the end zone. McGee had caught only three passes that whole season, but he snared seven

from Starr that day for a total of 138 yards.

The Chiefs tied the game in the second quarter on a pass from Len Dawson to Curtis McClinton, but Jim Taylor countered with a 14-yard TD run. A Mercer field goal for the Chiefs made it 14-10 at halftime.

Wille Wood broke the game open early in the third quarter when he intercepted a Dawson pass and returned it 40 yards to the Chiefs' five, where Elijah Pitts took it in for the score, making the Packers' lead, 21-10. Then came the second of McGee's touchdown catches and another Pitts six-pointer, and it was all over for the Chiefs. Final score: Packers 35, Chiefs 10.

Starr completed 16 of 23 passes for 250 yards and two touchdowns and was chosen the game's most valuable player.

Super Bowl II in Miami the next year was no

Sideline Conference. Bart Starr and his back-up, Zeke Bratkowski, confer with Lombardi during Super Bowl I in the Los Angeles Coliseum. The Packers beat the Kansas City Chiefs, 35-10. *Vern Biever photo.*

less emotionally draining on Lombardi. He still felt the terrific pressure to defend the traditions and reputation of the entire NFL in the Packers' meeting with the Oakland Raiders.

The Packer offense was in control of the game all the way against the Raiders. Don Chandler kicked four field goals; Herb Adderley returned an interception 60 yards for a score; and Starr completed 13 of 24 passes for 202 yards and one touchdown. While they only led by a 3-0 score in the first quarter, they padded that lead to 16-7 at halftime; then left the Raiders far behind with a 10-point third quarter as Donny Anderson scored on a two-yard run and Chandler kicked

Financial Security Comes at Last

Three events transpired in the year 1966 which served to cap Vince Lombardi's spectacular career with the Packers.

The merger of the National Football League and the American Football League was engineered that year, leading to Super Bowl I in January of 1967.

That same year the league put together the first television package, with CBS handling the games for the National Football Conference, NBC continuing with the American Conference, and ABC initiating Monday night football. The Packers received over $1 million in television revenues that year, which was a far cry above what they had been getting previously. The significance of the television bonanza became apparent to the Packers when they made their first big salary commitment to Donny Anderson, running back from Texas Tech, whom they had drafted as a junior in 1965. It was television money which enabled Lombardi to sign Anderson.

On the home front in Green Bay, with 13,800 orders for season tickets on the waiting list, the Packers replaced the temporary bleachers in the end zone at City Stadium with permanent seats, boosting the stadium capacity to over 50,000.

All of a sudden, the clouds lifted from the financial outlook of the Packers. Now they were really in the big league and heading into Super Bowl I.

his final field goal. The final margin was almost the same as that of Super Bowl I: Packers 33, Oakland 14.

The Packers had triumphed, but the game left Vince totally exhausted, mentally as well as physically.

At the next meeting of the Packer Executive Committee, Vince announced that he was retiring as head coach to devote full time to his remaining role as general manager of the Packers. Members of the Committee tried to persuade him to postpone that decision on the grounds that he was emotionally drained and not in a position to make good long-range decisions. Fred Trowbridge asked Vince, "What the hell are you going to keep busy with, Vince, besides opening the mail?" But Vince was adamant. He refused to reconsider at the next several meetings and said the subject was closed.

Trowbridge's question proved to be quite omniscient. Vince found that he really did not have enough work or responsibilities as general manager to occupy his tremendous energies.

One of his first acts was to promote Phil Bengtson to the head coaching job. Bengtson had built the defensive team that had carried the Packers to their five championships under Lombardi. Vince promised himself that he would abstain from any interference with Bengtson in coaching the team and would give Bengtson a completely free hand, but he found that resolution more and more difficult to keep as the training season approached, then arrived, and as the team went into the exhibition season and finally the regular season.

Lombardi ordered a special cubicle prepared for himself in the press box where he could watch the games in complete isolation, but even the sound-proofing in the walls, floor, and ceiling weren't enough to muffle his rantings and ravings as he watched the team perform on the field.

One season of watching the team from the sidelines was all that Vince could stand, and when the offer arrived from the Washington Redskins to become head coach, Vince couldn't refuse. To make the offer more attractive, Edward Bennett Williams, the Redskins owner, offered Vince a piece of the action. The chance to acquire five percent in the Washington football corporation impressed Vince greatly for all during his Packer career he had complained bitterly that as general manager he didn't even have a vote on the Executive Committee or even

The Packer Legend

the Board of Directors.

That situation was intentional on the part of Packer corporate management. Ever since the departure of Curly Lambeau from the organization, the officers and Directors of the Packer corporation had decided that never again would the operating chief have ownership rights or a vote on the Board of Directors or the Executive Committee.

There were times when the Committee and Lombardi differed on basic corporate policy. I remember one specific occasion very well when the question was whether or not to expand the stadium beyond its then current capacity of 42,000 seats. Lombardi was unalterably opposed to any expansion. He argued that we were selling out the stadium on a season ticket basis and that more capacity might well threaten that financial security. He also worried that the courts would void the practice of the league blacking out television broadcasts of games in their home territories, but the Committee felt it had a better perspective on the steady and prosperous growth of the Packer market in both Green Bay and Milwaukee and particularly the strong groundswell of support from Packer fans. When the Committee voted for an expansion of the stadium to 50,000 seats over Lombardi's vigorous objections, I remember his retort: "What the hell am I anyway around here? I am supposed to be general manager, and I don't even have a vote."

In early 1969, the Committee and Board of Directors released Lombardi from his contract so that he could become the head coach of the Washington Redskins, and as Paul Harvey would say, you know the rest of the story.

Lombardi found out, somewhat to his sorrow, that ownership of five percent of the stock in a closely-held corporation does not carry much leverage. Williams ran the Washington franchise, and Vince Lombardi was the head coach...period.

In his only season in Washington, Lombardi began much the way his first season had gone in Green Bay as he introduced the players to Lombardi discipline. The Redskins went 7-5-2 in that season, and it looked as though Lombardi was on his way to building another championship club in Washington.

It was during the training season of 1970 that Lombardi complained of abdominal pains and went into the hospital for tests. Exploratory surgery revealed a terminal cancer, and Lombardi went down hill very rapidly after that.

The entire Executive Committee of the Packers attended his funeral mass in New York's St. Patrick's Cathedral on September 7, 1970, then adjourned with a number of his close friends to one of his favorite little Italian restaurants on East 58th Street in New York.

There is a tragic epilogue to this story.

Not too long ago during one of my annual physical check-ups, my internist recommended a proctoscopic examination. Conferring with the doctor after the test, in which he gave me a clean bill of health, he remarked: "You know, we were treating Vince Lombardi for rectal problems before he left Green Bay, and he told me on one occasion, 'You are not going to shove that thing up my rectum.' And if we had done so, I am certain we would have found his cancer in its early stages when it could have been cured."

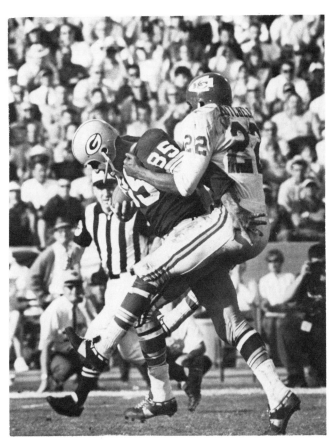

Super Bowl Hero. Aging Max McGee, the wide receiver from Tulane, came off the bench in the first quarter when starter Boyd Dowler was injured. McGee had only caught three passes during the regular season, but in Super Bowl I in Los Angeles against the Kansas City Chiefs, he snared seven Bart Starr aerials, two of them for touchdowns which helped defeat the Chiefs, 35-10. *Vern Biever photo.*

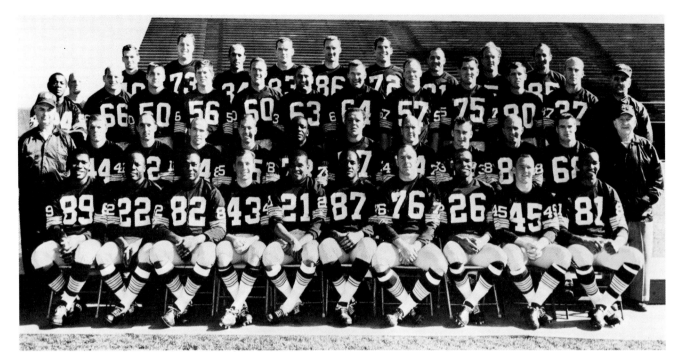

1966 Title Team. Won 12, Lost 2. Front row, left to right: D. Robinson, E. Pitts, L. Aldridge, D. Hart, B. Jeter, W. Davis, B. Skoronski, H. Adderley, D. Hathcock, M. Fleming. Second row: Trainer B. Jorgenson, D. Anderson, Z. Bratkowski, C. Dale, B. Starr, B. Brown, R. Kostelnik, H. Jordan, J. Grabowski, B. Anderson, G. Gillingham, eqpt. mgr. D. Braisher. Third row: W. Wood, R. Mack, R. Nitschke, B. Curry, T. Crutcher, L. Caffey, F. Thurston, J. Kramer, K. Bowman, F. Gregg, B. Long, P. VanderSea, asst. eqpt. mgr. B. Noel. Fourth row: T. Brown, J. Weatherwax, D. Chandler, A. Brown, B. Dowler, S. Wright, J. Taylor, P. Hornung, M. McGee. *Lefebvre photo.*

1967 Title Team. Won 9, Lost 4, Tied 1. Left to right, front row: D. Robinson, E. Pitts, L. Aldridge, D. Hart, B. Jeter, B. Skoronski, W. Davis, H. Adderley, W. Wood, M. Fleming. Second row: B. Jorgenson, T. Brown, R. Nitschke, Z. Bratkowski, C. Dale, B. Starr, R. Kostelnik, H. Jordan, D. Chandler, D. Horn, J. Rowser, B. Long, D. Braisher. Third row: D. Gentile, B. Brown, K. Bowman, J. Grabowski, J. Kramer, F. Thurston, B. Wilson, G. Gillingham, B. Hyland, C. James, B. Noel. Fourth row: D. Anderson, J. Weatherwax, T. Crutcher, J. Flanigan, A. Brown, B. Dowler, F. Gregg, L. Caffey, S. Wright, D. Capp, T. Williams, M. McGee. *Lefebvre photo.*

A Super Victory. Commissioner Pete Rozelle hands Vince Lombardi the trophy for winning Super Bowl I in Los Angeles. Lombardi was honored posthumously when the trophy was named for him after his death in 1971. Receiving the Lombardi Trophy is the goal of every NFL team each season because it represents the ultimate achievement in professional football, a pinnacle Lombardi reached five times in his career at Green Bay, winning two super bowls and three other NFL titles.

Vern Biever photo.

How's That Swing? Lombardi played golf as ferociously as he coached football. He loved the game and was supremely happy when he could get away and join his favorite foursome for a few hours at the Oneida Country Club.
Vern Biever photo.

Chapter Fifteen

LOMBARDI

THE

MAN

What manner of man was this Vince Lombardi who became a legend in his own time?

Lombardi literally had a magnetic personality. On many occasions, I witnessed this phenomenon. Every head would turn in his direction when he entered a room. I am speaking of public places such as restaurants or the clubhouse at the Oneida Golf Club where he enjoyed his few hours away from football. His very presence attracted everyone: their eyes, their ears, their total attention.

The secret of Lombardi's success in football was that basically he was a teacher. He was first a student, then a teacher of the basic fundamentals of the game: blocking, tackling, running, throwing, catching, and kicking a football.

He shouted that teaching at his charges with almost a maniacal voice, but Lombardi had the great gift of taking something off the end of his criticism. One day he was shouting at a rookie offensive lineman who was down in a three-point stance. Screamed Lombardi, "In that stance you can't move forward, you can't move to your right, you can't move to your left, all you can do is shit!" Henry Jordon put it this way, "When he tells me to sit down, I don't even look for a chair."

Lombardi inherited as the nucleus of his team a group of dispirited athletes who had decided that playing football in Green Bay might as well be fun if they couldn't win at it. Some of them thought they could get by with their old ruses during that first training camp.

One who found out Lombardi was no sucker was Max McGee, the fun-loving offensive end.

McGee, Hornung, Quinlan, and Currie were used to escaping from the training dorm at St. Norbert College after curfew and arriving back in the early hours of the morning. The first time Lombardi caught McGee in the act, he fined him $250; the next time, $500. The third time? Lombardi was waiting in the hallway when McGee was sneaking back to his room. He said to McGee, "This time, Max, it will cost you $1,000." Then he added with his inimitable grin, "And, McGee, if you have someone out there that's worth $1,000, I'll go out with you tomorrow night."

As the years went by in Green Bay and the victory string mounted, stories attributing almost mystical powers to Lombardi began circulating. On more than one occasion when rain threatened to turn the Packer stadium into a sea of mud and drench the 50,000 fans assembled therein, Lombardi would put his hands on his hips and stare up at the heavens, and miraculously, the rain would stop.

Lombardi was an intensely religious man, and maybe this lent credence to some of the tales. He went to mass every morning of the week at St. Willebrord's Church in Green Bay on his way to the Packer office. He told me that he had adopted the seven-day a week mass schedule because "it is the only way I can control my terrible temper."

That probably best describes the Lombardi personality. He was highly emotional, but he used those emotions to create the effect he desired.

Chuck Lane, the publicity man whom Lombardi brought to the Packers from the Harlem Globetrotters, said this about Lombardi's acting ability: "It was like watching the greatest Shakespearean character you have ever seen. He would come in mornings, and he would walk into the dressing room and would have one face on. The other coaches would be sitting out drinking coffee in the other room, discussing things, and you could just see him. It was like he was off stage then, and he would work himself into the proper mood. And boy, when he came out of that room he came on ready to go, and he was just like some kind of great actor taking the stage. I tell you it came off as a totally sincere performance, and it was a helluva performance to listen in on when he would go out there and get his troops around him. He laughed. He cried. He prayed. He motivated. I think he could motivate almost anybody to do almost anything. He

Meet Vince and Marie. Mr. and Mrs. Vincent T. Lombardi arrived in Green Bay on a cold February day in 1959 where Vince was to take over as head coach and general manager of the Green Bay Packers. Thus began the Lombardi Era in Packer history. *Lefebvre photo.*

Keeping The Faith

During a game in the 1981 season, one of the fellows who served hotdogs and hamburgers to the press showed me a light that has been stored away on a shelf in the cafeteria area of the press box at Lambeau Field.

"It's been sitting there ever since Vince left," he told me.

The light was the vigil light that Lombardi had installed in his personal cubicle of the press box the last year he was with the Packers, the year he was only general manager and Phil Bengtson was the head coach.

The Packer Legend

communicated with human emotions."

Paul Hornung used to tell the story on the banquet circuit about the time the Packers were preparing for a league championship game against the Dallas Cowboys in Texas. Lombardi thought he could dodge the terrible winter weather in Green Bay by training in Arkansas, but to his dismay, it snowed most of that week in Arkansas and Packer practice conditions were terrible. Hornung related that one day after practice Lombardi returned to his motel room, where his wife, Marie, was huddling under the covers to try to keep warm. Lombardi crawled in with her, and Marie cried, "Jesus, your feet are cold!" Vince responded, "Marie, you can call me Vince when we're alone."

Max McGee expanded on this in 1968 when a large testimonial banquet was staged for Vince. Just before the food was served, McGee brought out a platter, containing five fishes and nine loaves of bread, and set it before Lombardi at the head table. Lombardi almost rolled on the floor in laughter. It brought down the house.

Marie Lombardi, as do the wives of most great men, had a great deal to do with the success of Lombardi's career. She was strictly an Easterner when the Lombardis moved to Green Bay with their two teenage children. It was a difficult adjustment for her, but she was always there backing Vince up when he needed her.

She is quoted in the very fine book about Lombardi written by John Wiebusch as saying, "I always knew how far I could go with him. And, of course, he knew the same with me. I learned a lot about him and his pride in our 30 years. I used to make him say he was sorry, but I learned later on that he was more important than my silly little pride. The last 15 years or so he never had to say he was sorry for anything around."

Marie Lombardi carried on the fight against cancer which Vince had started, appearing each year in Milwaukee for the Vince Lombardi Memorial Golf Tournament and starting a similar fund-raising tournament in Washington. She herself died of lung cancer in April 1982.

There are two other facets to Lombardi's character that need detailing here.

Lombardi was "colorblind" as far as race or ethnic background was concerned. One of the greatest contributions he made to the Green Bay Packers was his insistence on eliminating any possible evidence of racial discrimination on his ball club. He made that clear at the outset of his

Post Game Prayer. The first thing Vince did after a game was to lead the squad in a prayer, win or lose. Lombardi was a practicing Catholic. He attended mass every morning of the week at St. Willebrord's Church. Stories circulated about Lombardi's mystical powers to make things happen, but he knew there was no mystery about the power of prayer.
Vern Biever photo.

The Packer Legend

career, and he instituted many practices with the Packer team which were pioneers in his time, one of them being mixing Blacks and Anglos in their rooming arrangements.

In the first meeting with the 60 players on the field he said: "If I ever hear nigger or dago or kike or anything like that around here, regardless of who you are, you are through with me. You can't play for me if you have any kind of prejudice."

Lamar McHan, the starting quarterback, found this out the hard way. After he had been replaced by Bart Starr in a game against Pittsburgh in mid-season, McHan was overheard calling Lombardi "that black dago sonofabitch" on the plane ride home. McHan was gone the next day.

Another facet of Lombardi's character was his outlook on injuries. He simply wouldn't admit that they existed. He said that pain was all in

Didn't You See That One? Vince makes a point to an official, quietly explaining his reasoning. He made a habit of restraining himself in such situations, realizing there was no sense in yelling at a referee and thereby possibly upsetting him. *Vern Biever photo.*

Concentration. Lombardi watches over his troops at the Packers' Oneida Street practice field, located just across the street from their headquarters and City Stadium. *Vern Biever photo.*

the mind. Jerry Kramer once said, "None of our injuries hurts him at all."

Art Daley, the retired sports editor of the Green Bay *Press-Gazette*, tells this story: "In 1963, Bart Starr broke his hand in St. Louis, and Lombardi was particularly vicious with the press. He didn't want to say it was broken. He just wouldn't talk, and then the week after, he even kicked a photographer off the practice field, fearing he would take a picture of Bart. After the season, Vince explained that the reason he acted like that was because 'as soon as you make a big thing out of a star player being hurt, the entire team can start to feel sorry for itself.' Vince would never let that happen, but he was afraid it could."

Under Lombardi, you simply played hurt.

I recently asked Bart Starr for his thoughts about Vince Lombardi. Starr thought for quite a bit, then told me, "I think the greatest thing about Vince was his sense of timing, which probably had as much to do with our success as anything else. The timing showed through on the practice field in his exhortations to the team, before the game, between halves, during the game, and most especially in his choice of the right play at the right time.

"I suppose that one of the marks that I will leave behind in this football game is the long pass to the free end on second and one for a touchdown. That was the timing I learned from Vince Lombardi. He would go along in a game, as he often said, hitting at their strength, but at just the right moment, he would call for an off-beat play which would completely take the other team by suprise.

"The same thing was true of him in his relations with the players, when he always knew when to lay it on them and then when to pull it back.

"Lombardi was a teacher; probably the greatest teacher I have ever known. He not only taught us football, but he taught us the building of individual characters, the will to succeed in life, and yet he taught us also humility to accept defeat and make something out of it.

"Vince Lombardi molded the character of every player who played under him and that character still shines through today."

Starr and Forrest Gregg, the coach who took the Cincinnati Bengals to the Super Bowl in 1982, are the outstanding proteges of Lombardi in the coaching ranks today, but there are a number of his former players who are still active as assistant coaches in the National Football League. Norb Hecker had a stint as head coach at Atlanta and now is with the Super Bowl champion San Francisco 49ers. Boyd Dowler is a receiver coach with Tampa Bay. Babe Parilli has been a quarterback coach with New England as Lamar McHan has been with New Orleans. Elijah Pitts is a backfield coach with Houston, and Willie Wood was an assistant coach at San Diego. Jim Ringo is an assistant with Los Angeles, and John Symank was with Baltimore. Zeke Bratkowski is now with Baltimore, and Lew Carpenter continues on the Packer staff.

Anytime one of Lombardi's players is interviewed and asked about his success in football or any other endeavor, he will pay tribute to the character building experiences that he acquired under Lombardi.

Two Billoti brothers, Ray and Ron, ran a very good Italian supper club called *The Forum* a few blocks from Packer headquarters, and it was one of Lombardi's favorite haunts. The Billotis

considerably enlarged the facility, prospering from their intimate relationships with the Packers and Lombardi, and named one of their private dining rooms the Lombardi Room. Significantly, it was in this room that the Packer directors met in 1969 to hear Vince say that he was leaving the job as Packer general manager to become head coach of the Washington Redskins.

The Billotis do not operate *The Forum* anymore, but they do have a supper club called the Celebrity House, and one wall of the dining room is dedicated to pictures of Lombardi throughout his Packer career. I think that the paragraphs which are displayed below these pictures tell the story of Lombardi the Legend as well as anything I have ever seen written about him. They read:

"In times when our nation and the world so desparately needed heroes, Vince Lombardi shown brilliantly above all others. It wasn't just the victories, it was the lessons he left, the greater values, strength of character, the indefatigable will, his intense dedication to excellence, mental toughness, and love of them.

"All of these qualities inspired the men who followed his leadership. Men followed Vince Lombardi. They loved him; they respected him because he exuded leadership and confidence. We of the Green Bay Packers and the National Football League feel privileged to have brushed shoulders with his greatness."

Mobbed by Fans. Fans dashed onto the field to congratulate Lombardi after the Packers beat the Bears, 9-6, in Lombardi's first league game as head coach in 1959. *Vern Biever photo.*

Marie Tosses the Coin. Vince's widow Marie did the honors at the opening ceremony in Super Bowl XV in New Orleans. Oakland became the first wild card team to win the Lombardi Trophy, beating Philadelphia, 27-10.

Vern Biever photo.

The Packer Legend

THE MANY MOODS

OF

VINCE LOMBARDI

Pensive

Elated

Confident

Concerned

Teacher

Puzzled

Drained

But Happy

GREEN BAY PRESS-GAZETTE

VOLUME LVI, No. 67   48 PAGES   FOUR SECTIONS   GREEN BAY, WIS., THURSDAY EVENING, SEPTEMBER 3, 1970   PRICE 15¢

Vince Lombardi . . . As Packer Coach

Coaching Great Succumbs to Cancer

Legendary Lombardi Dies

WASHINGTON (AP) — Vince Lombardi, Washington Redskins coach and onetime ruler of a football dynasty with the Green Bay Packers, died today of cancer. He was 57.

A spokesman at Georgetown University Hospital said Lombardi succumbed at 6:12 a.m. CDT, his wife, Marie, at his side.

Lombardi, the only man in the history of the National Football League playoffs to win three straight championships, had undergone two operations within a month in his battle with the disease.

Had Confirmed Gravity

Mrs. Lombardi had confirmed Wednesday the gravity of the ailment. She said the cancer was "extraordinarily virulent."

An hour and 40 minutes after her husband died Mrs. Lombardi left the hospital looking strained but composed.

As she left by a side exit, she kissed a nurse goodbye and said "Thank you for everything," forcing a smile.

News of Lombardi's death had spread rapidly in the hospital where patients and workers were following the coach's fight for survival closely.

His name became legendary for the feats he accomplished at Green Bay.

His motto: "Winning isn't a

big thing. It's the only thing."

"He had a covenant with greatness, more than any man I have ever known," said Redskins President Edward Bennett Williams in a statement. "He was committed to excellence in everything he attempted. Because he was so committed, he was able to lead other men to commit and discipline themselves to reach heights of which they had never dreamed.

Called Inspiration

"Our country has lost one of its great men. The world of sport has lost its first citizen. The Washington Redskins have lost their leader. I personally have lost a beloved friend."

Bill Austin, interim Redskins coach, added in a statement:

"Words are inadequate to express my deep sorrow and regret at the passing of Coach Vince Lombardi, a great leader and a greater man.

Features on Vince Lombardi

Reaction from the Packers	Page C-1
Reflections from Mrs. Lombardi	Page C-1
Lombardi Era in Green Bay in pictures	Page C-3
Bob Woessner's reaction	Page A-2
Lombardi as seen by Art Daley	Page C-2
A close look at Lombardi the man	Page C-2
Out of Bounds? column	Page C-2
The living Lombardi legend, an editorial	Page A-4

"He was and always will remain in my memory a man of unequaled ability, character, drive and integrity. He was an inspiration to those of us who were privileged to have worked for and with him."

Pete Rozelle, pro football commissioner, said, "The death of Vince Lombardi is a deep, personal loss to all in professional football, but those who will miss him the most are those who still had yet to play for him, who might have been taught by him, led by him, and counseled by him.

"Vince Lombardi was a very rare person, a citizen whose achievements and principles were recognized and honored far beyond the framework of his role in society.

Col. Earl "Red" Blaik, former coach at Army and an associate of Lombardi at West Point, said:

"Vince Lombardi epitomized 20th century America by his devotion to his family and dedication to his church and country. He was recognized as a strong willed man whose extraordinary success in life came from a seriousness of purpose and hard work."

"This coupled with a remarkable intellect made him the peer of his profession. He was a volatile, sometimes gruff, lovable, loyal friend who somehow seemed indestructible. I am shocked and grieved at the passing of the great coach."

George Halas, 75-year-old owner of the Chicago Bears, lauded the "unforgettable personality" of Vince Lombardi and said his former Green Bay coaching rival's death "is a great loss not only to football, but to the entire country."

'I Loved Him'

"I regret that I really became closer to Vince only within the last five years," said Halas. "That was all too short a time to enjoy and admire his great qualities. We understood each other. I loved him as a friend and as a man.

"I am sure Vince would have been a leader in any field and in any era."

Halas said Lombardi's death was regrettable also because

"he had so many years of his life and career ahead of him when he was stricken.

"All too few men are around to match his forceful leadership and competitive qualities."

The New York native arrived in Green Bay in 1959, one year after the Packers posted its worst record, 1-10-1. He forged a 7-5 season his first year, won the divisional championship in 1960, and then proceeded to capture NFL titles in 1961, 1962, 1965, 1966 and 1967.

His Packers won the first two Super Bowls which pitted the NFL against the AFL.

Lombardi retired from coaching in 1968 to serve as general

TURN TO PAGE A-2, COLUMN 1

Funeral Services

The funeral Mass for Vince Lombardi will be said at St. Patrick's Cathedral in New York at 10 a.m. Monday (CDT) by Terence Cardinal Cooke. Friends may call at the Galler Funeral Home, Wisconsin Ave., in Washington starting at 2 p.m. Friday, and the following day (Saturday) at 2 p.m. at the Abbey Funeral Home, 66th St. and Lexington Ave., in New York. Burial will be at Mount Olivet cemetery near Redbank, N.J.

The Green Bay Years

Vince Built a Dynasty, Legend Here

By LEE REMMEL
Press-Gazette Sports Writer

Vincent Thomas Lombardi, claimed today by the ravages of cancer, forged the greatest dynasty in pro football history — in the sport's smallest city.

"A native New Yorker, he was lured to Green Bay in 1959 by the promise of sweeping authority in resuscitating the Packers, then at the lowest ebb in their 40-year existence.

His subsequent rise from the role of an obscure assistant coach with the Giants to an awesome legend in his own time is a story unparalleled in the annals of sport.

A man of formidable purpose and total dedication, Lombardi restored the Packers to respect-

ability in one season, then set about creating a dynasty.

Produced Triple Crown

Explosively volatile yet rigidly self-disciplined, he drove them to the National Football League's Western Conference championship the following year, then to five league titles in seven years, an unprecedented reign that may never be matched.

The last three came in succession, 1965-66-67, a parlay without equal since the NFL adopted the divisional system in 1933 and one which earned him pre-eminence among pro football's coaches.

Spent by the strain of producing that "triple crown," Lom-

bardi decided to retire in February of 1968. Obviously affected by deep emotion, he announced that he would devote himself to his duties as general manager, with the explanation he felt it impossible to do both jobs "because of the nature and growth of the business and the corporate structure of the Packers."

Breath of Life

The Brooklyn-born Italian, who joined the Redskins in February of '69, relinquished his Washington coaching mantle to assistant Bill Austin on what was then called an "interim" basis late last month when it became apparent he could no longer coach.

New Success

Ironically, he appeared on his way to new success, having last year brought the Redskins, perennial also-rans, their first winning season since 1955.

During his nine-year Packer tenure, the brawny, square-cut son of a patriarchal meat retailer directed the Packers to an imposing 141-39-4 record, a .766 winning percentage.

His teams won 42 of 50 post-season games, amassed an 89-29-4 record in league play and, significantly, won 10 of 12 post-season games, including five of six NFL championship games. They also won both Super Bowls in which they appeared.

Devout Catholic

A daily communicant, Lombardi was a devout Catholic and made that belief a part of his professional life.

Each year, he told his players, "There are three things that should be important to you: Your religion, your family and the Green Bay Packers, in that order."

Although his coaching system once was characterized as "complex simplicity," Lombardi adopted a basic approach. "Some people try to find things in this game or put things into it which don't exist," he said, summing up his philosophy. "Football is two things. It's blocking and tackling. I don't care anything about formations or new offenses or tricks on defense. You block and tackle better than the team you're play-

"When I retired a year ago, I certainly had no intention of going back into coaching," he explained. "It was a truthful retirement. It wasn't six months after I decided to retire . . . that I realized I had made a bad decision. But, as far as Green Bay is concerned, there was no way I could come back to coach here without hurting a lot of people."

But coaching was the very breath of life to Lombardi and, after one year of chafing on the sidelines, he abruptly ended his retirement to become part owner, executive officer and head coach of the Washington Redskins after the Packers granted him a release from his contract as general manager.

Officials, Friends Mourn Death of Vince Lombardi

Tributes to the late Vincent T. Lombardi flowed in today as the word spread rapidly of the death of the man who became a legend while leading the Green Bay Packers to unprecedented glory in the National Football League.

Government officials, clergymen, congressmen and men who cherished his friendship expressed sorrow and a great sense of loss.

Tributes included:

Dominic Olejniczak, president of the Packer Corp.: In the passing of Vince Lombardi, I sense a great personal grief at the loss of a warm and close friend with whom I was privileged to work an intimate terms during the "heyday" of his remarkable career. His genius as a coach was in no small degree the result of the many attributes of his personal character.

"Vince Lombardi will forever be identified closely with the golden period in the history of the Green Bay Packers for it was here that his career as a head coach began and blossomed into universally recognized greatness, until both the

record of achievement never equalled in all the annals of sports, a record that will probably never be surpassed.

"To those of us who were privileged to know him well his loss is indeed a deep one."

Gov. Warren Knowles: The passing of Vince Lombardi is a great loss to professional football and to all people who enjoyed and respected the competitive spirit that he championed.

"The citizens of Wisconsin will always remember the exciting championship years of the Green Bay Packers under his leadership. He brought the Packers to the pinnacle of professional excellence and made himself and his teams a legend in their own time.

"Vince Lombardi was a winner. He won the respect, loyalty, and love of all Wisconsinites and millions of football fans throughout the nation. Courage and dedication to excellence characterized his life to the end."

Mayor Donald Tilleman: "Vince Lombardi was a winner among men. He made a lasting mark wherever he went and

second home — but throughout the nation where his example provided inspiration to millions.

Bishop Aloysius J. Wycislo: "I visited with Marie and Vince Lombardi recently and assured them how much we all loved them in Green Bay. They were very much consoled by our prayers and told me how much consolation they received from that moment of silence and prayer at the Bishop's Charities Game. I am sure that all of us in the Green Bay area will be praying for the repose of Vince's soul and for consolation to Marie and the family."

Harry Masse, local businessman and close friend: "Like so many others, I feel very deeply the loss of a great American and a close friend. Vince Lombardi was a very unusual man, deeply religious, blessed with great talent and ability. He followed Teddy Roosevelt's advice: 'When you work, work hard. When you play, play hard.' He was a stirring example of the type of man our country needs so sorely today, in the history of football he will stand alongside the immortals.

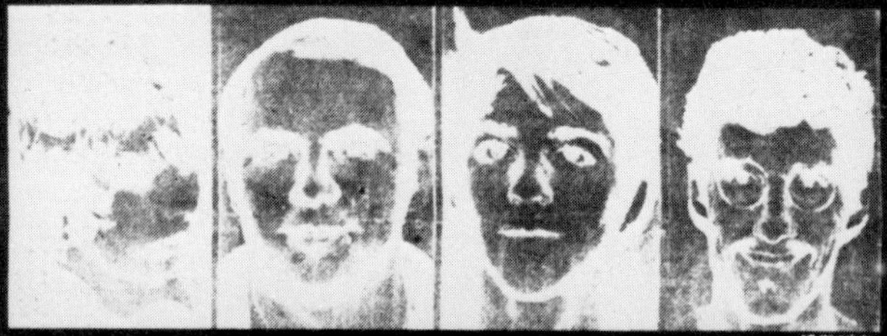

Nationwide Search Begun for Four Charged in Bombing at UW
From left: Dwight Armstrong; his brother, Karleton; David Fine; Leo Burt   —AP Wirephoto

4 Charged, Sought in UW Blast

WASHINGTON (AP) — A nationwide search has been launched for four young men charged in the bombing of the Army Mathematics Research Center at Madison. One man died and three were injured in the blast.

One of the four charged in the Aug. 24 bombing was linked by the FBI to Students for a Democratic Society. Three had attended the University of Wisconsin where the research center

was located. The fourth was identified as a high school dropout.

The FBI said fugitive warrants and charges of sabotage, destruction of government property and conspiracy have been filed against Karleton Lewis Armstrong, 22; his brother, Dwight Alan Armstrong, 19; David Sylvan Fine, 18, and Leo Frederick Burt, 22.

An FBI agent investigating the blast filed an affidavit

Wednesday in Madison, saying the Armstrong brothers had told a friend they had a large cache of explosives and planned a series of bombings.

Agent George P. Baxtrum Jr. said in the document the Armstrongs had visited Maxim Silter in Minneapolis prior to the research center bombing. The affidavit alleged the brothers told Silter the bombings would be done late in the evening and no one would be hurt.

"The boys advised him that they had a great amount of explosives in their possession, namely nitrate and primacord," Baxtrum said.

In the affidavit, the FBI agent said the Armstrongs told Silter they were responsible for the Jan. 1 bombing of the Badger Army Ammunitions Plant. Authorities said an undetonated bomb was found on the grounds of the ammo plant.

Karleton Armstrong rented a trailer and bought 100 gallons of gasoline Aug. 16, the agent quoted a Madison service station employe as saying. According to the document, another man reported the elder brother purchased 1,700 pounds of nitrogen fertilizer three days later.

Karleton Armstrong rented a trailer and bought 100 gallons of gasoline Aug. 16, the agent quoted a Madison service station employe as saying. According to the document, another man reported the elder brother purchased 1,700 pounds of nitrogen fertilizer three days later.

The fertilizer and gasoline could be combined to make an explosive device.

Baxtrum said the four men charged were stopped by police shortly after the research center was bombed, but were allowed to pass. A friend of the four received a letter postmarked Aug. 28 in which they said they were in New York City en route to Canada.

The FBI said the university's Sterling Hall, in which the gov-

'Whole World Crashes Down' On Father of 2 Accused Bombers

MADISON (AP) — "I just feel like the whole world has kind of crashed down around us," the father of two young men accused of bombing a University of Wisconsin building, killing three other children's father, said Wednesday.

Karleton L. Armstrong, 22, and his brother, Dwight, 19, both of Madison, where the university is located, are among four young men sought by the FBI in connection with bombing at Sterling Hall Aug. 24.

The other two are David S. Fine, 18, of Wilmington, Del., and Leo F. Burt, 22, of Haverford, Pa.

'Didn't Preach'

"He wanted to be in on it, he thought it was the wave of the

few SDS meetings, like we all do once in a while. He didn't preach to the rest of us. He just sort of made comments, like a lot of people do, like 'kill the pig.'"

Dwight dropped out of East High School in 1968.

"He probably was a 10th grader at the time of the withdrawal," said Principal Wayne Benson. "He wasn't doing his work; he wasn't passing his subjects."

Was on Rowing Team

Dwight was "very much a follower," said a fraternity house resident. He hung around with college kids and might have done things to impress them. He thought of his brother as an idol.

dent; but he took a few courses because he was "much interested in the media as instruments of social change," said Harold Nelson, director of the university journalism school. "He was a very good student."

Burt was known as a writer of radical stories in the Daily Cardinal — a paper with strong radical leanings. He had gone to summer school to complete work on his bachelor's degree.

Was Night Editor

Fine was one of four night editors on the Cardinal staff. He resigned in April because of a "personality conflict."

"He was intensively concerned about the Vietnam war, but no more intensely than other children or adults," said the

PART IV

THE

LEGEND'S

LEFTOVERS

1968 - 1974

DEE-FENSE. Coach Phil Bengtson departs from his usual placid expression as he wills the Packers to "hold that line." The felt hat was a Bengtson trademark. *Vern Biever photo.*

Chapter Sixteen

IN

THE

SHADOW

"How's Bart Starr's arm?" the man asked in perfect American.

The question and the language would not have been unusual anywhere in Wisconsin or the United States for that matter. What made it unusual was that it was asked of me in a fishermen's *taberno* in Italy.

My wife and I had gone to Europe to meet our youngest son in Venice after he had completed a semester of studying abroad. We were spending several days there before going to Greece and taking a tour of the Greek islands.

I had read in Gourmet Magazine that if you wanted one of the finest fish meals in Italy, you should take the ferry from Venice over to the Lido, a peninsula sticking out into the Adriatic Sea, not unlike our own Door County Peninsula here in Wisconsin. Many commercial fisherman

have their home ports on this peninsula, and we went to a *taberno* where the fishermen tied up at the nearby dock and brought their fresh fish in to be served in the restaurant.

I had tendered my American Express card in payment for a sumptuous luncheon to the owner of the *taberno*, who by this time was sitting in a booth with two other cronies. The gentleman who asked me about the condition of Bart Starr's arm was a Cuban who had spent some time in Canada and who owned a glass factory in Venice at the time.

Before I could answer, the proprietor said, "Have an *ouzo*," and I was invited to join the conversation.

It turned out that the gentleman in question was particularly interested in the Packers at that time because he was going to sponsor a professional basketball team in Venice and he wanted to name them the Packers. He inquired of me what channels he would have to follow to get permission from the Green Bay football corporation to use the name. One *ouzo* led to another, and suffice it to say that the conversation from that point deteriorated.

I recall the conversation particularly now because Bart Starr's arm had a great deal to do with Phil Bengtson's unsuccessful career as head coach of the Green Bay Packers, succeeding Vince Lombardi.

Recall, if you will, that when Vince decided to exercise the option in his contract to divest himself of coaching duties and remain as general manager, he gave Bengtson a contract as head coach, and I already related the problems Lombardi had in secreting himself in a small soundproof cubicle in the press box, forcibly restraining himself from interfering in any way with the coaching.

Bengtson was the man who had constructed

the defense which probably won as many games for Lombardi as did Lombardi's offense. I still see Bengtson on the sidelines dressed in coat, tie, and matching pants, a felt hat perched on his head, signaling the defensive formation with very precise movements of his hands, hat, feet, or ever present cigarette.

Phil had been an All-American at the University of Minnesota and had been an assistant coach with several teams in the National Football League, coaching the defense for the San Francisco 49ers before Lombardi brought him to Green Bay. I still think that he was one of the better head coaches the Packers have had, but injuries to Starr, which befell him in his first season, and problems with Vince's other aging performers spelled his doom.

Let's face it. Lombardi was a realist. When he bowed out of the head coaching job, he knew full well that the team which had won three consecutive championships and two Super Bowls was growing old. He also knew that as the league

Bengtson Named Head Coach. General Manager Lombardi picked his defensive coordinator, Phil Bengtson, to succeed him as head coach. Packer President Dominic Olejniczak applauds. *Vern Biever photo.*

High Priced Stepper. Donny Anderson of Texas Tech was the highest paid ballplayer on the Packer roster at that point in time. He played for Lombardi, Bengtson, and Devine until the latter traded him to St. Louis for MacArthur Lane after the 1971 Season. That's Gale Gillingham blocking out ahead. *Vern Biever photo.*

The Packer Legend

had expanded it had become more difficult to acquire new talent through the draft or by trade. Lombardi knew what he was doing when he stepped aside as head coach in favor of Bengtson.

Starr told me recently that he had secretly been having troubles with his passing arm in the 1967 season, and when Bengtson took over under General Manager Lombardi in 1968, Starr was badly injured in mid-October. While he was warming up for the Los Angeles Ram game, he pulled a muscle in the biceps of his throwing arm and told Bengtson that he simply could not throw the ball. At that point, he was out for three weeks. Zeke Bratkowski, whom Lombardi had acquired from Chicago, took over at quarterback.

Despite Starr's injury and a freak accident to Jim Taylor when he burned his foot while cooking in his kitchen at home, the Packers were in the thick of the title season all the way in 1968. They lost some really tough ones, 23-17 to Detroit, 16-14 to the Rams, 13-10 to the Bears, 14-10 to the Vikings, and were still in the championship race until the last three games of the season when they lost to the 49ers, 27-20, and Baltimore Colts, 30-16. Even at that, they beat the Bears in the final game, 28-27 and wound up with a 6-7-1 record.

In regard to those close scores, Bengtson had inherited another major problem from Lombardi. The Packers had Don Chandler, one of the most reliable place kickers in the league during Lombardi's triple championship seasons. But Chandler by this time had established himself in a lucrative business back home in Kansas City, and he told Bengtson that he would only play for the Packers if he could report on Fridays, work out for two days, and play on Sundays. Lombardi told Bengtson he wouldn't go for any such arrangement. He conveniently forgot that Paul Hornung had played for him on Sundays when he was in service and his pal, Pat Martin would fly down on Saturdays, bring him to Green Bay or wherever so he could play on Sundays, then fly him back to camp after the game.

Bengtson must have tried out a dozen kickers in that first season, and he never did come up with a capable one. One candidate was a disc jockey in neighboring Appleton who had done some kicking in high school. That's how desperate Bengtson was.

And as you look back at those scores by which the Packers were defeated in his first season, you can understand his frustration. The Packers lost five games by a total of 22 points and tied another. So 23 points in six games, or four points a game, would have given them a record of 12-2.

By the time the 1969 season rolled around, other teams in the league knew about Starr's arm. They began to give the Packers the long passing game, pulled in their secondaries to stop the short passes, and applied tremendous pressure on Starr. In one game he was sacked eight times, and in the succeeding game, Bengtson finally pulled Bart out in favor of rookie quarterback Don Horn.

Even at that, Bengtson compiled a record of 8-6 in 1969 and again was in the thick of the championship battle all the way. He still had not solved the kicking problem, although he finally brought in the aged veteran, Ben Agajanian. Again they lost three crucial games by a total of 16 points. They were 5-1 at one point in the first half of the season until Starr's arm went bad again and the kicking game fell apart.

In the third and last season under his contract, Bengtson went into the hospital that spring with a bleeding ulcer. Phil couldn't take the pressures of the dual responsibilities like Lombardi did. Lombardi was the emotional Italian who could and did blow his stack when he was troubled or irritated. Phil was the taciturn Norwegian who kept all his emotions bottled up inside of him, eating at the walls of his stomach.

There were suggestions made that Bengtson should resign that spring for his own health's sake, but he toughed it out that fall for a 6-8 season.

That wasn't good enough for the Executive Committee, however, which still had the Lombardi golden decade firmly in mind, and Bengtson resigned in mid-December, soon after the last game of the season, knowing full well that his contract would not be renewed.

I have always felt that we in Packer management didn't really do right by Phil Bengtson. Realistically, Lombardi as general manager wasn't a great deal of help to Phil in shoring up obvious weak spots on the roster, notably quarterback and kicker. How many head coaches in the league have broken even without top notch performers at these two vital offensive positions?

Secondly, I was opposed at the time to imposing the duties of general manager on Bengtson when Lombardi left for Washington, and I got into trouble with other members of the Executive Committee over that matter. I was interviewed on a sports show on WLUK-TV,

The Packer Legend

Channel 11 in Green Bay, and I expressed the opinion publicly that the head coach had all he could handle in directing the football operations and that making him general manager also, in name if not in fact, didn't make any sense. We had to give Lombardi full charge or he wouldn't have come to Green Bay. Bengtson really didn't want to be general manager.

Packer Vice-Pres. Dick Bourguignon blew up at me at the next committee meeting. He said I intimated that I spoke for the committee, which I didn't intend. He also objected to the fact that I appeared on a station owned by the company for which I worked, Post Corporation, and he thought that represented a conflict of interest.

Packer Pres. Dominic Olejniczak settled the matter. He said he thought we had to give Bengtson the same prestige which we had given Lombardi by naming him to the dual jobs. I have long respected Ole's judgment, and as I have mentioned elsewhere, the committee always hashed their opinions out in advance, then reached a unanimous concensus.

I went along for the sake of harmony, but it would have solved some major problems down the road if we had bitten the bullet then and divorced the duties of corporate management from those of coaching the football team.

Phil has led a good life since leaving Green Bay. After several seasons as personnel director for New England, then San Diego, he settled in that beautiful California area, made some investments in real estate which have turned out well, and now is a comfortable retiree. His wife Kay suffered badly from arthritis during Wisconsin winters, so she is very happy. The Bengtsons still return to Green Bay on occasion to visit children who still live here. They are warmly welcomed whenever they do.

Phil is one of the finest gentlemen I have ever known, and he was a damn good football coach. He was just in the wrong place at the wrong time.

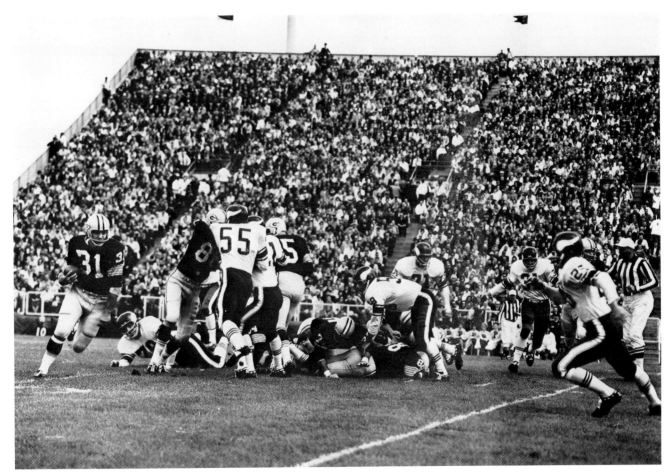

Look Out, Here I Come. Jim Taylor sees plenty of daylight as he picks up yards against the Vikings. This was in 1967, his last season with Green Bay and Lombardi's last year as head coach. *Lefebvre photo.*

How Many Draft Choices for Tittle? Dan Devine meets the press in Green Bay for the first time after being named head coach in 1971. When he traded five top draft choices for sore-armed quarterback John Hadl, he put a mortgage on the Packers future that his replacement, Bart Starr, spent five years paying off. To make matters worse, he made the deal without conferring with Packer management, a move which did not exactly endear him to the Board of Directors. *Vern Biever photo.*

Chapter Seventeen

THE

GREAT

GIVEAWAY

There was something prophetic about the first game Dan Devine coached in the National Football League. Early in the opener against the New York Giants, a wide receiver took a sideline pass and smashed into Devine. The Packer head coach was carried from the field on a stretcher with a broken leg.

Dan Devine came to Green Bay with one of the most impressive records of anyone in the ranks of college coaches at that time. He left Green Bay four years later with the wolves howling at his heels.

But Devine did have the last laugh on his Green Bay detractors. That's getting ahead of the story, however, so let's start at the beginning.

When the Packers were seeking a new head coach in January of 1971 to replace Phil

Bengtson who had resigned, they finally narrowed the choice down to two outstanding college coaches: Devine, from the University of Missouri; and Joe Paterno of Penn State. There was a division of opinion among the Executive Committee between the two.

Paterno reminded some of the members of Vince Lombardi. Of Italian extraction, he was also an Easterner and had many of the dramatic characteristics of Lombardi. He particularly impressed those members of the Committee who had been close to Lombardi, primarily Vice-Pres. Dick Bourguignon and Tony Canadeo.

Pres. Dominic Olejniczak leaned toward Devine. Both men were interviewed by the full Committee in Green Bay, and Olejniczak felt that Devine's experience as athletic director as well as head coach at Missouri gave him the upper hand on qualifications. He had supervised the building of a fine new stadium and field house during his tenure at Missouri, while Paterno had been strictly a football coach.

The Committee went along with Olejniczak, and the job was offered to Devine.

I agreed. I felt strongly that the president of the corporation should be supported in his choice since he was elected to carry out that responsibility.

Another factor was that we never really knew whether Paterno would have taken the job if it had been offered to him. He had been wooed by other NFL clubs before and had turned them down. We knew that Penn State alumni would have put up a stiff fight to keep him. Paterno flattered the Packers, though, when he told us that if he decided to make the switch into the pros, the Packers were the only NFL team he would consider. Paterno has been sought by a

number of other teams since then also, but he is still at Penn State.

The first meeting between the new head coach-general manager and the Executive Committee was a rather strange affair. Olejniczak thought it would be nice to invite Devine and his wife Jo to the Olejniczak's home for a social evening with members of the Committee and their wives.

The youngest two of the Devine's four children had arrived in Green Bay, and they were invited to join the group, although no other young people were present. Devine had made the point to Olejniczak that his family was very important to him, even more important than his job, and this was a way of demonstrating it. The trouble was he carried the demonstration a bit far. There was a pool table in the Olejniczak family room, and Devine spent a good part of the evening playing pool with his children. It didn't sit very well with Committee members.

Fallen Coach. Dan Devine was carried from the field with a broken leg which he sustained in the first league game in which he coached the Packers. A wide receiver out for a sideline pass crashed into him, causing the injury. The Packers lost that day, 42-40, to the New York Giants. Maybe the fracture and the outcome of the game were omens for Devine's future with the Packers. *John Biever photo.*

Devine got off to a good start with his first draft in 1971, however, picking up John Brockington, the fine fullback from Ohio State, as his first draft choice. He also chose a quarterback, Scott Hunter from Georgia, in the sixth round.

Bart Starr had undergone surgery on his ailing arm during the winter, right after the end of the 1970 season, and he was a question mark for 1971. As it turned out, Zeke Bratkowski opened the campaign at quarterback, but Hunter came along rapidly and took over the starting job by mid-season. Starr saw only limited action toward the end of the year, then retired.

Brockington turned out to be a great fullback in his rookie year, rushing for over 1,000 yards, but the Packers wound up with a 4-8-2 record for the season.

Coach on Crutches. Devine was able to return to the sidelines on crutches by the third game of the season against the Cincinnati Bengals, which the Packers won, 20-17. *Vern Biever photo.*

During the off season, Devine swung a trade for Donnie Anderson and acquired the big running back MacArthur Lane to pair with Brockington in a big-back backfield. The move paid off handsomely, and with Hunter taking over as the starting quarterback, the Packers breezed to a 10-4 season in 1972 and won the Central Division title. They came away a cropper, however, when they played the Washington Redskins in the playoffs in the nation's capital. Washington coach George Allen came up with a defensive alignment the Packers had never seen before, stationing one of his biggest defensive lineman on the Packer center's nose. The maneuver completely halted the Green Bay

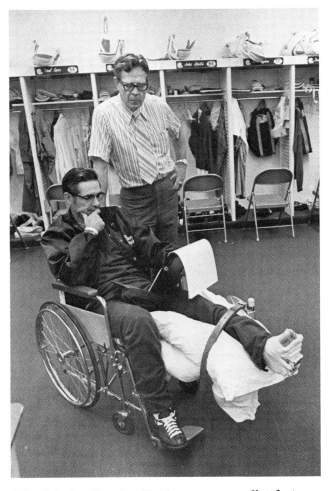

Wheelchair Coach. Devine was confined to a wheelchair for a few weeks after having his leg broken in the opening game against the Giants. Here he goes over a scouting report in the dressing room with scout Wally Cruice. *Vern Biever photo.*

The Packer Legend

running game, and the Redskins won, 16-3.

Bart Starr was engaged as a quarterback coach by Devine in that 1972 season, and many fans credited the Packers' success that year to Starr's offensive strategy. The story came out after they lost to Washington that Starr had recommended some changes in the game plan to counter the unique Allen defense, but Devine did not take Starr's advice. At any rate, Starr did not return to the staff after that season.

That was the zenith of Devine's career with the Packers. After that, it was all downhill.

I felt that the Dan Devine of 1971 and 1972 was a completely different man from the Devine of 1973 and 1974. During mid-1973, his wife was diagnosed as having multiple sclerosis, and I have always felt that this had a great effect on Devine's subsequent performance in Green Bay. The Devines were a very close family, as I mentioned earlier, and the diagnosis was a great shock to them. Jo Devine first noticed early that summer that she was having difficulty with her golf game. She had always been an excellent golfer. It got to the point where she was actually fanning the ball on some shots. A trip to the Mayo Clinic brought the fateful diagnosis.

Devine's relations with the press deteriorated considerably about this time also, another facet of the change in his personality. He became defensive, particularly in regard to numerous

Another Devine Acquisition. MacArthur Lane came to the Packers from St. Louis in a trade for Donny Anderson and joined Brockington in a big-back backfield which won the Western Division title their first year together, 1972.   *Vern Biever photo.*

From Boom to Bust. John Brockington, the Ohio State fullback, was a sensation his first three years, exceeding 1,000 yards rushing in all three seasons, but after Devine gave him a no-cut contract the next year his play steadily deteriorated.
Vern Biever photo.

The Packer Legend

rumors circulated around town about him and his family. On one occasion, Devine declared that the family dog had been shot, presumably by an irate fan, and he complained that his children were being heckled on the school bus. The Devines had built a beautiful new house out in the country west of Green Bay, and the dog had been raiding a neighboring farmer's chicken coop. The farmer had taken matters into his own hands and shot the dog.

Devine was interviewed by *Time* magazine about some of these rumors, and he was quoted extensively with some rather derogatory remarks about the people in Green Bay. That didn't help his relations with members of the Executive Committee.

It was about that time that Chuck Lane decided he had had it with Devine and resigned as Director of Public Relations. He was replaced by Lee Remmel, long-time sports writer for the *Press Gazette*. Of greater concern to the Committee were some of the personnel moves made by Devine.

The Packers had fallen to a 5-7-2 record in 1973, and in 1974 Devine made some rather startling deals which appeared to be motivated by sheer desperation. One of these was the acquisition of quarterback John Hadl from San Diego, but Devine paid a tremendous price for a quarterback who, as it turned out, was over the hill.

I remember watching the sports news on television the night it was announced that Hadl had been acquired for the Packers' five top draft choices the next two years. I was astounded at the price we had paid and called Pres. Olejniczak on the phone to inquire what he knew about it. He told me that he too had been watching television and that was the first he learned of the trade.

Mr. Quarterback Retires. Bart Starr hung it up as an active player after the 1971 season. He joined Devine's staff as an assistant coach for one year in 1972, the only winning season Devine had in his four years at the helm. Starr's wife Cherry shows the anguish of the moment, and Devine's expression seems to say, "What am I going to do now?" *Vern Biever photo.*

The Packer Legend

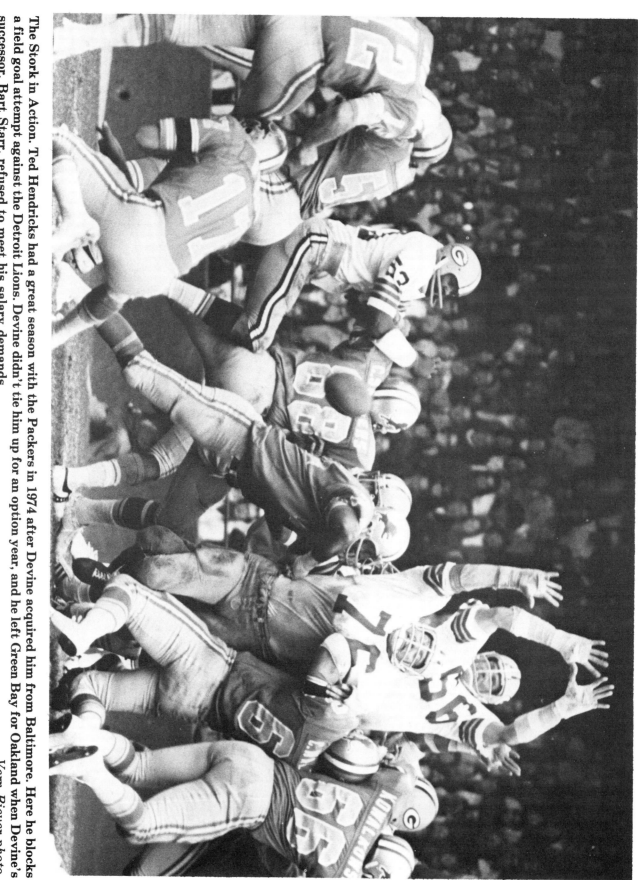

The Stork in Action. Ted Hendricks had a great season with the Packers in 1974 after Devine acquired him from Baltimore. Here he blocks a field goal attempt against the Detroit Lions. Devine didn't tie him up for an option year, and he left Green Bay for Oakland when Devine's successor, Bart Starr, refused to meet his salary demands.

Vern Biever photo.

The Packer Legend

Hadl Gets It Away. John Hadl barely got this pass off ahead of the Atlanta Falcons' Claude Humphrey's rush. There were 48,000 no shows at Atlanta for this game played in bitterly cold weather. It was Devine's last game, and the Packers lost, 10-7, and finished with a 6-8 record for the year. Devine's record for his four seasons in Green Bay was 25-27-4. *Vern Biever photo.*

The Packer Legend

Just Before the End. Devine's last game as Packer head coach was in Atlanta. He called Packer President Dominic Olejniczak from Atlanta and requested an immediate meeting to talk about his status with the Packers for 1975. The Packer Executive Committee decided quickly that they had had enough of Dan Devine and his mishandling of his authority as general manager. He was gone a week later. *Vern Biever photo.*

It had long been and still is the policy of the Packer Executive Committee not to dictate selections of playing personnel to the coaching staff, but previous coaches and general managers had always consulted the president of the organization if they were trading away future assets of the corporation, i.e., high draft choices. Devine had given up the first, second, and third choices for 1975 and first and second choices for 1976. As it turned out, Devine really mortgaged the future of the Packers for several years down the road in acquiring Hadl.

Another instance of poor judgment involved the re-signing of Brockington for the 1974 season after his three-year contract had expired. The World Football League had come into being that year, and a team known as the Chicago Fire acquired the rights in that league to dicker with Brockington. Devine pushed the panic button and told the Executive Committee that he simply had to have Brockington in his backfield that season at any price. The Packers wound up paying Brockington the most handsome salary they had ever paid a player and, in addition, gave him a three-year guaranteed contract, something they had never done before. Brockington was a total disappointment that season and the next two. He wound up being traded to Kansas City after his three-year contract ran out.

The Committee became more and more disenchanted with Devine as the 1974 season wore on. The Packers wound up winning only four games and losing 10. Devine still had a year to go on his five-year contract, and at the moment, the sentiment of the Committee seemed to be to let him finish it out. This was not to be, however.

The Packers wound up the season playing the Falcons in Atlanta, and that Sunday night, Devine called Pres. Olejniczak from Atlanta and said he wanted to meet with him when the team got home. He told Olejniczak he had to know what his status was for the 1975 season. Olejniczak told him that he would not be available that night but would be glad to meet with him the following morning.

He did so, and Devine reiterated that he had to know immediately what his status was with the Packers. Olejniczak informed him that the Committee had not discussed the subject, but that he would call the Committee together if Devine insisted on it.

Devine did so insist, and Olejniczak asked the Committee members to come to his home that Monday evening.

The Committee was reluctant to make such a critical decision on such short notice and decided to put the matter off until their regular meeting later that month, but Devine kept insisting to Olejniczak that he needed a decision immediately. So Olejniczak called the Executive Committee into special session, and we finally had had it with Dan Devine, deciding to pay him off for the fifth year of his contract.

As I recall now, I don't think we had any suspicions that Devine had something up his sleeve, but his intransigence about the following season cemented our opinion that we didn't want to go through another year with him in charge.

We met in Fred Trowbridge's office first thing that Saturday morning, and afterward Pres. Olejniczak and Trowbridge met with Devine and his attorney to arrange the legal details of paying him off for the final year of his contract. We had done this before. Olejniczak always insisted on arranging a clean break so there would be no legal entanglements hanging over afterward.

The four men shook hands on the deal, and Devine and his attorney left. It was only a minute later, however, when Devine returned and popped his head into Trowbridge's office, saying, "Oh, by the way, I am going to Notre Dame."

When I got to my office in Appleton, our sports editor told me that rumors had been circulating all morning that Devine was out with the Packers and was going to Notre Dame. Lee Remmel, Packer public relations chief, had established that the athletic director at South Bend had called a press conference for that afternoon.

He had the Notre Dame job in his pocket while he was negotiating to be paid off for another full year with the Packers.

So Devine took a year's salary from the Packers with him and became the head coach at Notre Dame. As most of you know, he went on again to have a distinquished career in college football at Notre Dame, reaching the pinnacle of the college game by guiding the Fighting Irish to a national championship in 1979. That success was galling to many Packer officials and fans, for Devine left the Packer team in extremely poor shape when he departed after the 1974 season.

When he retired from Notre Dame after the 1980 season, Devine said he was considering a return to professional football, but there was one thing for certain: it would never be with the Green Bay Packers.

The Think Tank. Adjoining City Stadium is the headquarters of the Green Bay Packers. The business offices are located here. Also here are the ticket office, film studio, film library, coaching and scouting staff offices, sophisticated computer equipment, locker rooms, training quarters, weight room, and a number of classrooms.

Giordana photo.

The Packer Legend

Chapter Eighteen

THE

OVERSEERS

The somewhat sudden departure of Dan Devine and the unpleasantness surrounding his leaving once again posed the question to Packer management of what the title "general manager" really meant. It was basically a misnomer.

I have related how the Executive Committee took over most management functions in Curly Lambeau's last few years in Green Bay and how they resolved at that point in time that future head coaches would not be elected to corporate office or have a vote in the management of the corporation.

Even though Vince Lombardi was the general manager as well as the head coach, he did not have a vote on the Board of Directors or on the Executive Committee. Phil Bengtson was the general manager in name only. Devine usurped authority he did not have when he traded away

five top draft choices to get quarterback John Hadl. He disposed of corporate assets without approval of the owners of those assets, and that eventually led to the complete break with the Executive Committee.

This small, close-knit group of officers and Directors has preferred over the years to operate in the background, leaving the publicity and kudos to the players and coaching staff. The Packers' business is putting a football team on the field. That is the job of the coaches and players. It takes financial resources to do so, and that is the job of the officers and Directors of the football corporation. I don't mind saying that they have not done such a bad job of doing so either. The Packers' cash reserves totalled some $15 million in 1981.

The football corporation is incorporated under

the laws of the State of Wisconsin as they apply to non-profit corporations. The *Articles of Incorporation* are rather standard in form, except for the unique provisions, outlined in an earlier chapter, dealing with the no-dividend policy and arrangements for disposition of assets in the unlikely event of the Packers going out of business.

The by-laws spell out the duties of the officers, the composition of the Board of Directors, and provide for the appointment by the Board of an Executive Committee which shall carry out the responsibilities of the Board at all times when the Board is not in session. The statutes provide that there are three functions that the Executive Committee cannot perform for the Board: election of officers, election of Directors to fill vacancies, and the declaration of dividends. The latter is a moot point as far as the Packers are

New Packer Prexy. Judge Robert Parins succeeded Olejniczak as president of the football corporation in May 1982. He has served on the Board since 1966 and the Executive Committee since 1979.

concerned, since the articles provide that no dividends can ever be paid. In all other matters, the Executive Committee has full and complete authority.

The Executive Committee consists of the four officers plus three additional Directors. Members are elected each year at the annual meeting of Directors.

The Executive Committee has provided the Packer corporation with the free talents of the community's best business and professional brains over the many years it has been in existence, dating back to 1923. With only one recent exception, officers and Executive Committee members serve without salary, and as a matter of fact, they have even paid for their own tickets to the games all these years. Only in the last few years have they been given two complimentary tickets to games in Green Bay but not even that for home games in Milwaukee.

Long-Time President. Dominic Olejniczak served as Packer president from 1958 until May of 1982 when he became chairman of the Board of Directors. He was mayor of Green Bay when first elected to the Packer board in 1950.

Ex-Player, Now Vice-President. Tony Canadeo was an active player for 10 seasons with time out for military service in the Army during World War II. He has served on the Board of Directors since 1955, as a member of the Executive Committee since 1958, and was elected vice-president in May 1982.

At various times in the development of the corporation, Executive Committee members played active roles in management and administrative functions.

Curly Lambeau was vice-president and general manager of the corporation, but he served on a part-time basis along with his insurance office secretary. At that time, the Executive Committee met every Monday noon to handle corporate affairs and had a number of sub-committees to assist Lambeau. There was a stadium committee which oversaw all matters relating to the grandstands and the playing field. Chief of Police H. J. (Tubby) Bero handled policing, ticket-takers, and ushers. The finance committee at that time consisted of the general managers of the two largest paper-making concerns in the city and several bankers.

When George Strickler was fired as publicity director at the end of the Lambeau regime, a former Packer great, Francis (Jug) Earp, was hired to handle that job, but since Jug had never written a press release in his life, I took over that job and spent several hours each day at the Packer office helping Earp.

When Gene Ronzani replaced Lambeau as coach, he was hired strictly as a coach and the Executive Committee at that point took over complete charge of management affairs. As pro football grew in size and stature, it became obvious that part-time volunteers could no longer handle these chores, and this led to a reorganization of the management structure in 1954. Another former Packer great, Verne Lewellen, was hired as a full-time business manager. As a matter of fact, it was Lewellen who then recommended hiring Lisle Blackbourn as head coach to succeed Ronzani.

Corporation Treasurer. John S. Stiles succeeded Fred W. Trowbridge as treasurer in 1981. He has been a Board member since 1958 and a member of the Executive Committee since 1980.

The Packer Legend

Veteran Member. John B. Torinus was elected to the Packer Board of Directors and Executive Committee in 1949 and became secretary of the corporation in 1955.

The Executive Committee gradually turned more responsibility over to Lewellen, and in his second year on the job, the corporation ended up in the black financially for the first time ever. This led to another reorganization in the late 1950s when the Committee was reduced in size to the present seven members and began meeting monthly rather than weekly.

It was at this point that Vince Lombardi came on the scene. The only condition under which he would accept the Green Bay job was if he was given total authority over football operations. He was made general manager as well as head coach, and he retained Lewellen as his business manager.

Recalling the position they had taken at the end of the Lambeau regime, however, the Board of Directors refused to make Lombardi a director or even an officer, and he often chafed under this situation. He represented the corporation at

league meetings but only as an aide to the president, Dominic Olejniczak.

Dominic Olejniczak was first elected to the Board of Directors while he was still serving as the mayor of Green Bay and at a time when the Packers realized they would have to do something about replacing the old City Stadium. Ole, as Olejniczak is called by those who know him, began putting together the plan of action to have the city build the Packers a new facility, but even more important, he was chairman of the search committee which brought Lombardi to Green Bay. He served as president longer than any predecessor, 23 years.

During most of those years, one of Olejniczak's principal jobs was financial manager of the corporation's assets, which are considerable. His background in real estate management well-equipped him for the job.

Long a Packer Backer. Jerry Atkinson became actively involved in "Backing the Pack" when he managed Green Bay's largest department store. He has served on the Board of Directors since 1950 and on the Executive Committee since 1958.

His predecessors were not always as fortunate. Their principal duty often revolved around trying to "beg, borrow or steal," as the saying goes, enough money to keep the corporation alive.

I have related how Lee Joannes loaned the club $6,000 to get them out of receivership and took the franchise as collateral. In the late 1940s, I recall walking over to the Kellogg-Citizens National Bank with Packer Pres. Emil Fischer when he personally guaranteed a $50,000 note to avert bankruptcy.

Olejniczak was named chief executive officer as well as president when Lombardi left Green Bay for Washington. The title of general manager was transferred to head coach Phil Bengtson, but Bengtson really didn't wish to become involved in corporate affairs.

Olejniczak was paid the handsome sum of $10,000 a year to assume those duties and he

Newest Member. Phil Hendrickson is the newest member of the Executive Committee, having been elected to that post in May 1982. He is president of the Krueger Metal Products Company in Green Bay.

hasn't had a raise to this day.

Dan Devine was also given the title of general manager as well as head coach, but Olejniczak continued to function as chief executive officer,

This arrangement broke down in the last year of Devine's tenure, however, to the point where there was little communication between the two. The John Hadl trade was an example. Devine consulted no one, not even Olejniczak, when he traded away five top draft choices over the next two years for the sore-armed quarterback.

Other violations of proper procedure cropped up after Devine left. When Bob Harlan started negotiating a new contract with MacArthur Lane, he found out through Lane's agent that Devine had given him a contract guaranteeing him a salary of $20,000 a year as a scout for ten years after Lane retired from football. There wasn't even a copy of the contract in the Packer office files.

Events like these have made Packer officers and directors more and more leery of turning over complete authority to a general manager. When Starr was given that title in addition to being named head coach in 1975, his

Recent Addition. John Fabry was elected to the Board of Directors in 1980, then to the Executive Committee in 1981.

Assistant to the President. Tom Miller played for the Packers in 1946 and became their publicity director in 1956. He now supervises all administrative functions as assistant to the president.

responsibilities were very carefully outlined in his employment contract.

The relieving of Starr of his duties as general manager in December of 1980 appeared to the news media and outsiders as a radical new departure in corporate management, but in reality it didn't mean that much. Starr really functioned only in a minor way as general manager. Olejniczak retained full authority as chief executive officer.

Under the mandate given the Committee by the Board of Directors at that meeting, the Committee formulated a comprehensive written plan of corporate responsibilities in early 1981 which was outlined to stockholders and Directors at the annual meeting in May.

The statement said in essence that considering the unique structure of the Packer corporation as a community enterprise, owned by some 1600 community stockholders, authority over corporate affairs simply cannot be turned over

to a hired general manager. That authority must rest with the elected officers of the corporation, headed by the president who is in fact the chief executive officer.

Pres. Olejniczak was given the additional title of Chairman of the Board by the Directors in October of 1981, and Vice-President Robert Parins was named chief executive officer. It was a prelude to Parins' election as president of the corporation at the annual meeting in May 1982. Subsequently, he retired as a circuit court judge for Brown County and became a full-time CEO of the Packers.

Along with Parins moving up, the Board of Directors elected Tony Canadeo as vice-president and Phil Hendrickson to the Executive Committee at the annual meeting in May 1982.

Judge Parins will be a forceful and thoughtful leader of the Packer organization. A long time professional associate and personal friend of the retiring president, he can be regarded as Dominic

Assistant for Personnel. Bob Harlan is the other assistant to the president, handling all personnel matters. It's his job to negotiate player contracts.

The Packer Legend

Olejniczak's protege and hand-picked successor. His judicial temperament and experience equips him uniquely well for the job as the Packer chief executive officer where he can listen out the opinions, advice, and counsel of the Directors and Executive Committee members, then make the necessary and sometimes tough decisions.

The president has two full-time administrative assistants. Bob Harlan handles all personnel matters, including player contracts, and Tom Miller handles all administrative duties, including ticket sales, stadium facilities, travel arrangements, office management, and public relations. Each has a full-time staff to carry out those various functions.

One other very important cog in the Packer management machine is Dick Corrick, the director of player personnel. His job is to find the best player talent available, whether from the college ranks through the NFL draft or through trades and free agent acquisitions.

Director of Player Personnel. Dick Corrick is the man who comes into focus every spring when the NFL draft is held. It's his job to evaluate the talent coming out of the colleges, then to make the best choices for the team.

The Green Bay Packers football corporation is a smooth-working organization, from the president and his assistants through the Executive Committee and the Board of Directors, the coaching staff and trainers, the publicity department headed up by Lee Remmel and the office people down to the men who keep Lambeau Field in top playing condition. All do their part to make the Packers a successful operation, both on the field and off.

The whole object of the Executive Committee, the president and his aides in managing the corporation's affairs is to provide the coaching staff with everything it needs to produce a representative football team in the National Football League. That takes money, and today it takes a lot of money.

The annual budget of the Packer corporation totals over $12 million. A huge portion of this is player salaries, which continue to increase every year. A single free agent who only comes in for a week of practice with the team and still gets released makes more than the entire 1919 team made for a whole season.

The Executive Committee oversees player contracts only in a general sense through the annual budget, and in the past, the Committee has been accused of being a little tight with the purse strings. It might be more appropriate to say that the Committee has been cautious in paying players because of the responsibility and accountability the Committee has to the Board of Directors, the stockholders, and Packer fans in general. However, in this age of escalated player salaries and multi-million dollar television revenues, the Committee is attempting to compete with any of the other 27 franchises in the NFL for the services of the best talent on the market. The best example of that is how the Packers obtained John Jefferson, the All-Pro wide receiver they picked up from the San Diego Chargers in 1981. Another example is how James Lofton's contract was negotiated that same year.

In the latest accounting, the corporation had a net worth in the neighborhood of $19 million. It isn't the wealthiest franchise in the NFL, but it is on solid financial footing, probably the most firm foundation it has ever been on since the team was founded in 1919.

Thus, the basic mission of the Board of Directors, the officers, and the Executive Committee is to safeguard those financial assets to insure that the Packer football franchise will always remain a viable one in Green Bay.

The Packer Legend

Miles of Tape. This will give you some idea of the amount and sizes of tape used by trainer Dominic Gentile on the average day, whether it is a practice or a game day. Trainers have to know more than just how to get the tape on and off the players. They are well-versed in human anatomy, physical therapy, and injury prevention and rehabilitation.

Vern Biever photo.

Chapter Nineteen

TELL ME

WHERE

IT HURTS

The Packers have only had three trainers in their 60-plus year history: Carl (Bud) Jorgenson, Dave Woodward, and Dominic Gentile. The man who holds the record for longevity is Bud Jorgenson. Although retired now, he is still one of the Packers greatest boosters at age 75 today.

Jorgenson actually started working for the Packers as a teenager in 1924. It was only a part-time position, mainly running errands for George Whitney Calhoun and helping to take care of the team's equipment. In those early days of Packer history, the Packers traveled mostly by train, of course, and sometimes by bus. It was Bud's job to make sure that all of the equipment went aboard with the players.

Gradually, Bud started taping some of the players, mainly at their instruction, before games and practices. By this time, many of the players

had played a considerable amount of college ball and were somewhat familiar with their taping requirements.

In 1935, the Packers hired a professional trainer. Dave Woodward was the trainer for the University of Minnesota and actually taught courses in training methods at that college.

According to Jorgenson, the greatest thing that happened in his career was the arrival of Woodward on the Green Bay scene, for Woodward immediately took Jorgenson in hand and began teaching him the trade. It was fortunate that he did because Woodward died suddenly of a heart attack in 1940, leaving Jorgenson as the head trainer.

Bud can sit and recount by the hour his experiences with the Packers going back to those early years. He remembers particularly the first time they played in New York, meeting the Giants in the Polo grounds in 1928. The Packers were billed as the big team from the little city out in Indian country. They leaped into national prominence that day when they beat the Gotham Giants, 7-0.

The first thing Monday morning after the game, Calhoun sent Bud on the subway to the office of Dr. Harry Marsh, who was the secretary of the Giants ball club, to pick up the Packers' check. Bud recalls watching people reading the newspaper on the subway and thinking to himself, "I wonder how many of them know where Green Bay is." When Bud picked up the check from Dr. Marsh, it was for the magnificent sum of $3,000, which was the Packers' share of the gate from the day before.

This was the Prohibition Era, and one of Bud's

Meet the Nautilus. This is the weight room at the Packer training headquarters next to Lambeau Field. It is equipped with the finest weightlifting equipment available, known as Nautilus machines. *Vern Biever photo.*

The Packer Legend

Team Physician. Dr. Eugene Brusky is the Packers' doctor. He is on duty at all Packer games and has regular office hours in the Packer training room during the week. *Vern Biever photo.*

The Packer Legend

sideline jobs was to make sure there was a goodly supply of "Ma Kline's moonshine" secreted among the baggage. Ma Kline ran a saloon out on the Cedar Creek road north of Green Bay, and she made the best moonshine in the territory.

Bud recalls when the Packers played in the first ever All-Star game in 1929. They had won the National Football League Championship for the first time that year and were meeting a team of All-Stars from the rest of the League in Memphis. They took the early morning train from Green Bay to Chicago, and Johnny Blood started working on the moonshine the first thing that morning. By the time they got to the old Illinois Central Station in Chicago, Blood was rolling in his usual fine style, and after they had boarded the train for Memphis, the conductor came to Curly Lambeau and said, "You have got to do something about that player of yours." Blood had taken a knife and cut the vein in his wrist and he was dipping his finger in the blood and had painted a sign which read: "I am the famous Johnny Blood." And to make matters worse, he was parading the sign up and down the passenger cars. It was to be an all-day trip, and Curly was not quite sure what to do about Blood. Lambeau learned that there was an empty sleeping car at the end of the train, so he arranged with the conductor to put his drunken player to bed in one of the berths with orders not to let Blood out of it until they got to Memphis, which they did close to midnight.

In those days, the trainer's duties were pretty much limited to taping up the players before practice or a game, but gradually as standards improved in the NFL, Jorgy found himself with more and more to do.

The Packers made a great acquisition in 1953 when Bud persuaded Verne Lewellen, the general manager, to hire the late Dad Braisher as their equipment man. Braisher had just retired after 30 years of coaching football and basketball at DePere High School, and he also was a former manual training instructor. So he was ideal for the Packer job. In no time at all, he constructed various shelves and lockers for the equipment and had the place looking neat as a pin.

Braisher also had the facility of serving as a father confessor to many of the players. He was a quiet, almost bashful man. In later years when Vince Lombardi appeared on the scene, he and Braisher became the greatest of close personal friends.

I asked Bud to give me his impression of Lombardi, and he did so in very few words.

"Everybody hated his guts," Bud said, "but they all respected him."

Jorgenson went on to say that working with Lombardi was the greatest thing that ever happened to him in his life. Lombardi taught him what discipline really means. "Lombardi would bawl you out for almost nothing at all once a week on a regular basis just to make sure he had your attention."

He said that Lombardi very seldom complimented you on a job well done in the belief that it was what you were being paid for. But just slip up once and he would come down on you like a ton of bricks.

Dominic Gentile, who had been the football coach at West DePere High School, began working as the assistant trainer under Jorgenson in 1961 and became head trainer when Jorgenson retired in 1970. A visit with Gentile in the Packer training quarters today is a far cry from those memories of Bud Jorgenson.

Gentile explains that the training staff has two primary jobs: the first being to aid in the rehabilitation of injured players, and the second to prevent injuries as much as possible. Detailed medical records are kept of each player, and detailed reports are made of each injury situation to the National Athletic Injury Reporting System. That agency was hired by the National Football League to conduct a comprehensive study into player injuries, specifically how they occur and how they might be prevented. There is a similar research project also going on at Stanford University.

Gentile works under treatment prescriptions from the team physician when handling injured players. Five different modalities are used in hastening the healing process: ultrasound, orthotron, diathermy, galvanic, and whirlpool baths. When the player's injury has begun to heal, he is then put through a prescribed program of exercise and weightlifting to build up the injured muscles.

I have personal knowledge of the completeness of Gentile's treatment programs.

About 12 years ago, I had both of my hip joints replaced with stainless steel total hips. I had been on crutches for eight years with a severe case of osteoarthritis in both hip joints, actually to the point were the joints were practically fused. Obviously, the very large muscles which activate the joints were badly deteriorated. It was those muscles that I had to rebuild if I was going to resume an active life.

I had begun a physical therapy program in the hospital, but upon release, I went to Gentile and asked him to design a complete program of rehabilitation for me. This was, of couse, right up his ally.

The surgery and hospital stay was in February and March, and by the first of June, I threw away the crutches.

Gentile has figured out that he uses about 200 miles of tape in any given season. On game days, he and an assistant begin taping the 45 active players at 8:30 in the morning, and they usually finish just before the pre-game warm ups around 12:20 p.m.

One of Gentile's most important duties obviously is to get out on the field to an injured player as rapidly as possible and first determine whether the services of the team doctor are needed or not. The doctor is always on the sidelines and accompanies the team to all of its games. With his wealth of experience, Gentile

Packer Trainer. Dominic Gentile became assistant trainer under Bud Jorgenson in 1961, then succeeded Jorgenson as head trainer in 1971 when Jorgenson retired. *Packers file photo.*

can diagnose the normal injury situation rather rapidly, and if possible the player is assisted to the sidelines as soon as he is able. In serious situations, the player is taken immediately to the locker room, where x-ray equipment is available if the doctor needs it.

The training room is actually equipped like a small hospital so that most injury situations can be taken care of by the team doctor right there.

The trainer is also the right-hand advisor to the coaching staff on the condition of any given player at any given time, and the question of whether a player is ready or will be ready to play in a given game is obviously of great importance to the coaching staff.

The profession of professional football team trainer has come a long way since Bud Jorgernson's career started back in the 1920s, but Gentile will tell you that they are still learning how to prevent injuries and how to hasten the rehabilitation of injured players. Through the research being carried on by the NFL, great improvements have been made in players' equipment to minimize the danger of injury, and all the efforts of the league, team doctors, coaching staffs, and trainers are being directed toward the elimination of as many injuries as possible.

As any player who has suffered an injury that has prevented him from performing up to his usual standard can tell you, the team's trainer is an integral part of the organization. He is almost a 12th man on the field. Without him and his knowledge, many players would have their careers shortened or ended long before their time.

Hard Work Pays Off

When Lynn Dickey had his leg broken by the Los Angeles Rams, there was doubt that he would fully recover and resume his NFL career. Dickey did recover, however, and a large part of that rejuvenation was due to Packer trainer Dominic Gentile. He put Dickey through a rugged rehabilitation course that got the sure-armed quarterback back on the playing field.

Gentile's most recent challenge has been running back Eddie Lee Ivery who has suffered two knee injuries. Ivery has been working hard under Gentile's instruction, but only time will tell whether he can come back.

President Dedicates Hall of Fame. President Gerald Ford came to Green Bay in 1976 to dedicate the Packer Hall of Fame. Looking on are Bart Starr, left, and Tom Hutchison, right, president of the Hall of Fame corporation.

Lefebvre photo.

The Packer Legend

Chapter Twenty

WHERE

LEGENDS

LIVE ON

A visit to the Packer Hall of Fame in Green Bay is a must for anyone visiting Green Bay for other purposes. It is worth a trip in itself to see this wonderful, moving story of the history of the Green Bay Packers.

The Hall of Fame had humble beginnings, but it has since moved into its own building adjacent to the Veterans Memorial Arena across Oneida Street from City Stadium, Lambeau Field. That building has recently been doubled in size to accommodate the large number of visitors who come to the Hall on a year-around basis.

Back in 1964, the Green Bay Visitor and Convention Bureau decided to put a portable information center in the Lambeau Field parking lot. Some 10,000 visitors were given information on the Green Bay area that summer, and almost every last person sought more information about

the Green Bay Packers. This motivated the Bureau to explore the possibilities of creating a Packer Hall of Fame.

Coach Vince Lombardi was one of the prime movers in getting the project off the ground. Mayor Donald Tilleman of Green Bay, Bill Brault, and Harry Huebner of the Bureau met in Lombardi's office with Lombardi and Packer President Dominic Olejniczak and requested permission to construct and operate a Packer Hall of Fame in the arena. The only space available was in a lower concourse, and that was only available during the summer months.

But the Hall of Fame opened on May 15, 1967, and as many as 60,000 people visited it that summer. Almost immediately, the Bureau set out on the task of building a permanent Hall of Fame building because of the terrific interest

Packer Hall of Fame. This is the entrance to the only hall of fame devoted to one pro football team. It is open daily from 10 a.m. to 5 p.m. every day of the year except Christmas. The Hall was originated in the 1950s and was first housed in a concourse at the arena. It features a fine gift shop, several exhibits on individual players and coaches in Packer history, and participatory exhibits that include testing your skill at place-kicking. In the gift shop, a visitor can purchase almost every book ever written about the Packers as a team or about the men who have played or coached for the Packers.

The Packer Legend

shown in the meager exhibits in the arena those first few summers.

Brown County, the Packer corporation, and Packer fans all combined to raise the $350,000 needed to erect the building and equip it with exhibits. Over 5,000 individuals bought $25-lifetime memberships, and major business sponsors came up with over $160,000 to provide the major exhibits.

President Gerald Ford presided at the cornerstone laying in April of 1976, and the new Hall of Fame opened officially to the public on July 12th of that year.

Previously, the citizens group responsible for establishing the Hall of Fame had begun an annual ceremony at which Packer greats were selected for induction. The first banquet was held in mid-1969 and was an instant success. The committee adopted a five-year plan for selecting inductees, taking 10 players from the 1920s the first year, 10 from the 1930s the next, and so on until the 60-year history of the Packers had been covered. After that, the number was reduced to five a year, with one from an old-timer's list,

several from later years, and at least one non-player who has contributed significantly to the Packers. Jack Vainisi, the Packers' first talent scout, was honored posthumously in that category in 1982. The list of inductees along with plaques representing each of them is one of the principal exhibits in the Hall.

The Hall of Fame building was doubled in size in 1981 when the Packers came up with another $150,000 contribution, and the Hall of Fame itself was able to raise another $250,000 for the addition to the building and the new exhibits.

The Hall of Fame is far more than just a collection of old jerseys and helmets and pictures. It features a large number of audio-visual exhibits. In the original Hall, there were 21 35-millimeter projectors and four 16-millimeter ones. In the new addition, there are 15 more 35-millimeters and three video tape projectors.

The visitor is first ushered into the Locker Room, a small theater, where he witnesses a 30-minute multi-media presentation of the history of the Packers from 1919 through 1976.

Hall of Fame Exhibit. Marie Lombardi left all of Vince's collection of football memorabilia to the Packer Hall of Fame. At one point, she threatened to give everything away if the Hall was not given a permanent home of its own. This is his picture gallery.

The Packer Legend

Dramatic lighting effects highlight most of the exhibits. The effects are achieved by maintaining almost complete darkness throughout the display area and controlling the lighting individually within each exhibit. Using this technique, the building interior is de-emphasized, and each exhibit takes on a personality all its own. Some of these exhibits offer a close-up look at present Packer players, their families, and the coaches. For the weekend football widow, there are recorded interviews with the wives of Packer players, and for the card-collecting enthusiasts, there is a special projector that lets them call up their favorites from among the 74 inductees into the Hall of Fame. These are not only players but include other individuals who have contributed over the years to the building of this sports legend.

Vince Lombardi's widow, Marie, carried on the campaign to build the Hall of Fame after Lombardi died. A collection of 17 crates of his personal memorabilia had been stored for several years in the vault at the Peoples Marine Bank. At one point, Marie threatened to remove the collection from Green Bay and disperse it elsewhere if the Packers and the county did not get going on building a permanent home for the Hall. This collection now dominates the Lombardi Room in the Hall of Fame.

Visitors can also test their skill at kicking field goals or their passing accuracy in two of the participatory exhibits. The Hall of Fame is

History of Equipment Told. Old and modern shoes, helmets, and footballs form another exhibit in the Packer Hall of Fame. The Hall not only tells the history of the Green Bay Packers but also presents the past of the National Football League in general. The average annual attendance of 65,000 visitors attests to the popularity of football and the Packers.

The Packer Legend

Canadeo and Michalske Honored. Tony Canadeo's award for having surpassed 1,000 yards in 1952 is among the items in this collections honoring him. Mementos from the career of "Iron Man" Mike Michalske highlight his display.

designed to be an attraction for the entire family, mother included.

There is a very fine gift shop in the Hall of Fame. All sorts of Packer memorabilia can be found there; everything from T-shirts to Packer football jerseys, from jewelry to ashtrays, blankets to books, including this one as well as every book ever written by or about a Packer player or coach or the team. Don G. Herbel is the man in charge of the Hall of Fame, and according to him, the Hall carries the largest line of Packer mementos in the country.

At a recent luncheon with James A. Van Matre, Director of Tourism for the Green Bay Area Visitor & Convention Bureau, I learned some rather amazing facts about the Hall, facts which point out its popularity with Packer fans of all ages. Over 65,000 people visit the Hall every year. During the winter months, January through March, when Green Bay is at its coldest, the Hall still attracts an average of 35 people each week day and 200 each Saturday and Sunday. As the weather warms up in the spring, those numbers increase weekly until around July 4th when it begins growing to its peak. With the football season, it really explodes, reaching proportions that make it the number one attraction in northeastern Wisconsin.

The Packer Hall of Fame is open 364 days of the year from 10 a.m. to 5 p.m. daily. The only day it isn't open is Christmas.

As halls of fame and museums go, the Packer Hall of Fame is the only one in the world dedicated to reviving the memories of one professional sports team. Its uniqueness equals that of the team for which it was established. As an entertainment medium, the Packer Hall is an excellent value, making it well worth a trip to Green Bay anytime of the year.

Starr's Jersey Retired. Jersey No. 15 is part of this historical exhibit in the Packer Hall of Fame. Don Hutson's No. 14, Tony Canadeo's No. 3, and Paul Hornung's No. 5 are the only other Packer jerseys to be retired.

Bart Starr Named New Packers Coach-GM

By CLIFF CHRISTL
Press-Gazette Sports Writer

"To every man there comes in his lifetime, that special moment when he is figuratively tapped on the shoulder and offered the chance to do a very special thing, unique to him and fitted to his talents; what a tragedy if that moment finds him unprepared or unqualified for the work which would be his finest hour."

Borrowing that quote from Winston Churchill, Bart Starr opened his first press conference as general manager and head coach of the Green Bay Packers. He was officially introduced, this morning as the Packers' eighth coach in the 56-year history of the franchise by President Dominic Olejniczak at the team's Lombardi Ave. office building.

Starr will be in complete charge of the football operations and operate with a three-year contract, which is all he asked for.

Starr, who toiled in a Packer uniform for 16 years, said, "I'm absolutely ecstatic about this opportunity. I'm extremely thrilled and

very honored . . . but I'm not awed by it."

He asked the fans for their prayers and patience, and then pledged to them, "Our number one objective will be to create a very solid front. We'll have a fresh start built around cooperation and unity. In order to build anything successful for a period of time it has to be built on a rock solid foundation."

Because of his "great love affair with the Green Bay Packers," Starr admitted he's been hurt by the way the franchise's image has been tarnished in recent years.

"I've been a little disappointed the last few years — travelling around the country — to see the respect somewhat slip for the Green Bay Packers," he said.

Obviously alluding to his lack of experience as a coach, Starr said, "I'm not as qualified as I'd like to be, but I'm willing."

Monday will be his first official day on the job and he implied his first items of priority will be preparing for the college draft and hiring his staff.

He said he hasn't given much thought to

assistant coaches, although he would hope Dave Hanner remains on as a defensive aide. "I'd certainly like for him to stay," Starr said.

Otherwise, he added, "One of the things I hope to do is surround ourselves with assistant coaches or associate coaches from diverse backgrounds."

The front office structure he said would be "designed to allow us to concentrate more on football." He explained that Bob Harlan, assistant general manager, and Tom Miller, assistant to the general manager, consequently, will be given added responsibilities.

Starr wouldn't indicate whether or not Chuck Lane, former public relations director of the Packers and now a business employe of his, will rejoin the organization.

He also said he was unqualified at this point to make an overall evaluation of the team's personnel. Nor would he comment specifically on Dan Devine's prediction the Packers would win 10 games next year. "I only want to talk about things in the past that will help us in the future," he said.

Hadl Calls Pick Great

Beginning with quarterback John Hadl, most of the Green Bay Packer players are greeting the news that Bart Starr will be their next head coach with enthusiasm.

"I think it's great," said the 34-year old Hadl. "He's obviously a highly qualified individual who knows the game of football. I'll be looking forward to playing with him. That's great.

"I don't think there is any doubt we'll have a good relationship and get this thing going in a positive direction. I

know we'll have a perfectly workable situation."

Hadl said that he has met Starr on a number of occasions and they've always been on friendly terms.

"What can I say?" wide receiver Jon Staggers rhetorically asked. "It sounds good. He's certainly knowledgeable about the game, that's for sure."

Clarence Williams, a teammate of Starr's in 1970 and '71, said, "I never heard anybody speak negatively of Bart — not any of the ballplayers."

Williams added, "To me, I think he's going to be a great coach, just like he was a ballplayer. I have confidence in him as a coach because I know what he did for us the year we won the divisional championship. I think he's the man. He's the best man available."

Williams agreed with those who contend Starr played an extremely influential part as an offensive assistant in the Packers' successful '72 season. "I think he played a big role," Williams said. "He knows more about the offensive game than those other coaches did. I think he had a tremendous influence on us winning that year."

Quarterback Jerry Tagge, who received his tutoring from Starr as a rookie in '72 said, "I think he's a great choice. Our defense has a great future, and it's in the offensive area that Bart is most capable and that's the area I think he'll be concentrating on."

Appraising it from an individual standpoint, "I think I'm in a good situation. My attitude is that I'm going in shooting for the number one job."

Coach Bart Starr

P-G Photo by Ken Behrend

Pack Hitched to Starr From '56 Through '72

Bart Starr's ties with the Packers date back to 1956, when he was drafted in the 17th round after an inauspicious college career at the University of Alabama.

After serving a three-year apprenticeship under two head coaches and a handful of more experienced quarterbacks, Starr started the final four games in 1959, Vince Lombardi's first season as coach.

Then in 1960, Starr established himself as the regular and led the Packers to the Western Division championship, although they lost in the National Football League championship game to Philadelphia.

Thereafter, he became recognized as one of the greatest quarterbacks of all time. Certainly he was one of — if not the — winningest quarterbacks in the history of the game.

He led the Packers to world championships in 1961, '62, '65, '66 and '67.

In the latter years of his ca-

are: He was selected the all-time Packer quarterback in a Press-Gazette poll of the fans in 1969, the 50th year of the NFL. He was the league's leading passer in 1962, '64 and '66. He was the NFL's MVP in '66. He was the MVP in the Super Bowl in '67 and '68.

He played in the Pro Bowl in '61, '62, '63 and '66. And he still holds a host of league passing records. His 57.42 completion percentage for a career is still the best in the NFL. And he holds the mark for passes thrown without an interception, 294.

Starr Commands Respect

When Bart Starr walks into a room, the atmosphere changes.

People pause in mid-conversation. The noise becomes a hush. Heads turn. There's a new excitement. People feel his presence.

Overly dramatic?

Maybe. But if you have ever been in a room when Bart dropped in, you know the scene.

He commands respect. He doesn't demand it. But his very appearance commands him.

Even now. Years have his glory days as the on-field leader of the championship Green Bay Packers, he has retained his legion of admirers, perhaps even increased.

The aura about him is one of those qualities few men have. It's an unexplainable thing but it's there. It says you must respect this man.

Lombardi had it. He had it in his glare and in his walk and in his voice. he radiated authority. You didn't have to like him but you felt him and, whether through fear or admiration, you had to respect him.

Some of this has passed on to Starr. Indeed much of it has. Not the fear so much as the admiration. The glare isn't there. Neither is the walk. Neither is the voice. And authority doesn't radiate but it is there. You just know it is there.

Unlike Lombardi's aura, Starr's is not natural. It is acquired. It has been earned through a diligence and self-discipline that has become a classic story in American sports. As Starr matured from a

OUT OF BOUNDS?

By Len Wagner
Press-Gazette Sports Editor

shaky rookie to a mature leader, recognized as a man at the epitome of his chosen profession, that aura grew with him.

Perhaps because of the manner in which this aura was earned, though performance rather than imparting fear, it may be even stronger than that which belonged to Lombardi.

Unlike Lombardi, Starr is likeable. He may not be as perfect as his reputation would lead you to believe, but he is class. That's the word pros like to use for a man they respect.

And respect is the most vital ingredient in leadership. Don't make the mistake of underestimating it in light of his relatively soft speech and pleasant personality.

Starr has it.

He is a leader.

Unseld, Hayes Top Bucks in OT

MILWAUKEE (AP) — The Milwaukee Bucks were too busy writing a traffic ticket against Elvin Hayes, and Wes Unseld was allowed to park overtime.

Unseld tied the score 99-99 in overtime Monday to pave the way to Washington's 106-103 National Basketball Association victory over the Bucks.

Hayes' two baskets in the final minute were decisive, but it was Unseld's performance that left the Bucks exasperated with themselves.

tello said Unseld, 6-foot-7 and 245 pounds, determined the outcome with his three-tip domination of the show.

"We figured Unseld wouldn't be shooting, so we had Kareem go out and put pressure on Hayes," Costello said. "That meant Warner had to do the best he could with Unseld underneath."

"It just didn't work out in our favor," Abdul-Jabbar said.

Unseld, converting 50 per cent of his field shots, finished with 16 points. Bullet coach K.C. Jones called him "just a

Detroit Gives Forzano Three Year Contract

Pro Football Notes —

Lions Coach Rick Forzano has been given a new three year contract . . . Las Vegas oddsmakers favor Oakland by six points over Pittsburgh and Minnesota by four points over the Rams . . . An attorney says the NFL can save its draft from the Kapp Decision by putting a one or two year limit on the amount of time a team is allowed to keep rights to a player without actually signing him.

Rommie Loudd, managing general partner of the WFL Florida Blazers, has been arrested on charges of embezzl-

Starr Record

STARR'S NFL RECORDS
Career Passing Efficiency
First — 57.42 per cent, 1956-71. (1,808-3,149)
Season Passing Efficiency
Third — 64.74 per cent, 1966. (109-171)
Fewest Interceptions, Season
First (tie) — 3, 1966.
Most Consecutive Passes, None Intercepted
First — 294, 1964-65

Career
Lowest Percentage-Interceptions
Third — 4.28 per cent, 1956-71. (138-3,149)
Lowest Percentage Season Interceptions
Second — 1.20 per cent, 1966. (93-171)
Second — 1.47 per cent, 1966. (4-272)
NFL CHAMPIONSHIP GAME RECORDS
Most Passes Attempted
First — 142, (83 completions), 6 games
Most Passes Completed
Second — 83, (142 attempts), 6 games
Passing Efficiency, Career
Second — 58.5 per cent, (19-28), 1966. Green Bay vs. Dallas
Passing Efficiency, Game
Second — 1.060, 6 games
Most Touchdown Passes, Career
First — 9, 6 games
Most Touchdown Passes, Game
Second (tie) — 4, 1966, Green Bay vs. Dallas
Fewest Passes Intercepted, Career
First (tie) — 1, (142 attempts), 6 games
Attempts Without Interception, Game
First — 34, 1960, Green Bay vs. Philadelphia
Consecutive Attempts Without Interception
Second (tie) — 6 games, 1960-61, 1961
SUPER BOWL RECORDS
Passing Yards, Game
First — 250 yards, 1967, Green Bay vs. Oakland (Super Bowl I)

We Wish You A

PART V

THE

LONG

ROAD

BACK

1975 - 1982

Starr Faces Press. It was a happy occasion when Bart Starr faced the press for the first time after his selection as head coach in late 1974.

The Packer Legend

Chapter Twenty-One

THE

PEOPLE'S

CHOICE

The Packer Executive Committee did not pick Bart Starr as head coach and general manager when Dan Devine suddenly left in December 1974. Packer fans did. A quiet conspiracy had been building for some time in the latter part of the 1974 season to draft Starr for the head coaching job, and the campaign came out into the open in full force within hours after Devine's resignation was made public.

Chuck Lane, the publicity chief when Devine became the head coach, didn't hit it off with Devine. He resigned and promptly went to work for Starr who, in addition to other business interests, headed a firm known as Bart Starr Enterprises which specialized in the sale of Packer souvenirs, things like Packer watches, pennants, and so forth. Lane was quietly putting together the campaign to promote Starr to head

coach during the latter part of the 1974 season.

The Packer Executive Committee interviewed two people for the job: Dave Hanner, the long-time defensive coach and former defensive star of the Packers; and Starr. They felt they owed it to Hanner to at least give him consideration in view of his long service as a player and as an assistant coach.

Starr's presentation at his interview was impressive. He handed out typewritten brochures, which had been prepared by Lane, outlining his qualifications and also a rather complete plan of action if he were named to the job. There was really little the Executive Committee could do but confirm the desire of 99.9 percent of the Packer fans who were clamoring for Starr. Bart made the situation easier when he told the Executive Committee

Starr's First Quarterback. Starr inherited John Hadl as his number one quarterback when he took over in 1975. Dan Devine had given away five top draft choices to get Hadl, and the sore-armed passer only played two years in Green Bay.

Vern Biever photo.

that he would hire Hanner as his top assistant in charge of co-ordinating the defense.

The signing of Starr to a three-year contract as head coach and general manager came on December 24, 1974. There couldn't have been a nicer Christmas present for Packer fans. Starr issued a statement asking for "the prayers and patience of Packer fans everywhere; we will earn everything else."

Starr inherited the mess which Devine had left. For quarterback, he had the sore-armed John Hadl for whom Devine had traded away five top draft choices over the next two years. He was backed up by Jerry Tagge, the Green Bay West and Nebraska star who had been drafted by Devine, and Jack Concannon, a veteran quarterback acquired by Starr soon after he took over. He did have John Brockington, MacArthur

Lane, and Barty Smith as three big running backs, and Chester Marcol for place-kicking, the league's leading scorer in 1974. But Brockington had peaked several years before that, and Lane and Barty Smith were also getting on in their careers.

One of the first tough decisions that Starr had to make concerned the very talented linebacker Ted Hendricks, whom Devine had acquired from Baltimore in a trade in 1974. Typical of Devine's handling of player contracts, Hendricks only had a one-year contract and was a free agent coming up for 1975. Starr refused to meet his contract demands, and Hendricks was picked up as a free agent by the Oakland Raiders. He went on to star with that team and was one of the main factors in their winning Super Bowls XI and XV in 1977 and 1981. Starr later admitted that letting Hendricks get away was one of his worst mistakes. It was a case of standing pat on a principle and losing a game-breaking performer.

Starr put together the nucleus of a very fine coaching staff, however. In addition to Hanner, he brought in John Meyer as defensive coach,

The Stork. Ted Hendricks played for the Packers only part of Dan Devine's last season. He was a free agent when Starr took charge, and Starr refused to give him a no-cut contract, so he went to Oakland and led them to two NFL titles. *Vern Biever photo.*

Steady Linebacker. Jim Carter wasn't very popular with Packer fans when he replaced Ray Nitschke as middle linebacker in the early 1970s, but he was well established in that position when Starr took over.

his old friend Zeke Bratkowski as quarterback coach, and the former Packer star, Lew Carpenter, as receiver coach.

As a result of the Hadl trade, Starr had no number one pick in the 1975 draft, so he took a tackle by the name of Bill Bain as an alternate second choice, Willard Harrell as an extra third choice, and Steve Luke in the fourth round. From that initial draft, Luke was the only player to last with the club for any length of time.

Bart lost his first four ball games before nipping the Dallas Cowboys, 19-17, then lost four more before mauling the New York Giants, 40-14, and the Bears, 28-7. There were two more losses before the Packers finished the season on an up note by defeating the Atlanta Falcons, 22-13. Winning three of their last five provided reason for hope, even though the Pack had only a 4-10 record on the season.

One of Starr's initial problems, probably attributable to his lack of experience, was that he got rid of a number of players whose character he thought left something to be desired. Unfortunately, he was unable to replace these people as fast or as quickly as he thought he could, and from his first season on, he suffered from a serious lack of depth in key positions on both offense and defense.

Starr became convinced in that first season, however, that he needed a quality quarterback, and in April of 1976, he swung a trade with the Houston Oilers, bringing Lynn Dickey to the Packers in exchange for Hadl, cornerback Ken Ellis, and several minor draft choices.

Dickey was a third round draft choice from Kansas State in 1971 and had understudied Dan Pastorini at Houston, but he sat out the entire 1972 season with a dislocated hip. Dickey moved immediately into the number one spot with the Packers in 1976 and was off to a good start in that position when he suffered a shoulder separation in game No.10 in Chicago, requiring surgery and sidelining him for the rest of the year.

Dickey's career to date with the Packers has been one of continually overcoming serious injuries. He suffered a broken leg on the last play of the game against the Rams in Milwaukee in November of 1977, and sat out the rest of season and all of 1978. In fact, he did not regain the number one quarterback spot until the last three games of 1979, climaxing a long period of rehabilitation after three separate operations on his leg.

The trade for Dickey started looking good the fourth week into the 1976 season. The Packers lost their first three games, then turned it around in the next three, beating the Detroit Lions, 24-14, the expansion Seattle Seahawks, 27-20, and the Philadelphia Eagles, 28-13. A narrow defeat to the Super Bowl-bound Raiders, 18-14, was considered a moral victory. Then the Lions got some revenge, defeating the Packers, 27-6. Another win, this one over the New Orleans Saints, 32-27, gave the Pack a 4-5 record, and there was reason to hope for a .500 season.

Then Dickey suffered his first injury as a

Middleton Sweeps. Terdell Middleton ran for over 1,000 yards and helped the Packers to a winning season in 1978. Blockers Barty Smith (33), Derrel Gofourth (57), and Tim Stokes (76) lead him around end in the famous Packer sweep.
Vern Biever photo.

The Packer Legend

Packer, and the Bears pulled off a 24-13 win over the Pack. Dickey's leadership and arm were sorely missed in the next two games as the Pack lost narrow encounters with the Minnesota Vikings and the Bears, each by a touchdown. Another loss to the Vikings and a season-ending win over the Falcons gave Starr a 5-9 record for his second year at the helm, and there was room for optimism among Packer fans for the 1977.

Starr said all along that he would build the new Packer team on the draft, and after he got over the penalties from the Hadl trade, he started to pick up some quality ballplayers in 1977. Having two first round draft choices that year, he chose two defensive ends: Mike Butler from Kansas and Ezra Johnson from Morris Brown. He picked up a fine offensive tackle, Greg Koch from Arkansas, in the second round and running back Terdell Middleton from Memphis State in the third round. In the seventh round, he got another offensive lineman, Derrel Gofourth from Oklahoma State, and in the eighth round, he took quarterback David Whitehurst from Furman.

In 1978 his first round choice was the fine wide receiver from Stanford, James Lofton, and in the next two rounds, he picked up two linebackers, John Anderson from Michigan and Mike Hunt from Minnesota. He added linebacker Mike Douglas from San Diego State in the fifth round.

The addition of these quality ballplayers started to make itself felt in the 1977 season. When Dickey went down with a broken leg on the last play of the Ram game, Whitehurst took over as the quarterback, starting the next game against the Washington Redskins. He gave it his all and showed that he had a future in the NFL as the Packers lost a squeaker, 10-9. He lost his next start, 13-6, to the Vikings, then slipped past the Lions, 10-9. Another loss to the Bears, 21-10, was followed by a final game win over the San Francisco 49ers, 16-14. Winning two of their last three gave Starr another 4-10 season, which could easily have been 6-8 if Dickey had been able to complete the year.

With Dickey still out all of the 1978 season recovering from his broken leg, Whitehurst was thrust into the starting post. The other players Starr drafted in 1977-78 began showing their talents as the Packers won six of their first seven games, losing only to the powerful Oakland Raiders, 28-3. The Packers rattled off wins against the Lions, 13-7; the Saints, 28-17; the San Diego Chargers, 24-3; the Lions again, 35-14; the Bears, 24-14; and the Seahawks, 45-28. A win

over the Tampa Bay Buccaneers, 9-7, after a loss to the Vikings, 21-7, guaranteed the Pack a winning season.

With their record standing at 7-2, the Packers looked like a sure thing for the playoffs. Everyone connected with the Packers and the fans were certain their trust and faith in Bart Starr had paid off. The Pack was back!

Then the roof fell in. The Packers lost five of their last seven games, only beating the second-year Bucs, 17-7, and tying the Vikings, 10-10. They were finally eliminated from the playoff picture on the last day of the season when the Rams whipped them, 31-14, in Los Angeles. A lack of depth caused the second half collapse as Starr's fourth season ended up at 8-7-1, however, it was the Packers first winning year since Devine had taken them to the playoffs in 1972.

Terdell Middleton wound up as only the fourth running back in Packer history to exceed 1,000 yards in a season, gaining 1,116 yards in 284 carries. His play startled the entire National Football League, and there was once again hope for the next year.

Packer fans began to have visions of more winning seasons after that fine performance in the early going of 1978. Another draft and a year of experience for the young players figured to give the Packers a real shot at the playoffs in 1979.

Then Starr startled the football world by firing Dave Hanner as his defensive co-ordinator during the 1978 Christmas holidays. He also discharged Chuck Lane as publicity director. He did not elaborate on his reasons in either case. There was a further blow in early 1979 when Bill Curry, the offensive line coach, left to become head coach at his alma mater, Georgia Tech.

Losing Curry became a minor matter, however, compared to the injury jinx that struck Packer running backs in the 1979 season. One after another, all of Starr's starting backs went out for the season with knee injuries.

It began with first round draft choice, Eddie Lee Ivery from Georgia Tech, in the opening game of the season with the Bears in Chicago when he twisted a knee and required surgery. One after the other, Barty Smith and Steve Atkins also required knee surgery, and Terdell Middleton was out most of the year with a series of ailments. Walt Landers had suffered knee problems in 1978 and missed the first half of the 1979 season.

To replace these players, Starr picked up

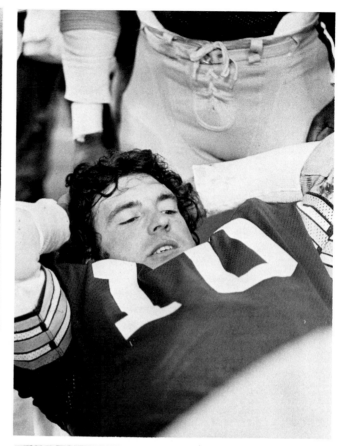

What Now? The concern on Bart Starr's face is quite evident as he sees his starting quarterback go down hard on the last play of the game against the Rams in November 1978. Dickey suffered a broken leg which caused him to miss the rest of that season and all of 1979. He tries to hide his agony as he is carried off the field on a stretcher. David Whitehurst was a rookie when Dickey went down for the count. He started the next game against Washington and was the starter the next year. *Vern Biever photos.*

Sammy Lee Johnson and Ricky Patton as free agents in mid-season, but the injury jinx wasn't limited to players who started the season in Green Bay. Johnson lasted one play, suffering a knee injury on a kickoff return in his first and only game with the Packers. Patton finished out the season but the next year went to the 49ers. He started for them in Super Bowl XV.

There was some light on the horizon, however, as even with a 5-11 season, the Packers were extremely competitive. Some of the losses were by very close scores: to the Bears, 6-3 and 15-14; to the Minnesota Vikings, 27-21 in overtime; to the New York Jets, 27-22; and to the Buffalo Bills, 19-12. Those five losses could easily have been wins, and Starr would have had his second winning season.

That same injury jinx bedeviled Starr again in the 1980 season, although this time it struck in a new spot: the defense, primarily linebackers and linemen. All four starting linebackers went down for the season: Rich Wingo with back surgery, George Cumby with two successive knee injuries, John Anderson with his third broken arm in three seasons, and Mike Hunt

with a neck injury which forced him to retire from the game. The three starting defensive linemen, Mike Butler, Ezra Johnson, and Charles Johnson, in the Packers' new 3-4 alignment were also hampered by injuries most of the season.

Compounding Starr's problems was the loss of Bruce Clark, his first round draft choice from Penn State. A domineering nose tackle in college, Clark signed with Toronto of the Canadian Football League.

There were some spurts of genius, however, during that season. The Packers won the opening game in overtime against the Bears, 12-6, when Chester Marcol had his field goal attempt blocked only to have the ball bounce back into his hands. He promptly ran it in for the winning touchdown. That victory was followed by successive losses to Detroit, Los Angeles, and Dallas. The Cincinnati Bengals, coached by former Packer great Forrest Gregg, came to town only to have the Packers nip them, 14-9. Two missed field goal attempts kept the Packers from defeating Tampa Bay in overtime as they had to settle for a 14-14 tie. A last second touchdown pass gave the Cleveland Browns a

Man With a Mission. Steve Odom didn't toss the ball into the stands after he returned the opening kickoff against Seattle in 1978 for a touchdown. He presented the ball to a boy in an Appleton hospital who had lost both his legs in a farm accident. Odom had visited the lad the week before and had promised him a football if he returned a kick for a TD. *Vern Biever photo.*

The Packer Legend

A Helmet for the Chief. President Gerald Ford visited with Bart and Cherry Starr when he dedicated the Packer Hall of Fame in 1976, and the Starrs returned the favor by presenting the president with a Packer helmet. *Vern Biever photo.*

narrow 26-21 win over the Packers, then the Packers humbled the Vikings, 16-3, in Green Bay. The Packers then went to Pittsburgh to play the Super Bowl champs and fought them to a standstill, losing 22-20. A victory over San Francisco, 23-16, was followed by a narrow defeat to the New York Giants, 27-21, then the Packers once again outplayed the Vikings, 25-13. A winning season was still within reach, but the roof fell in on the Packers the last three games as they lost to the Bears, 61-7, in Chicago; to the Houston Oilers, 22-3; and to Detroit, 24-3. The Pack finished with a dismal 5-10-1 record.

Packer fans' patience with Bart Starr started to wear thin during the latter part of the 1980 season. The press became much more hostile, and some of this feeling was reflected to some extent by the Packer Board of Directors. The Board was called into a special session in late December, and it was obvious that at least some of the Directors were after Starr's scalp.

The Executive Committee had discussed informally on several occasions the idea of separating the jobs of head coach and general manager in order to allow the coach to concentrate 100 percent of his time and energies on football operations. At the Directors' meeting, Vice-Pres. Robert Parins read a prepared statement from the Executive Committee, recommending that Starr finish out the last year of his contract as head coach but suggesting that the Executive Committee be given authority to study a possible realignment of management duties. This was not good enough for a majority of Directors, however, and in order to save Starr's job, the Committee agreed to proceed immediately with the separation of the responsibilities of head coach and general manager.

After the vote was taken, some of the Directors realized that Starr had not been informed of the possibility of such action being taken at this meeting. A large group of media representatives with their tape recorders and cameras were waiting in the locker room where publicity director Lee Remmel was presiding until the meeting adjourned. Pres. Dominic Olejniczak summoned Starr into the meeting and informed him of the Directors' decision. It was one of the few times in Starr's career that he was

Lombardi Protegees Succeed. Starr chatted with his old pal Forrest Gregg when the Packers played Cleveland in a pre-season game in 1977. Gregg went from the Browns to the Cincinnati Bengals and took them to the Super Bowl in 1982. *Vern Biever photo.*

obviously distraught. He had prepared a statement to be read to the Directors, but it did not jibe with what the Directors had just decided. He recovered to some extent, however, and went on with his statement, saying generally that he would devote his full energies to the coaching of the football team in the 1981 season. Starr was obviously still upset, however, when he and Olejniczak met the press in the locker room.

The Executive Committee and most of the Directors fully intended the separation of responsibilities as a positive measure to help Starr meet the challenges of the coaching job, particularly in the last year of his contract. They felt he should be given the best possible shot at pulling off a winning season. Unfortunately, it did not come out that way at the news conference and subsequently on the air and in the press. Cliff Christl, the sports reporter for the Green Bay *Press-Gazette*, wrote a by-line story the next day calling it a stupid decision on the part of the Directors.

Starr recovered his usual composure during the next few weeks and began to devote himself

exclusively to the 1981 season. His first round draft choice in the 1981 draft was testimony to Starr's dedication to the Packer organization. He picked Rich Campbell, a quarterback from the University of California. It was obvious to one and all that Campbell would not be a great deal of help to the Packers in winning football games in 1981. Starr could have taken some very fine linemen who probably could have stepped in immediately and been of help, but he still insisted that the way to build a winning football team in Green Bay was through the draft. He knew very well that the Packers badly needed a young quarterback who could replace Lynn Dickey some years down the pike. It was typical of Starr's integrity, and the move reinforced his image with most Packer fans.

Starr and his staff and players headed into the 1981 training season with a great deal of verve. They all felt that with a healthy squad they were on the verge of a winning year.

The 1981 season presented another great drama in Packer football history. It was do or die for Bart Starr, and most Packer fans were sincerely hoping that Bart could pull it off.

The Packer Legend

Mr. Quarterback. Starr's greatest asset as a passer was his accuracy. He threw 284 passes without an interception, a record yet to be beaten. Not bad for a 17th round draft choice. *Lefebvre photo.*

Chapter Twenty-Two

MISTER

QUARTERBACK

Bart Starr has been criticized by fans for being ultracautious about giving playing time to rookie quarterbacks, or even second and third-year signal callers. But he knows from personal experience whereof he speaks. It may seem inconceivable now, but "Mr. Quarterback" spent a very frustrating three years with the Packers before Vince Lombardi took charge, and those three years may very well influence how he handles young quarterbacks as a head coach.

As mentioned previously, Starr was a 17th round draft choice out of Bear Bryant's football factory at Alabama, and being drafted in the 17th round itself was not a confidence builder for the young quarterback. He had suffered a back injury at Alabama, and that dissuaded pro scouts from drafting him earlier.

His first four seasons with the Packers were spent playing behind Tobin Rote, then Babe Parilli, and finally Lamar McHan. Rote was Lisle Blackbourn's quarterback in Starr's first season, 1956, and then Blackbourn traded Rote to Detroit and brought Parilli back from Cleveland to become his number one quarterback in 1957 and 1958. Lombardi traded Parilli in 1959 but brought in McHan.

Starr got in a little playing time in his first season and actually started against San Francisco in mid-November, but after going three for six passing and scoring a touchdown, he was replaced by Rote in the second half and watched the Packers lose a tough one, 17-16. Starr didn't appear again until the last quarter of the last two games of the season on the coast. Both were lost causes when he went in.

His prospects started looking up in the pre-

Out With the Old. Here's a great view of the famous Packer sweep. Lamar McHan is the quarterback handing off the Paul Hornung, Jim Taylor throws a block into the left side of the Cardinals' line in a 1960 exhibition game. Jerry Kramer (64) and Fuzzy Thurston (63), the legendary "Guardian Angels" of Packer running backs, lead the way. McHan was replaced in mid-season by Starr. *Vern Biever photo.*

In With the New. After McHan was overheard calling Vince Lombardi "a black dago" so-and-so, he was traded immediately, and Bart Starr became the regular starting quarterback. Here Starr hands off to Hornung who is led by blockers Jim Taylor (31), Forrest Gregg (75), Jerry Kramer (64), and Fuzzy Thurston (63). Other Bear defenders to the right are already out of the play. *Green Bay Press-Gazette photo.*

Bart's Backup. Zeke Bratkowski, a former Bear, was Starr's backup from 1963 through 1968, then Phil Bengtson reactivated him from the coaching staff when Starr was hurt in 1971. *Vern Biever photo.*

season the next year, however. He replaced Paul Hornung in a September game at Boston when the Pack was behind 10-0 and brought the team out a winner, 13-10. It was their fifth straight victory in the exhibition season, and he started the last one against Pittsburgh and played the entire game in a 10-10 tie.

Then came the climactic game with the Bears to dedicate Green Bay's new stadium and open the league season. Starr started at quarterback, but when he didn't get the offense moving, Parilli came on and pulled the game out of the fire, 21-17.

Bart played more and more that season but mostly in losing causes. He threw for two touchdowns against Detroit and Baltimore in October games, but the Pack lost both games, 21-14 and 45-17. He started against the Giants in early November, but again the Pack lost, 31-17. He threw for the only points against the Bears, but it wasn't good enough in a 21-14 loss. Finally, Bart played the entire game against Pittsburgh in late November, and the Pack won at last, 27-10. It was their third and last win of Blackbourn's last season.

Things went from bad to worse when Ray McLean took over in 1958. Starr was snake-bitten along with the entire team. He had a pass intercepted by Baltimore in Milwaukee in the last minute and returned 54 yards for the winning touchdown. He went three of 14 in Baltimore the next Sunday, and Parilli came in and completed five passes and had five intercepted. Baltimore humbled the Pack, 58-0.

Against the Bears, he fumbled in the end zone, and the Bears recovered for a score. They intercepted his next pass for another touchdown in a 24-10 loss. Against Los Angeles in November, Starr played only the last quarter after Parilli again had five interceptions, and he didn't play at all against San Francisco in Milwaukee.

The Packers again went to the Coast for their last two games. Starr started against San Francisco, had his first two passes intercepted, and was replaced by Parilli. Against Los Angeles, rookie Joe Francis started the game, was replaced by Parilli, and Starr didn't play at all.

Record Receiver. Carroll Dale ranks right behind Don Hutson in several all-time Packer pas receiving categories. Lombardi acquired him in a trade with Los Angeles in 1965, and he was one of Starr's favorite targets. *Vern Biever photo.*

Bart Starr Day. President Richard Nixon came to Green Bay to join in honoring Bart and Cherry Starr in October 1970. Henry Jordan was the emcee. Bart's parents are at the left. On the right are head coach Phil Bengtson, NFL commissioner Pete Rozelle, Packer President Dominic Olejniczak, and Wisconsin Governor Warren Knowles.

Vern Biever photo.

The Packer Legend

That's a summary of Starr's first three years with the Pack. Now contrast that with this record in nine seasons under Lombardi during which he became the most productive quarterback in pro football history: five world championships; eight playoff games with seven wins and two Super Bowl titles; most valuable player in Super Bowls I and II; led the league in passing in 1962, 1964 and 1966; played in the Pro Bowl four times; Most Valuable Player in NFL in 1966; set four NFL passing records, one of which still stands. His 16-year career was the longest in Packer history. He was inducted into the Pro Football Hall of Fame in 1977, and his No. 15 jersey has been retired by the Packers and hangs in their Hall of Fame.

Starr became the number one quarterback in the ninth game of Lombardi's first season. He took the Pack to four straight victories; over Washington, 21-0; Detroit, 24-17; then conquered the West Coast nemesis, beating Los Angeles, 38-20, and San Francisco, 36-14. It was the Packers' first winning season in 12 years.

What turned Starr almost overnight from a frustrated, losing quarterback into the cool, calculating engineer of a football machine which revolutionized the game itself?

What was the difference between McLean and Lombardi?

I asked Bart that question, and he responded with one word: "Leadership." Then added, "A sense of direction, organization, dedication, but those are all elements of leadership. That's what Vince brought to the team."

Starr admits to a total sense of frustration that year under McLean. He had not expected to play much his rookie year with Tobin Rote at the controls, but when Blackbourn traded Rote and brought in Parilli, it created a real conflict in Bart's loyalties, for Parilli had been his hero as a high school quarterback. As a matter of fact, in his senior year at Montgomery High, he went to Kentucky and Parilli gave him an intensive two-week training course in the basic skills of quarterbacking. Competing with Babe for the starting job in Green Bay was tough on Bart.

He had a similar loyalty problem with McLean, for it was Scooter who went to Tuscaloosa after the 1956 draft and signed Starr to a Packer contract. The players loved Scooter, but they soon learned even in the training season that there was a paucity of organization, a total lack of leadership.

I have gone into considerable detail over these early years of Starr's career because in my years on the Executive Committee I have been trying to identify those minute factors which make the difference between winning and losing, and once identified, then asking the question: How can a coach manipulate those factors to produce a winning team?

I asked Starr if he could relate his contrasting experiences with McLean and Lombardi to his own situation now as Packer head coach. Now that his team has had a taste of winning in the second half of the 1981 season, would they maintain that momentum in 1982?

"Winning is an infectious thing, as is losing," Starr continued. "Once a team wins a few ball games in a row, it begins to gain confidence, it executes better, and more and more it hates to lose.

"Our coaching staff and a lot of our players knew deep down inside at the start of last season that we were a better football team than we had been showing. We went out to win in the exhibition season because we wanted our players to realize that. And when we beat Dallas and Cleveland and Oakland and then won our opening game with the Bears, we had that momentum going.

"Then came that debacle with Atlanta, and it took the stuffing right out of us. It really took us until the second half of the season to get things back on the track.

"After we won those six games and had a shot at the playoffs, we were all terribly disappointed over our loss to the Jets in that last game. Some unfortunate things happened to us early, and we had to play catch-up. Our game plan went out the window, and with our offensive line badly weakened, their defensive people just poured in on us.

"A team doesn't realize what getting into the playoffs means until it's been there. You talk and talk about it all season, but when it happens, it has a lasting effect on the team. The Giants will benefit more from getting into the playoffs last year than from all the top notch players they acquire in the draft. It's an invaluable experience."

From his remarks, it was obvious that Bart feels the Packers will make it in 1982. The jury is still out as to whether he can provide that mysterious ingredient which will turn this team into a consistent winner. Bart certainly can identify that ingredient. Only another season will tell whether he can provide it.

Gazing into the Future? Starr watches his team perform in the Silver Dome against the Detroit Lions. Maybe he is really looking ahead to 1982 when the Packers may again reach the playoffs. *Vern Biever photo.*

The Packer Legend

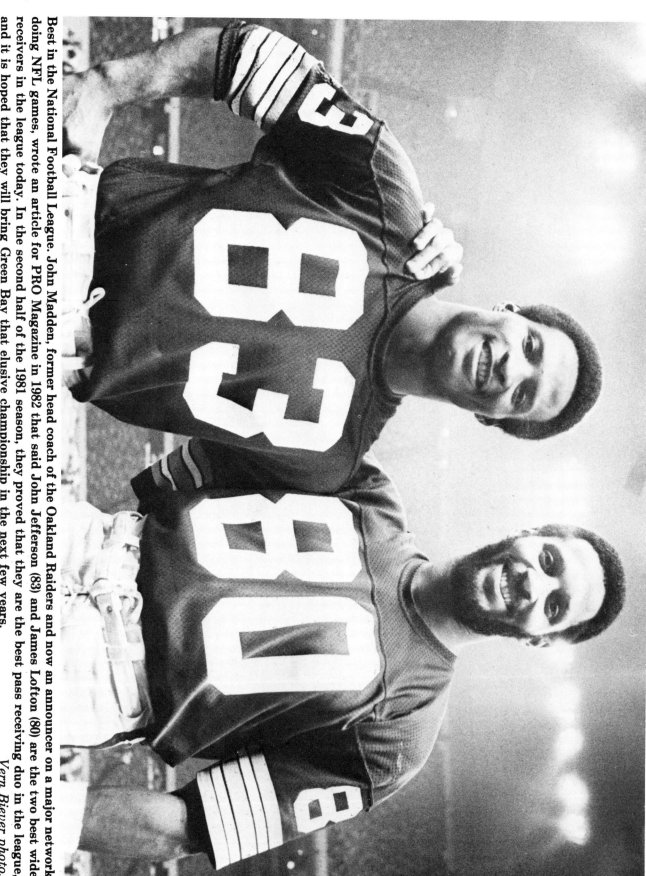

Best in the National Football League. John Madden, former head coach of the Oakland Raiders and now an announcer on a major network doing NFL games, wrote an article for PRO Magazine in 1982 that said John Jefferson (83) and James Lofton (80) are the two best wide receivers in the league today. In the second half of the 1981 season, they proved that they are the best pass receiving duo in the league, and it is hoped that they will bring Green Bay that elusive championship in the next few years.

Vern Biever photo.

Chapter Twenty-Three

THE

RENEWAL

OF

STARR

Bart Starr had to wait three extra days for his Christmas gift from the Packers after the 1981 season.

Back on December 24, 1974, he was given a three-year contract as head coach and general manager. It was by unanimous vote of the Executive Committee and Packer fans everywhere.

On December 28, 1981, he was given a new two-year contract as head coach, and while the vote on the Executive Committee was again unanimous, his support among the fans was not all that clear-cut.

In arriving at that decision, the Committee had to consider two opposing factors: first, Starr's record over seven seasons of 39 wins, 65 losses, and two ties; and secondly, the 1981 season when his team had a 2-6 record for the first half of the

season and turned that around for a 6-2 record in the second half and almost made it into the playoffs.

So, in effect, the Executive Committee was saying, "We have to give him the opportunity to see if he can keep his winning momentum going."

One of the factors which made the decision so difficult is that Bart Starr is as fine a person as ever you will meet, in athletics or out. He is honest, forthright, clean as a whistle, as we used to say. He is a "workaholic," usually getting to the office between 5 and 6 a.m. He has a fine football mind and a talent for organizational work.

The question which had grown in the minds of fans and Packer Directors was whether Starr could motivate his players to give him total

The Packer Legend

Bart in the Classroom. Bart Starr always said the secret of Vince Lombardi's success was his great ability as a teacher. In his efforts to restore the glory of winning NFL titles to the Green Bay Packers, Starr has tried to emulate Lombardi's classroom teaching techniques. The second half success the Packers enjoyed in the 1981 season may be the first dividends of Starr's approach.
Vern Biever photo.

The Packer Legend

dedication and performance, particularly on a consistent level.

Starr's teams had won some impressive victories against the better teams in the league, particularly in the last few seasons, but then they had fallen flat on their behinds in crucial games, like the final one in 1981 against the New York Jets in New York when they lost the game when the coin was flipped. They were humbled, 27-3, when a victory would have sent them into the playoffs as a wild card team. Their fans even had visions of the Packers doing what the Oakland Raiders had done the year before when they posted a fine second half, then won the Super Bowl as a wild card.team.

Putting the seven seasons in perspective, there were a number of factors to be considered.

Starr took over the head coaching duties with only one year of experience as an assistant under Dan Devine. He asked for the fans' patience and

Lofton Off and Running. James Lofton takes off after catching a pass against the Atlanta Falcons. He's a great open field runner as well as one of the best pass receivers in the NFL. *Vern Biever photo.*

The Packer Legend

understanding, and he received it.

His inexperience showed in his constant changing of assistants, the losing of a number of experienced players on matters of principle without any real opportunity of replacing them with quality ballplayers. Ted Hendricks is an example. It showed up in his drafting. He was shorn of top draft choices through Devine's deal for John Hadl, but he didn't make very good use of what he did have.

Starr was completely honest with his employers on that score. "Men, you have given me on-the-job training, and I appreciate it greatly," he told the Executive Committee when they extended his original contract with a year to go on it. "But you have a considerable investment in me, and I feel I am now ready to make it pay off for you," he continued.

That year, his fourth, it looked like the experience was paying off. The Packers won six of their first seven games and were leading their division by a good margin at the halfway mark. Then injuries started happening to key players, and the Packers' lack of depth became apparent. They won only two more games, tied one, and wound up 8-7-1, a half game out of the playoffs.

The fans had a taste of the old glory, and they eagerly anticipated the 1979 season, especially when Starr drafted a sensational running back, Eddie Lee Ivery, in the first round. Then Ivery caught his foot in the sticky astroturf in Soldiers Field in the opening game with the Bears, twisted his knee, and was out for the season. The injury plague continued that year, particularly to the offensive backfield. In the latter part of the season, the two starting running backs were

Heading for the Record. Placekicker Jan Stenerud set an all-time efficiency record with his field goal kicking in the 1981 season. He made an incredible 22 of 24 attempts. That's Ray Stachowicz, the Packers' punter, holding and George Cumby blocking Bill Currier of the New York Giants. *Vern Biever photo.*

The Packer Legend

free agents Starr had picked up when all his veterans went out with injuries. The Packers wound up back at 5-11 for the season.

Starr undertook some drastic changes at season's end. He fired Dave Hanner as defensive co-ordinator; Hanner, the hero of the defensive line under Lombardi, Starr's teammate, the only other man interviewed for the head coaching job when Starr was selected. As a sidelight, he also fired publicity director Chuck Lane, who worked for Starr in his private business after Lane couldn't stomach Dan Devine any longer and who really was the architect of the powerful fan movement to install Starr when Devine's days were numbered.

John Meyer was put in charge of the defense, and disaster started striking his troops even before the season began. The Packers lost their number one draft choice, Bruce Clark of Penn State, to the Toronto Argonauts, ostensibly because Clark didn't want to play nose tackle in the new 3-4 defense which Meyer was installing. There were other factors involved, but that was the one which was featured by the press.

The Pack went 0-4-1 in the pre-season as they experimented with their new defense, including a final loss to Denver at Green Bay, 38-0, when the fans finally turned on Starr.

There were other complications. Bill Curry, the respected offensive line coach, left to return to his alma mater, Georgia Tech, as head coach, and the defensive line coach, Fred von Appen, quit early in the season when he didn't think Starr was tough enough at disciplining Ezra Johnson for having munched on a hot dog on the bench, a sandwich given to him by a fan in the stands.

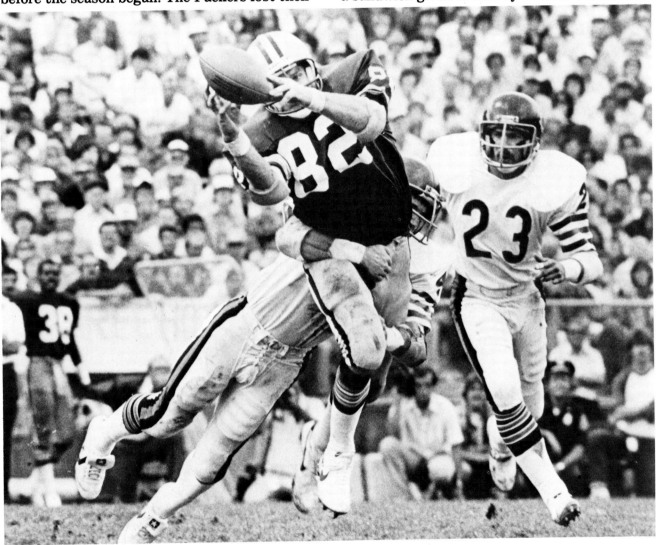

Underrated Tight End. Paul Coffman hasn't received the accolades due to him so far in his career. Here he makes a catch in traffic against the Bears' Lenny Walterscheid (23) and Doug Plank. *Vern Biever photo.*

The Packer Legend

Stacking Up Hofer. The 49ers didn't get anywhere on this running play against Mike Butler (77), Mike Douglass (53), and Ezra Johnson (on ground). All three Packer defenders will be returning for the 1982 campaign to lead what should be one of the finer defenses in the NFL. *Vern Biever photo.*

The team played well in its first eight games, going 3-4-1, and were even 5-6-1 with four games left. They lost all four and wound up 5-11-1. Injuries came in bunches during the second half, and by season's end, the team had 27 players on injured reserve.

The media became increasingly vitriolic over Starr's performance as the season progressed, and dissatisfaction mounted among the fans.

A special meeting of the Board of Directors was convened on December 27, and the Executive Committee was aware that certain Directors at least were out for Bart's scalp. The Committee attempted to counter the opposition by recommending that Starr finish out the last year of his contract as head coach but also mentioned that the Committee had been studying the possible separation of the duties of head coach and general manager. They asked to be allowed to come back to the Directors at a later date with a recommendation in that regard. The Board voted to separate the duties right then and there, but Bart's tenure as head coach

didn't come up for a vote. In effect, the Committee, by conceding on the general manager issue, had saved Starr's job.

It was embarrassing to Starr, however, the way it came out publicly. To the press, Bart had been demoted when actually the Committee and Starr's other supporters had been trying to say, "We have relieved him of those other duties so

The Fickle Fates of the NFL Draft

Here's an oddity about John Jefferson that most fans and some experts quite often overlook.

When the Packers were preparing for the 1978 draft, they knew they needed a top-notch wide receiver for their quarterbacks to throw to. The wide receivers they had at the time left quite a bit to be desired. So coach Bart Starr and his staff decided to take one in the first round.

There was more than one excellent prospect available that year. One of the most highly regarded was James Lofton of Stanford. Another was John Jefferson of Arizona State. The Packers' brain trust rated them one-two, respectively.

Starr felt certain that Lofton would be gone by the time the Packers' turn to pick came along. Much to his delight, Lofton was still available, and Starr took him without hesitation.

Just in case Lofton was gone by the time the Packers got their turn, Starr was prepared to play his ace-in-the-hole. He was all set to take Jefferson. Either way, he figured he would be getting a receiver who would be a game-breaker.

The oddity is that the San Diego Chargers had made the same plans as the Packers. They wanted Lofton first and Jefferson second, but they figured both would be gone by their turn. They were half right.

To complete this tale, Jefferson still wound up in a Packer uniform in 1981 when the Chargers traded him to the Packers for a player and three draft choices. So in effect, the Packers still got Jefferson through the draft, albeit four years later.

Huckleby Blossoms. Running back Harlan Huckleby from Michigan came into his own as an NFL runner and receiver in the 1981 season. He got his chance to start when Eddie Lee Ivery went down with a knee injury that required surgery in the opening game against the Chicago Bears in Soldiers Field. Leotis Harris (69) and Derrel Gofourth lead the blocking for him. *Vern Biever photo.*

he can spend 100 percent of his time on football operations." At the least, the move transferred some of the heat to the Committee and off Starr's back.

The media started all kinds of speculation as to who would become the new general manager. As I explained in a previous chapter, there really hadn't been a functioning general manager since Vince Lombardi, except possibly Dan Devine. The Committee really had no intention of hiring a general manager, and not long afterwards, it said so. In a public statement, the Committee said that given the unique nature of the public ownership of the Packers, the president elected by the stockholders is the chief executive officer; that's the way it has always been and that's the way it's going to continue to be.

So Starr set out on his do-or-die season free of other entanglements, and he made a smart strategic move with his first choice in the draft. The selection of Rich Campbell said that Starr was thinking about the future of the Packers rather than his own skin. He could have drafted a lineman or a running back who would have been of immediate help that crucial season, but Bart was counting on a healthy Eddie Lee Ivery after a year of recuperation from knee surgery, a healthy offensive line, and a healthy linebacking corps.

In the pre-season, it looked like he had just that. Starr went out to win those games, to instill a sense of winning in his club, and they beat Oakland, Dallas, and Cleveland before losing a close one to Denver. All had been in the playoffs the previous year, Oakland being the Super Bowl winner.

Came the opening game with the Bears in Chicago and down went Ivery again on that damnable Soldiers Field astroturf. He injured the same knee and was out for the season. By the end of the year, it became quite apparent what Ivery would have meant to the Packers.

The Packers eked out a win over the Bears, 16-9, then let the next two games slip away from them when Atlanta and Los Angeles came from behind to beat them. By mid-season, the Packers were 2-6, only one game ahead of the last place Bears.

Then something happened. Exactly what it was is hard to pinpoint, even in retrospect, but the Packers did a complete turnaround. They handily beat the Bears, Detroit, New Orleans, Seattle, Minnesota, and the New York Giants and came away with an 8-8 season.

These were some of the factors the Executive Committee considered in their two long deliberative sessions during the holidays that December. Most fans don't realize the many hours these volunteers put in on the job, even at holiday seasons.

The regular quarterly meeting of Directors was timed to coincide with the end of the playing season. It was held on the Monday after the team came home from its Sunday disaster in Shea Stadium against the Jets.

Judge Robert Parins, who had been installed as chief executive officer by the Directors at their October meeting, opened up the discussion by asking for a full and open meeting at which every Director would have an opportunity to speak his piece. He asked that no final action be taken that day and also requested the Directors to hand the matter back to the Executive Committee after the Committee had the benefit of the Directors' feelings.

Parins handled the matter in the same manner with the Committee, which met informally for lunch the next day. He suggested they try to assess what the Directors wanted them to do, exchange frank opinions, but take no immediate action. Later in the meeting, Starr was invited in, and the discussion continued on that informal basis. The Judge had been quite open with Starr after the Directors' meeting and had told him the Directors were divided in their support of him.

Starr told the Committee that he wanted his long association with the Committee and the friendship which had developed in seven years to be left out of their decision-making. He said he wanted the decision made strictly on what was good for the Green Bay Packers, but he asked that a decision be made in a reasonable amount of time so that his assistant coaches could seek employment elsewhere if the Committee decided against him.

The Committee again considered the complete turnaround the team engineered in the second half of the season. Their play had created emotion among the fans at games in both Green Bay and Milwaukee, feelings which the fans had not experienced since the glory days of Lombardi.

The game against the Detroit Lions in Green Bay in early December was the high point. The Packers fell behind, 10-0, in the early going but came back strong in the second quarter to win going away, 31-17. Fan emotion built as the game progressed, reaching the point where the entire stadium stood and applauded and gloried in the victory, the celebration lasting up to a half hour after the final gun sounded. Starr joined the team at mid-field, then the players and coaches went around the lower rows of the stands shaking hands with their delirious supporters.

I asked Bart during that meeting of the Executive Committee if he could explain what happened between the first and second halves of the season. He said the major factor was a psychological one, that the team won two games in a row, then three, and suddenly they realized they could win. "Success," he said, "breeds confidence, and confidence makes for better execution, fewer mistakes. The whole thing snowballs."

In my opinion, there were other factors. Probably the major one was the acquisition of the very fine wide receiver, John Jefferson, from the San Diego Chargers early in the season. Jefferson was a hold-out at San Diego, insisting on a renegotiation of his contract. Starr swung the deal with the Chargers: Jefferson for one first and two second round draft choices but only one

Great Stiff Arm. Fullback Gerry Ellis gives a solid stiff arm to Fred McNeill of the Minnesota Vikings in this 1981 game. Ellis, a castoff of the Los Angeles Rams at the beginning of the 1980 season when the Packers picked him up on waivers, was the leading ground gainer for the Packers in 1981. *Vern Biever photo.*

The Packer Legend

of them each year for three years. He took the proposal to Judge Parins, who called a special Executive Committee meeting along with Starr and presidential assistants Harlan and Miller. We agreed to go for it, and Harlan went to Los Angeles with the team for the game there that Sunday. He met with Jefferson's agent on Saturday. Jefferson had said publicly he wanted to be paid the same as other top wide receivers, like James Lofton for example. So Harlan took Lofton's contract along, a new one he had negotiated with Lofton's agent earlier in the year, laid it out on the table, and told Jefferson's agent, "We'll match it." The agent tried for some extra concessions. After all, he had to do his thing. But after a nerve-wracking few days the

Airborne Defender. Defensive back Mark Lee (22) really gets up in the air to bat down this pass aimed for Leonard Thompson of the Detroit Lions. The Packer secondary held its own against most opponents during the 1981 season and looks forward to doing even better in 1982. *James Biever photo.*

The Packer Legend

Ready to Blitz. That's linebacker Rich Wingo (50) about to tee off on Steve Bartkowski of the Atlanta Falcons in the 1981 game in Green Bay. The Packers entered the fourth quarter of that game ahead, 17-0, only to see the Falcons pull off an incredible rally to win, 31-17. *Vern Biever photo.*

The Packer Legend

Picking His Target. Lynn Dickey can pick a defense apart if given enough time. In this play against Detroit, Greg Koch and Leotis Harris keep the Lions at bay.

Vern Biever photo.

The Packer Legend

next week, Jefferson came to Green Bay.

A San Diego sports writer wrote that week that "John Jefferson will no longer light up the San Diego stadium scoreboard."

But he lit up Milwaukee County Stadium when he first ran onto the field the next Sunday. Jefferson had arrived in Green Bay on Thursday, practiced with the team Friday and in a light workout Saturday, and crammed the Packer play book nights with Lofton's help. Most fans thought he wouldn't appear at all, or if he did only in spot situations. Jefferson not only started the game, he finished it, and he introduced the "high five" to the Packer team and Packer fans.

Jefferson was used mainly as a decoy in those first few games while quarterback Lynn Dickey was getting used to his moves and J.J. was learning Packer patterns. He started and finished every game the rest of the season, and there's no question but that he injected a new emotion into the team. Fans were calling him the "million-dollar decoy" until he caught eight passes for 113 yards in that emotional game with Detroit.

The story goes that Lofton and Jefferson went to Dickey and said, "Look, don't be afraid to throw the ball down field into that double coverage. You throw it to either one of us, and if we can't catch it, we'll make darn sure it won't be intercepted."

That's when Dickey began throwing the ball down field.

Another major factor was a healthy offensive line for the first time in several years. Mark Koncar finally came back from all his injuries and his emotional dispute with Starr before the Tampa Bay game, which he sat out. Leotis Harris, Greg Koch, and Derrell Goforth joined iron man Larry McCarren to give Dickey the kind of protection he needs to pick a defense apart. Gerry Ellis gave the Packers a semblance of a running game, helped out by Harlan Huckleby and Terdell Middleton, enough at least to keep defenses honest, but that's where Ivery was so badly missed.

Meanwhile, the defensive team had been mostly healthy all year, the exception being Johnny Gray's and Mike Holly's knee injuries which put both of them out for the season, but those happened early enough to work Mark Murphy and Maurice Harvey into the secondary. The coaching staff was finally able to rely on the defense to keep opponents in their own backyard and turn the ball over to the offense in good field position.

There was another major factor to be considered, an immigrant from Norway by the name of Jan Stenerud. He left his native country at age 18 to enroll at Montana State on a skiing scholarship, but he had also played a little soccer in his homeland. He wound up on the football

Welcome Back, Schnelker

One of the matters the Executive Committee discussed with Bart Starr when they gave him a new two-year contract in 1982 was the hiring of an offensive co-ordinator.

Starr had such an assistant, along with a defensive co-ordinator earlier in his coaching career, but when Paul Roach left the staff in 1977, Starr assumed that function himself. The committee felt he had enough to do as head coach and that he needed assistants as co-ordinators of the offense and defense.

Starr brought Bob Schnelker back to Green Bay to fill that position. Schnelker had been an assistant to both Vince Lombardi and Phil Bengtson and had been the offensive co-ordinator for Monte Clark at Detroit.

Lew Carpenter, up in the press booth, and Zeke Bratkowski, on the sidelines, called the offensive plays in Starr's set-up, and there had been some criticism of Packer play-calling, particularly in the second half of a number of games in the 1981 season when the team got off to a good lead in the first half, then let the momentum of the game get away from them in the second half.

Soon after Schnelker was signed, Bratkowski was offered the offensive co-ordinator job under the new head coach at Baltimore, Frank Kush, on a three-year contract. After being passed over for the same job in Green Bay, it became too good an offer for Bratkowski to pass up, and he accepted it despite his close personal friendship with Starr and his long-time residence in the Green Bay area. Starr and Bratkowski were across-the-street neighbors in De Pere.

Packer fans look forward to new offensive leadership in 1982.

team at Montana State, and from there he went into pro ball with the Kansas City Chiefs. He played in the first Super Bowl against the Packers in 1967 and kicked one field goal and one PAT.

Starr was having his troubles with Chester Marcol back in 1979 when Marcol was having his troubles with the bottle. Starr was patient with Chester almost to the point of absurdity, but he finally lowered the boom in mid-season of 1980. In desperation, he tried one other kicker who had been cut by another team, then got in touch with Stenerud. He talked Stenerud out of retirement, and Jan joined the Pack late in the season. That solved the Packer kicking problems.

In 1981, Stenerud set an NFL record for kicking efficiency. He booted 22 field goals in 24 attempts for a percentage of 91.67, breaking the previous mark of 88.45 set by Lou "the Toe" Groza in 1956 when he made 23 of 26 attempts. His first attempt at a PAT was blocked by the Bears in the opening game, but after that he was successful on 35 straight attempts. Stenerud is now the sixth ranking scorer in pro football history. He's tied with Jim Turner with 304 lifetime field goals, second only to George Blanda with 335.

That kind of consistent kicking was another major factor in the second half successes, and best of all, Stenerud announced he would be back in 1982.

1982: That now becomes the magic year for the Green Bay Packers. It will be their 62nd year as a member of the National Football League, the only franchise dating back that far which is still located in the same city. (The Bears moved from Decatur to Chicago in 1923.)

These questions remain to be answered at this writing:

Was the emotional kind of football the Packers played under Bart Starr in the second half of the '81 season a preview of another championship flag flying over Lambeau Field in 1982?

Will the 1982 Packers repeat what their

Name of the Game: Publicity

Lee Remmel, the Packers' publicity director, has the reputation of having a computer memory as far as Packer facts, figures, names, and dates are concerned, and if he can't come up with an answer from memory, he has a whole reference library to consult. He has been of tremendous help in researching this book.

Like the five men between Remmel and the original Packer publicist George Calhoun, he inherited the traditions set by Cal as the guardian of all things having to do with Packer history. Remmel also has the same training as Cal in that he spent many years in the sports department of the Green Bay *Press-Gazette*.

I related earlier how Calhoun learned that he was being replaced by George Strickler. He only lasted in the job as long as Lambeau was around. Then the former Packer great, Jug Earp, took over.

When Earp retired, the Packers hired former University of Wisconsin publicist, Bonnie Ryan, who was replaced by Tom Miller, now administrative assistant to the president of the corporation.

Vince Lombardi promoted Miller and brought Chuck Lane into the job. Lane had been with the Harlem Globetrotters, and he served under Phil Bengtson and Dan Devine until he broke with Devine and left the Packers. He then went to work for Bart Starr in his private business in Green Bay.

Remmel was hired at that point, but Starr brought Lane back when he was hired as head coach. Lane and Remmel divided the duties, but it didn't work out very well. Starr finally let Lane go, leaving the entire job to Remmel.

Lee Remmel

forebears accomplished 11 times previously in 1929, 1930, 1931, 1936, 1939, 1944, 1961, 1962, 1965, 1966, and 1967?

As they say every year: "Wait'll next year!"

Touchdown Twins. John Jefferson is about to give James Lofton the "high five" after Lofton scores a touchdown against the Lions in Green Bay. Jefferson brought a new spirit to the team when the San Diego Chargers traded him to the Packers for draft choices and wide receiver Aundra Thompson in the early part of the 1981 season. Everyone, from the Executive Committee down to the littlest fan, is hoping that Jefferson's enthusiasm will continue to infect his teammates in the years ahead. *Vern Biever photo.*

The Packer Legend

The 1982 Draft: Hope

During the 1981 season, coach Bart Starr and corporate general manager Bob Harlan transacted a significant deal for the Packers which had a distinct bearing on the 1982 draft. They traded wide receiver Aundra Thompson, a four-year veteran from East Texas State, to the San Diego Chargers for All-Pro wide receiver John Jefferson. Included in the bargain were the Packers' second round draft choice in 1982, their first round choice in 1983, and their second round choice in 1984. Also, the Packers had to exchange places with San Diego in the drafting order in the first round of 1982, thus retaining a first round pick albeit the 23rd turn, 22nd if you discount New Orleans losing their pick for taking a player in the supplemental draft the year before.

Many fans considered the 1982 draft to be an exercise in futility before it began. The amount of talent available didn't appear to be very great, especially when the Packers needed immediate help at running back and in the offensive line, the same areas several teams ahead of them in the drafting order also needed help. Drafting as low as they would have to, everyone thought the few quality college players that were available would be gone. It didn't quite turn out that way, however.

The Packers drafted for need, just as they had planned. They took a huge offensive lineman from Iowa in the first round. Although he stood 6'6" and weighed 286 pounds (some say closer to 300) and he was an All-Big 10 selection in his senior year, Ron Hallstrom was unheralded by most scouts. He played defensive tackle in junior college and during his junior year at Iowa before switching to the offensive line for his final season.

Packer personnel director Dick Corrick said Hallstrom graded well in toughness, intensity, and productivity, adding Hallstrom has "a mean streak, he's tough." Some scouts remarked that he is a good trap blocker and exceptionally good on pass protection.

Coach Starr indicated that he expects Hallstrom to be a starter in the 1982 season or to at least give the man ahead of him a good run for his position. Starr said he loved Hallstrom's competitiveness and above all his productivity. "He's one of the few guys we saw in our preparation for the draft who

Top Prospect. The Packers wanted to strengthen their offensive line in the 1982 NFL draft, so they picked All-Big 10 offensive guard Ron Hallstrom from the University of Iowa. According to Packer scouting reports, Hallstrom has the most important ingredient necessary to make it in the NFL: the right attitude. He has the size for the pros, standing 6'6" and weighing close to 300 pounds. That's a lot of meanness.

for a Winning Future

we consistently saw get the job done."

The Packers didn't have a second round choice, having traded it to San Diego the year before.

In the third round, the Packers tried to fill their other need: a running back to complement fullback Gerry Ellis, providing halfback Eddie Lee Ivery can't make a comeback from his second knee surgery. Corrick and Starr opted for Del Rodgers from Utah. Rodgers was a 1,000-yard rusher his senior year, leading the Western Athletic Conference in rushing. Scouting experts referred to him as being a quick, strong, explosive runner with adequate hands. He was a three-year starter and played quite a bit as a freshman. His nickname is Popcorn.

In the fourth round, the Packers took Bob Brown, a defensive end from Virginia Tech. One scouting report described him as being a quick, explosive pass rusher, a very good athlete, aggressive, and possessing good football instincts. He was also a junior college All-American. It is expected that the coaching staff will try to convert him to a linebacker.

Mike Meade, a 5'10", 220-pound fullback from Penn State, was a darkhorse (he wasn't even listed in most scouting reports) choice in the fifth round. The Packers' brain trust recalled how the Pittsburgh Steelers took All-Pro Franco Harris, who was also a fullback from Penn State, in a late round.

The Packers tapped Penn State again in the sixth round, taking linebacker Chet Parlavecchio. Coach Joe Paterno of Penn State has been known for turning out superior football players, and Parlavecchio believes he is no exception to that tradition. According to him, he is the greatest linebacker of all time. That's what I call confidence.

Defensive coach John Meyer of the Packers felt one more man in the defensive secondary wouldn't hurt, so the Packers chose Joe Whitley from Texas-El Paso in the seventh round. Whitley's size appears to be going against him as a cornerback.

The Packers eighth round choice was Thomas Boyd, a linebacker from Alabama. Boyd had some trouble in his final year under Bear Bryant, but Starr is gambling that is all behind him.

Charlie Riggins, a defensive end from Bethune-Cookman, was the ninth pick. Eddie Garcia, a fine place-kicker from SMU, was taken in the 10th round. John Macaulay, a center from Stanford, was chosen in the 11th round. The Packers final choice was Phillip Epps, a wide receiver from TCU.

News media analysts raised several question marks about the overall selections. Some wondered why so many (five) defensive players were taken when the Packers' biggest needs were apparently on offense. Others wanted to know why Hallstrom was taken in the first round when players who had been rated higher by other experts were still available. The answers may lie in Starr's history as a coach.

Hallstrom will be joining eight other first round draftees, all taken since Starr has been head coach, on the Packers' 1982 roster. They include linebackers John Anderson from Michigan, taken in 1978, and George Cumby from Oklahoma, taken in 1980; defensive ends Mike Butler from Kansas, taken in 1977, and Ezra Johnson from Morris Brown, also taken in 1977; running back Eddie Lee Ivery from Georgia Tech, taken in 1979; offensive tackle Mark Koncar from Colorado, taken in 1976; wide receiver James Lofton from Stanford, taken in 1978; and quarterback Rich Campbell from California, taken in 1981. Hallstrom is the first offensive lineman taken in the first round since Koncar.

Overall, the 1982 draft has to be considered a pre-season success for two reasons. The Packers were able to fill two glaring gaps in their offense, and they got All-Pro wide receiver John Jefferson. After all, he was the price of their second round choice. Not a bad bargain.

Postscript

THE

PROMISING

FUTURE

In 1981, the Green Bay Packers achieved parity with their National Football League brethren, forging an 8-8 mark and a tie for second place in the NFC's highly competitive Central Division.

Although the record was not all they or their fans had hoped for, what intrigued the Packer faithful was the manner in which it was accomplished. It came by way of a dramatic comeback, which saw the Green and Gold rebound from an unhappy 2-6 start to finish with a 6-2 rush.

The big question remains whether Bart Starr can keep their winning ways going into the 1982 season.

History has shown that one year of reaching the .500-mark does not necessarily mean the beginning of a dynasty.

After four straight losing season (two under Curly Lambeau), the Packers broke even in 1952 under Gene Ronzani, only to fall flat again the next year with a 2-9-1 record.

Lisle Blackbourn reached the .500-level in 1955 after a 4-8-0 mark the season before, then his next two teams dropped back to sub-par seasons.

Dan Devine led the Packers to a division title and a playoff berth in 1972 after two losing efforts, one under Phil Bengtson.

And Starr has even had the ups and downs in his own history as the head coach of the Packers. After three straight years well below the .500 mark, his 1978 team finished 8-7-1, only to struggle through two more losing years in 1979 and 1980.

History has a habit of repeating itself, an old cliche for certain, but one that has proven true on too many occasions to be discounted.

This is not to say that the Packers' brain trust is concerned over the future. Confidence abounds in Green Bay for the 1982 season. There is every reason to believe that history will again repeat itself, but in the positive instead of the negative.

When Vince Lombardi became the head coach of the Packers in 1959, there was this feeling of great expectation quietly building in everyone connected to the Packers. The second half performance of the team in 1981 has once again created this tremor of good things to come.

In a sense, Bart Starr is a new coach taking the reins of the Packers for the first time. He now has the experience that is absolutely necessary to attain success in the NFL. For the first time in his career, he has a complete coaching staff that is well-versed in the game of football, and more importantly, he finally has the player personnel that is essential to winning. At every position, offensive, defensive, and special teams, the Packers have quality ballplayers, and they also have quality people behind them. No longer does Starr fear the injury jinx.

Starr has said, "We slipped offensively this past year (1981). I think you can either be enamored with or (be) too concerned about statistical perspectives. But, if you remain objective, there was a drastic slip offensively in our output from a year ago (1980). As you remember, in 1980 we finished 14th offensively, right in the middle of the league. This past year, we slipped to 23rd in total ranking.

"Defensively, we did just the opposite. In 1980, we were 25th defensively, a terrible position. This year, we climbed all the way to ninth, and that's the kind of improvement we need in every phase of our play. I'm not saying we can jump from 23rd to ninth offensively, but if we can maintain the level of consistency that we're seeking here, we'll show improvement, and by doing so, we not only will improve our productivity, but our record will improve right along with it."

Consistency is the name of the game for winning football, and no one knows this better than Bart Starr. He learned that principle under Lombardi, and he has attempted to instill it in his own players. At long last after seven somewhat frustrating years at the helm, Starr finally feels he has the people who will be consistent and who will provide Packer fans with the winner they so badly want.

Packer history is filled with some of the richest traditions in the history of the National Football League. Bart Starr has written several chapters in that history as a player, and now he feels it is his turn and obligation to write even more chapters as a coach.

Looking ahead to the 1982 season, Starr said, "We're optimistic and realistic. We're optimistic because of the way our people responded in the second half of the season last year and feel we have a real shot at our division this year. We're realistic by understanding that we have an extremely difficult schedule. I believe that will work to our advantage because we have some highly motivated people here and they respond accordingly."

The most highly motivated person with the Packers is Bart Starr, and if that accounts for anything, then "the Pack is back."

About the Author

John B. Torinus has been a professional newspaperman for 50 years and has been connected with the Green Bay Packers in one way or another for all of that time.

He became a volunteer assistant to the Packer publicity man, George W. Calhoun, while he was a student and summer intern at the Green Bay *Press-Gazette*, where he began his newspaper career in 1934.

Torinus was elected to the Packer Board of Directors and to the Executive Committee in 1949, a position he holds to the present time. In 1962, he became editor of the Appleton *Post-Crescent* but retained his executive positions with the Packers. He is currently the secretary of the Packer corporation.

Born in Stillwater, Minnesota where his family was in the lumbering business, he lived in Battle Creek, Michigan with his mother and her family after the death of his father, and moved to Green Bay after World War I when his mother married V. I. Minanhan, Sr., a Green Bay attorney who founded the Green Bay *Free Press* and later merged it with the Green Bay *Gazette*.

He attended De Pere public schools and graduated from Northwestern Military Naval Academy at Lake Geneva, Wisconsin and Dartmouth College in Hanover, New Hampshire. He served in World War II in this country and in the European Theater, retiring as a lieutenant colonel, U.S. Army.

This is his first book.